MW01258189

THE SCHOOL PSYCHOLOGY SUPERVISOR'S TOOLKIT

The School Psychology Supervisor's Toolkit provides accessible, adaptable strategies for supervising school psychologists at all points in the career span, from internship to advanced practice. The book covers a full range of key considerations for effective supervision, such as building strong working relationships, planning the supervision experience, providing constructive feedback, and addressing problems of professional competence. Features such as definitions of key terms, photocopiable handouts, tips for culturally responsive practice, and real-life case examples make this a rich and easily applied resource.

Meaghan C. Guiney is Assistant Professor in the School of Psychology at Fairleigh Dickinson University, USA. She is a licensed psychologist and Nationally Certified School Psychologist.

CONSULTATION, SUPERVISION, AND PROFESSIONAL LEARNING IN SCHOOL PSYCHOLOGY
Series Editor: Daniel S. Newman

Supervision in School Psychology: The Developmental, Ecological, Problem-solving Model
By Dennis J. Simon and Mark E. Swerdlik

The School Psychology Supervisor's Toolkit
By Meaghan C. Guiney

Technology Applications in School Psychology Consultation, Supervision, and Training
Edited by Aaron J. Fischer, Tai A. Collins, Evan H. Dart, and Keith C. Radley

CONSULTATION AND INTERVENTION IN SCHOOL PSYCHOLOGY
Series Editor: Sylvia Rosenfield

Becoming a School Consultant: Lessons Learned
Edited by Sylvia Rosenfield

Crisis Counseling, Intervention and Prevention in the Schools, Third Edition
Edited by Jonathan H. Sandoval

An Introduction to Consultee-Centered Consultation in the Schools
By Jonathan H. Sandoval

Handbook of Research in School Consultation, Second Edition
Edited by William P. Erchul and Susan M. Sheridan

Consultee-Centered Consultation: Improving the Quality of Professional Services in Schools and Community Organizations
Edited by Nadine M. Lambert, Ingrid Hylander, and Jonathan H. Sandoval

Consultation Across Cultural Contexts: Consultee-Centered Case Studies
Edited by Antoinette Halsell Miranda

Handbook of Multicultural School Psychology: An Interdisciplinary Perspective, Second Edition
Edited by Emilia C. Lopez, Sara G. Nahari, and Sherrie L. Proctor

International Handbook of Consultation in Educational Settings
Edited by Chryse Hatzichristou and Sylvia Rosenfield

Building Competence in School Consultation: A Developmental Approach
By Daniel S. Newman and Sylvia Rosenfield

For more information about this series, please visit: www.routledge.com/Consultation-Supervision-and-Professional-Learning-in-School-Psychology-Series/book-series/CSAPLISPS.

THE SCHOOL PSYCHOLOGY SUPERVISOR'S TOOLKIT

Meaghan C. Guiney

Routledge
Taylor & Francis Group

NEW YORK AND LONDON

First published 2019
by Routledge
52 Vanderbilt Avenue, New York, NY 10017

and by Routledge
2 Park Square, Milton Park, Abingdon, Oxon, OX14 4RN

Routledge is an imprint of the Taylor & Francis Group, an informa business

Library of Congress Cataloging-in-Publication Data
Names: Guiney, Meaghan (Meaghan C.), author.
Title: The school psychology supervisor's toolkit /
Meaghan C. Guiney.
Description: New York, NY : Routledge, 2019. |
Includes bibliographical references and index.
Identifiers: LCCN 2018039981 (print) | LCCN 2018051163 (ebook) |
ISBN 9780203728581 (eBook) | ISBN 9781138306080 (hardback) |
ISBN 9781138306103 (pbk.) | ISBN 9780203728581 (ebk.)
Subjects: LCSH: School psychologists–Supervision of.
Classification: LCC LB3013.6 (ebook) | LCC LB3013.6 .G85 2019
(print) | DDC 371.7/13–dc23
LC record available at https://lccn.loc.gov/2018039981

ISBN: 978-1-138-30608-0 (hbk)
ISBN: 978-1-138-30610-3 (pbk)
ISBN: 978-0-203-72858-1 (ebk)

Typeset in Bembo
by Swales & Willis Ltd

I dedicate this book to my husband, Brian Guiney, and my sons, Conor and Brendan. Thank you for your willingness to forgo home-cooked meals and play extra PlayStation while I was busy writing. Whether you knew it (Brian) or not (Conor and Brendan), you provided me with unwavering support and inspiration throughout this process. I am beyond grateful to have the three of you in my life and look forward to spending some free time with you again!

CONTENTS

Preface   *x*
Acknowledgments   *xii*
List of Contributors   *xiii*

Introduction   1

SECTION I
Building a Solid Foundation   **5**

1 Supervision Basics   7

2 Establishing a Strong Supervision Relationship   25

3 Supervision Planning   40

SECTION II
Navigating the Supervision Experience   **53**

4 Communicating Feedback   55

5 Evaluating Supervisees   70

6 Addressing Problems of Professional Competence   81

7 Providing Culturally Responsive Supervision   102
   Arlene Silva

SECTION III
Professional Issues in Supervision   **111**

8 Ethics and Supervision   113

9 Preventing Burnout through Self-Care   126

10 Technology and Supervision   147
   With Dan Florell

SECTION IV
Developmentally Responsive Supervision   **159**

11 Supervising Interns and Practicum Students   161

12 Supporting Early Career School Psychologists   173

13 Enhancing Professional Growth for Advanced Supervisees   186

Appendix A: Recommended Reading   202

Appendix B: Sample Professional Disclosure Statement   203

Appendix C: Sample Contract for Supervision   206

Appendix D: Self-assessment Tool   209

Appendix E: Sample Internship Training Plan   216

Appendix F: Sample Professional Growth Plan for Credentialed
School Psychologist   220

Appendix G: Intern Evaluation Form   224

Appendix H: Sample Remediation Plan   231

Appendix I: Developing Cultural Responsiveness   237

Appendix J: Letter of Recommendation for Strong Supervisee   240

Appendix K: Letter of Recommendation for a Supervisee Who
Struggled   242

Index   *244*

PREFACE

If you've picked up this book, you are likely a school psychologist. And if you are a school psychologist, you've probably had a number of supervisors over the years. Practicum supervisors, externship supervisors, internship supervisors, field supervisors, university-based supervisors, administrative supervisors ... whether you are still early in your career or a seasoned veteran, it is likely that you've worked with an array of other professionals to build your skills and hone your practice. In fact, supervision has been described as the *signature pedagogy* of psychology (Barnett, Cornish, Goodyear, & Lichtenberg, 2007). In other words, the most significant and powerful learning opportunities we have as school psychologists come through supervision. Personally, during my graduate training and years as a school-based practitioner I had at least seven different clinical supervisors, three administrative supervisors, and one designated mentor, each of whom shaped my career as a school psychologist in significant ways.

Looking back on your own supervision relationships, it is likely that some were extremely positive, while others may have been anxiety-provoking or even downright unpleasant. I have heard many examples of both extremes while teaching and presenting on supervision in recent years. What differentiates these experiences? Anecdotally, my students, who tend to be advanced doctoral students who are already practicing as school psychologists, indicate that their most effective supervisors were encouraging, accessible, patient, knowledgeable, and willing to openly address sometimes challenging subjects like cultural differences. On the other hand, those supervisors who are remembered less favorably are often described as unavailable, critical, or even downright harassing. Research supports these views: trainees sharing their impressions of their "best" supervisors described them as supportive, accepting, respectful, and open-minded, while the "worst" supervisors were remembered as busy, uncaring, critical, and lacking respect for boundaries (Ladany, Mori, & Mehr, 2013). Clearly the great supervisors can be distinguished from the not-so-great; how can we ensure we fall into the former category and not the latter?

This book was conceived as a practical resource for busy school psychologists who are providing supervision to trainees or colleagues at all stages of the career span. While teaching supervision to practicing school psychologists and working closely with practitioners in the field who supervise my interns, I have heard time and again that supervising school psychologists need "grab and go" resources that can be accessed easily and applied quickly. Whether you have just learned you will be supervising an intern for the coming year, have recently come to recognize that a supervisee is really struggling, or are realizing that a supervisee is exceptional and needs more of a challenge, *The School Psychology Supervisor's Toolkit* is meant to serve as your "one-stop shop" for practical basics that will help you start out on the right foot or address difficulties that may have arisen along the way.

The NASP (2010) *Principles for Professional Ethics* stipulate that contributing to the profession by supervising and mentoring is the responsibility of all school psychologists. I hope *The School Psychology Supervisor's Toolkit* will be a helpful resource to you in your efforts to support our field, whether you're embarking upon your first experience as a supervisor or have been at this for decades.

References

Barnett, J. E., Cornish, J. A. E., Goodyear, R. K., & Lichtenberg, J. W. (2007). Commentaries on the ethical and effective practice of clinical supervision. *Professional Psychology: Research and Practice, 38*, 268–275.

Ladany, N., Mori, Y., & Mehr, K. E. (2013). Effective and ineffective supervision. *The Counseling Psychologist, 41*(1), 28–47. doi:10.1177/0011000012442648.

National Association of School Psychologists (2010). *Principles for professional ethics.* Bethesda, MD: Author.

ACKNOWLEDGMENTS

Though I still have a lifetime of development to come, the many formal and informal mentors, supervisors, and colleagues in my "competence constellation" have profoundly influenced the professional I am at this point in my career. I will be forever grateful to the following school psychologists for teaching, supporting, and inspiring me from my earliest days in the field right up to today: Ron Dumont, Ted Feinberg, Sarah Guiney, Abigail Harris, Judith Kaufman, Danny Newman, Lara Monasch, Christine Petersen, J. T. Ridgely, Sylvia Rosenfield, Eric Rossen, Lee Rothman, Todd Savage, David Shriberg, Arlene Silva, Bill Strein, Joan Struzziero, Mark Swerdlik, Hedy Teglasi, Sarah Valley-Gray, Kate Viezel, Larry Wenz, and Jamie Zibulsky. I'd also like to thank the many wonderful supervisees and students who have put up with me over the past six years. It's a true privilege to have the opportunity to keep learning and growing by helping others do the same.

CONTRIBUTORS

Dan Florell, Ph.D., NCSP, Associate Professor, Eastern Kentucky University
Dr. Florell is a leading expert on the role of technology in school psychology practice and the webmaster for the National Association of School Psychologists. He teaches courses on child and adolescent development and provides supervision to school psychology practicum students and interns.

Arlene Silva, Ph.D., LEP, NCSP, Associate Professor, William James College
Dr. Silva is Chair of the School Psychology Department and Director of the School Psychology MA/CAGS program at William James College in Newton, MA. Her research interests and teaching relate to consultation and supervision in school psychology as well as diversity studies and culturally responsive practice.

INTRODUCTION

It's remarkable that there are so many wonderful supervisors out there, because most of them are likely self-taught. Although doctoral programs accredited by the American Psychological Association (APA) are required to include specific coursework in supervision (APA, 2006), it is not a component of the *Standards for Graduate Preparation of School Psychologists* that govern Specialist-level training for programs approved by the National Association of School Psychologists (NASP, 2010). It is therefore likely that many of the approximately 75% of school psychologists who do not hold a doctoral degree (Curtis, Castillo, & Gelley, 2012) have not had a formal graduate course on supervision. In fact, some studies indicate that only 15–20% of supervising school psychologists have completed graduate coursework on supervision (Cochrane, Salyers, & Ding, 2010; Flanagan & Grehan, 2011).

A recent survey of early career school psychologists found that just 15% of respondents had taken a graduate course devoted *partially* to supervision, and a slim 8% had had a course *solely* focused on supervision (Silva, Newman, Guiney, Valley-Gray, & Barrett, 2016). The overwhelming majority (63%) had no formal training in supervision whatsoever. This is not to say that these school psychologists are not great supervisors, but it does mean that they are likely teaching themselves, flying solo, and figuring things out as they go. Approaching supervision this way can be stressful at a minimum and potentially harmful to supervisees at the extreme. The goal of this book is to provide guidance and resources to support school psychology supervisors as they navigate this very important professional role.

What's in This Book?

The School Psychology Supervisor's Toolkit begins with essentials like definitions and key concepts of supervision that can be helpful for guiding practice. The first section of this book will also address important considerations for building a strong and successful supervision relationship, which undergirds all other supervision considerations. This includes a discussion of how to clarify roles, responsibilities, and expectations through the use of a supervision contract. Supervision planning is also addressed at the outset, as a strong supervision plan can help guide training experiences and professional development through the sometimes chaotic experience of working in schools.

The second section of the book is designed to help you navigate some of the challenges that are inherent to supervision. Because open and clear communication is essential for most successful interpersonal relationships, strategies for communicating feedback to supervisees will be addressed. There is also a chapter devoted to the evaluation of supervisee performance, which is one of a supervisor's most important (and often most intimidating) responsibilities. Although the vast majority of supervisees perform adequately or even exceptionally, the small minority who struggle to demonstrate competence can pose substantial challenges for supervisors; a chapter devoted to addressing problems of professional competence is included to assist supervisors who find themselves navigating these difficult situations. Finally, a chapter on culturally responsive supervision, an essential consideration for all supervisors in our increasingly diverse schools and society, provides guidance for supervising in a culturally responsive way and on developing culturally responsive supervisees.

The third section of *The Toolkit* covers several important professional issues related to supervision. One is ethics: this chapter will guide you in modeling ethical practice for supervisees and considers some ethical dilemmas that can arise within supervision relationships. One particular ethical imperative, self-care and the prevention of burnout for both supervisors and supervisees, is the focus of one chapter as well. Finally, a chapter on the role of technology in supervision is also presented.

The book concludes with chapters focused on the supervision of specific types of school psychologists across the developmental spectrum of the career span. First, considerations particular to the supervision of interns and practicum students are addressed, followed by a chapter dedicated to supervising and mentoring early career school psychologists. Finally, because even experienced school psychologists can benefit greatly from supervision, the book concludes with an examination of methods of supervision and support for advanced professionals.

Where's the Evidence?

As school psychologists we strive to make data-based decisions informed by research evidence. This should be as true for supervision as for any other domain of our practice. Although the professional literature on supervision in school psychology is relatively small, it is growing. Wherever possible, this book will direct you to research and scholarly sources that can provide more in-depth information about the topics addressed. But, as the title implies, this is not meant to be a textbook. It is designed to be a practical resource that can be consulted quickly in the limited time you have between evaluations, counseling sessions, and meetings (and other meetings and more meetings). For in-depth treatments of any of the concepts herein, you will need to turn to other sources.

If you have the luxury of additional time, I would highly recommend two excellent resources on supervision in school psychology by experts in the field. The first is Harvey and Struzziero's (2008) *Professional Development and Supervision of School Psychologists: From Intern to Expert* (2nd Ed.). This text covers virtually everything you could need to know about supervising both school psychologists and the delivery of school psychology services, and includes many helpful examples and handouts. The other essential source is Simon and Swerdlik's (2017) *Supervision in School Psychology: The Developmental, Ecological, Problem-solving Model*, which presents a detailed introduction to the only school-psychology specific model of supervision. These titles, along with a few others that should round out any supervisor's library, are included in Appendix A for your reference.

References

American Psychological Association. (2006). *Guidelines and principles for accreditation of programs in professional psychology (G&P)*. Retrieved from www.apa.org/ed/accreditation/about/policies/guiding-principles.pdf.

Cochrane, W. S., Salyers, K., & Ding, Y. (2010). An examination of the preparation, supervisor's theoretical model, and university support for supervisors of school psychology interns. *Trainer's Forum: Journal of the Trainers of School Psychologists, 29*(1), 6–22.

Curtis, M. J., Castillo, J. M., & Gelley, C. (2012). School psychology 2010: Demographics, employment, and the context for professional practices–Part 1. *Communiqué, 40*(1), 28–30.

Flanagan, R., & Grehan, P. (2011). Assessing school psychology supervisor characteristics: Questionnaire development and findings. *Journal of Applied School Psychology, 27*, 21–41. doi:10.1080/15377903.2011.540504.

Harvey, V. S., & Struzziero, J. A. (Eds.). (2008). *Professional development and supervision of school psychologists: From intern to expert* (2nd ed.). Bethesda, MD: National Association of School Psychologists.

National Association of School Psychologists. (2010). *Standards for graduate preparation of school psychologists*. Bethesda, MD: Author.

Silva, A. E., Newman, D. S., Guiney, M. C., Valley-Gray, S., & Barrett, C. A. (2016). Supervision and mentoring for early career school psychologists: Availability, access, structure, and implications. *Psychology in the Schools, 53*(5), 502–516. doi:10.1002/pits.21921.

Simon, D. J., & Swerdlik, M. E. (2017). *Supervision in school psychology: The developmental, ecological, problem-solving model*. New York: Routledge.

SECTION I

Building a Solid Foundation

1

SUPERVISION BASICS

Before we start looking at how to provide high-quality supervision, it's important to understand some basic ideas that underlie everything good supervisors do. This chapter will define supervision and present some "big ideas" to keep in mind as you use this book. It will also explain a bit about how a model of supervision can help you organize your approach according to your supervisee's level of development.

What Are We Talking About? Defining Supervision in School Psychology

A frequently cited definition of school psychology supervision comes from McIntosh and Phelps (2000):

> Supervision is an interpersonal interaction between two or more individuals for the purpose of sharing knowledge, assessing professional competencies, and providing objective feedback with the terminal goals of developing new competencies, facilitating effective delivery of psychological services, and maintaining professional competencies.
>
> *(pp. 33–34)*

The National Association of School Psychologists (NASP, 2018) distinguishes between *clinical* and *administrative* supervision (see Table 1.1), and emphasizes that both types are "provided through an ongoing, positive, systematic, collaborative process between the school psychologist and the school psychology supervisor or other school psychology colleagues" with a focus on "promoting effective growth and exemplary professional practice leading to improved performance" (NASP, 2010a, p. 11).

Together, these definitions highlight the core features of supervision designed to result in improved service delivery and outcomes for students, families, and school communities. These include:

- a long-term working relationship
- a well-planned approach with a focus on growth
- frequent feedback that supports learning.

The various terms and labels for types of supervision and supervision-like activities can be a bit confusing. Table 1.1 defines some of the different ways to support the professional development of school psychologists.

A few important factors differentiate the types of support defined in Table 1.1. First, unlike mentors, **supervisors retain responsibility for their supervisees' work**. For professional or clinical supervisors of pre-service, non-credentialed trainees (i.e., practicum students and interns), this means co-signing reports or other formal documents and consistently identifying supervisees as graduate students (NASP, 2010b). It also means supervisors must stay informed about all cases assigned to supervisees and all activities supervisees are engaging in at any given time. Second, **supervision typically**

TABLE 1.1 Types of Professional Support

Type of Support	Definition/Features
Administrative supervision (see Harvey & Struzziero, 2008; NASP, 2018)	Oversight of the "nuts and bolts" or logistics of service delivery with a focus on consumer satisfaction. Includes responsibilities such as hiring, firing, and assigning staff; conducting performance evaluations; assigning caseloads; and monitoring legal responsibilities (e.g., compliance with special education mandates). May be provided by a school psychologist or a professional not trained in school psychology.
Clinical supervision (see Bernard & Goodyear, 2014; NASP, 2018)	Supervision focused specifically on building professional skills with the goal of enhancing professional competence. Involves evaluating progress towards training goals and monitoring the quality of service delivery to ensure that supervisees are sufficiently well trained to practice independently at the end of the supervision relationship.
Mentoring (see NASP, 2016)	Similar in goals and purpose to clinical/professional supervision, but without an evaluative or "gatekeeping" component. Mentees are credentialed to practice independently and retain responsibility for their own work.
Postgraduate professional support (see NASP, 2016)	Broader term that incorporates both mentoring and supervision for in-service school psychologists who are credentialed to practice.

involves formal evaluation of supervisee competence, often with the added responsibility of "gatekeeping" for the profession, or providing input regarding whether or not the supervisee demonstrates sufficient knowledge and skills to function effectively. This aspect of supervision serves to protect clients and the public and promotes effective service delivery that benefits schools and communities. Whether you are providing clinical or administrative supervision, these are some important responsibilities! Finally, with these first two factors in mind a third important point becomes clear: **supervision involves a hierarchical relationship** in which the supervisor is in a position of greater power than the supervisee (Bernard & Goodyear, 2014). This will be important to recognize as we consider ways to build and maintain effective supervisory relationships (see Chapter 2).

Big Ideas

As you use this book to support your supervision practice, there are a few important points to keep in mind. Think of these as "big ideas" that underlie a successful approach to supervision.

Big Idea #1: Supervision Is a Distinct Area of Competency

> I thought that being a supervisor would come naturally. There is much more skill and practice involved than I expected.
>
> *(J. R., first-time supervisor)*

My students regularly tell me how surprised they are to discover that there is so much to learn about supervision. They often don't realize that there is more to being a great school psychology supervisor than just being a great school psychologist. Although experienced school psychologists typically have strong skills in domains such as assessment, consultation, and counseling, such expertise is necessary—but not sufficient—for effective supervision. Supervision guidelines published by the American Psychological Association (APA, 2014) highlight the fact that supervisors not only need to demonstrate competence in the domains of psychology practice they are supervising, but must also maintain competence in the practice of supervision itself. NASP (2018) also espouses the position that school psychology supervisors have formal or at least informal training in the practice of supervision. Becoming an effective supervisor takes training and practice, ideally including the opportunity to participate in supervision of one's supervision, otherwise known as meta-supervision. The fact that you've picked up this book suggests that you have probably already realized that supervisors need supervision training!

Big Idea #2: Quality Supervision Is Developmentally Responsive

> It is important to gauge the supervisee's level of competence...so that you
> will know what direction to take.
>
> *(D. T., first-time supervisor)*

While supervision is commonly thought of as a process of helping a novice learn and gain entry-level competence—and it often is just that—it should really be a feature of all stages of the career lifespan (NASP, 2018). Of course, what that supervision consists of and looks like will vary considerably depending on the development and needs of the supervisee. Based on interviews with 100 therapists, Rønnestad and Skovholt (2003) developed the Lifespan Development Model, which highlights common features of professionals throughout six distinct various phases in the career span. Table 1.2 illustrates how these findings apply to the development of school psychologists at different developmental stages. These features are not universally applicable; certainly there are individual differences and great variability in professional development. However, generally speaking, school psychologists move from being highly dependent and in need of substantial guidance early in their training to being highly independent, flexible, and able to solve problems efficiently by the latter stages of their careers. Supervision can support and enhance learning all throughout this progression of growth when approaches and techniques are selected based on the supervisee's needs and developmental level.

It is essential to remember that anyone can become a novice at any point when presented with a new challenge, such as working with a new population or adapting to a new role or responsibility. Such situations demand access to supervision. In contrast, sometimes supervisors must adapt to meet the needs of a particularly skilled supervisee who shows exceptional competence at a given developmental level. This ever-present need to approach supervision with supervisee development in mind is a central feature of the Developmental Ecological Problem-solving (DEP) model of supervision (Simon & Swerdlik, 2017) which is described briefly later in this chapter.

Big Idea #3: Supervision Is a Relationship

> I've had several supervisors throughout my training, and each relationship
> was vastly different ... [One] experience shaped my career in an extre-
> mely positive way. My supervisor was extremely knowledgeable and
> endlessly supportive, and I always felt that I could approach him for
> advice, suggestions, or just to learn from him.
>
> *(A. M., early-career school psychologist)*

As was noted earlier in this chapter, frequently cited definitions of supervision identify it as "an interpersonal interaction" (McIntosh & Phelps, 2000, p. 33)

TABLE 1.2 The Lifespan Development Model

Phase	Typical Features
Beginning student (practicum students, some beginning interns)	• Uncertain of competence, anxious • Dependent on professors and supervisors • Easily overwhelmed by complex cases • Eager to learn straightforward methods that can be easily applied to many situations • Highly attuned to encouragement and criticism from more experienced professionals
Advanced student (interns)	• More comfortable in professional role, but still vulnerable and insecure • Want to avoid making mistakes • Cautious, detail-oriented, thorough • Dependent on supervisors and role models • Benefit from observing experienced practitioners • Learn through modeling • Deeply affected by positive and negative supervision experiences • Can have strong affective reactions to supervisors
Novice professional (early-career school psychologists; first five years of practice)	• Exploring professional identity, defining professional role • More willing to express personality and display sense of humor • May feel overwhelmed by demands of independent practice • Disillusioned that "real-world" practice is different from graduate training ideals • Learning to set boundaries; may struggle to maintain work/life balance • Eager to acquire more specific professional development to learn new skills/techniques and fill recognized gaps in training
Experienced professional (mid-career school psychologists; next two decades of practice)	• More confident; more comfortable knowing there is not always a "right" or clear answer • Has defined a role that fits personal values, interests, attitudes • Has identified a more integrated and consolidated theoretical orientation • Applies techniques and methods more flexibly • Better able to maintain boundaries and "leave work at work" • Learns primarily from reflecting on experiences, both professional and personal • May feel there is not much new in the field and become disinterested in professional development workshops

(Continued)

TABLE 1.2 (Cont).

Phase	Typical Features
Senior professional (veteran school psychologists; 25+ years of experience)	• Experience personal and professional losses • May feel regret and/or anticipatory grief • May feel they've seen "reinventing the wheel" many times and become disengaged from the field • Sense of self-acceptance and satisfaction

Adapted from Rønnestad, M. H., & Skovholt, T. M. (2003). The journey of the counselor and therapist: Research findings and perspectives on professional development. *Journal of Career Development, 30*(1), 5–44.

and a "collaborative process" (NASP, 2018, p. 1). Whether it is clinical or administrative supervision, we are talking about a working relationship that requires a significant degree of trust. Many of my students exhibit significant anxiety as they embark upon internship experiences or other new challenges; I've seen time and again how a supportive supervisory relationship has been critical to helping these trainees deal with stress and successfully move forward. But it's not just graduate students who benefit from supportive supervision; a quality relationship can be helpful to supervisees at *all* levels for managing stress and promoting professional development.

A trusting relationship is essential to quality supervision. For example, take disclosure: supervisees need to be able to trust that they can safely admit mistakes to their supervisors. A study of therapists in training found that 44% of supervisees conceded they did not disclose clinical mistakes, often because they did not want to appear incompetent (Ladany, Hill, Corbett, & Nutt, 1996). Withholding such mistakes presents missed learning opportunities at best and at worst, serious risks for supervisors who are responsible for the consequences of their supervisees' work. A supervisory alliance that normalizes mistakes and embraces them as learning opportunities can protect a supervisor from being blindsided by unexpected problems. Supervisees also need to feel secure enough to discuss challenging subjects like cultural differences (Wade & Jones, 2015). Chapter 2 will address how supervisors can establish trusting working relationships.

Using a Supervision Model

We've established that supervision is a distinct area of competency in school psychology and that it takes more than just being a great school psychologist to be a great supervisor. Just as there are many different theoretical orientations available to guide the work of therapists and counselors, many models of supervision exist to help organize all the concepts and knowledge that will guide your approach as a supervisor. However, this section will focus on the only model of supervision designed specifically for school psychology: the Developmental, Ecological, Problem-solving (DEP) model. Several of the sources listed in Appendix A provide thorough overviews of other models of supervision from the clinical and counseling psychology literature.

Why Follow a Model?

As Simon and Swerdlik (2017) noted, without a "big picture road map, the supervision journey meanders along trails without a clear destination and no way of determining progress" (p. 81). Particularly for new supervisors, it can be quite helpful to have the structure of a supervision model as a guide. As the first reflection presented above indicates, there is a lot to learn and know about supervision. Studies of counselor development have found that therapists in the early stages of their careers gravitate towards easily applicable models of counseling or therapy to organize their approach (Rønnestad & Skovholt, 2003). With time and experience we become better able to think flexibly and apply concepts from multiple approaches to solve problems, but in the early stages of learning a new skill it can be extremely helpful to have the guidance and organization of a model to follow.

The Developmental, Ecological, Problem-solving (DEP) Model

The first model of supervision specifically designed for school psychology is Simon and Swerdlik's (2017) DEP model. Recognizing that the scope and setting of the practice of school psychology are quite complex, the DEP model incorporates the developmental knowledge that permeates our work with learners in schools, the ecological perspective that accounts for the many systemic variables that influence our daily practice, and the problem-solving approach that underlies all that school psychologists do. A particularly remarkable feature of the DEP model is its consideration of ecological factors related to diversity and multicultural competence. It is a comprehensive framework perfectly suited to the supervision of school psychology practice. Readers are strongly encouraged to refer to Simon and Swerdlik's book, *Supervision in School Psychology: The Developmental, Ecological, Problem-solving Model* for a comprehensive discussion of the DEP model.

Qualities of Effective School Psychology Supervisors

Quality supervision promotes maintenance and improvement of professional skills, can help to reduce stress and mitigate professional isolation, and has the potential to promote reflective practice (Harvey & Struzziero, 2008). But it's not conducted on paper or delivered by a computer; it's an interpersonal process. As supervisors we bring our own individual differences to the supervision relationship including our personalities, interests, habits, and culture. However, the knowledge, skills, and values summarized in Table 1.3 have been highlighted as the characteristics of effective supervisors (also see Falender et al., 2004; Harvey & Struzziero, 2008; Simon & Swerdlik, 2017).

Roles and Responsibilities: Who Does What?

A theme that will run throughout the foundation of this book is the importance of having clear behavioral expectations for everyone involved in the supervision interaction. Think about it: if supervision is a working relationship, isn't it important to know who is responsible for which aspects of the work? Let's

TABLE 1.3   Characteristics of Effective Supervisors

Good supervisors have knowledge of . . .	• The domain(s) of practice being supervised • Supervision theories, models, modalities, techniques, and research • Supervisee development • Best practices for supervisee evaluation • Ethical and legal practice • Diversity and culturally responsive practice • Schools as systems • Self-care
Good supervisors are skilled at . . .	• Supervision techniques and modalities • Building relationships • Communication • Assessing supervisee development and learning needs • Supporting and challenging supervisees • Providing and seeking feedback • Leadership • Teaching • Problem-solving • Respecting relationship boundaries • Promoting and modeling reflective practice and self-assessment • Self-care
Good supervisors value . . .	• Protecting client welfare • Promoting supervisee growth and learning • Individual differences • Diversity and cultural differences • Ethical and legal responsibilities • Evidence-based practice • Lifelong learning and professional development

consider what supervisors and supervisees can be expected to contribute to the supervision experience . . .

Supervisor Responsibilities: Be ... A TEACHER

Supervisors have a pretty extensive set of considerations to observe. Table 1.4 provides an overview of these responsibilities, along with expectations we are likely to have for supervisees. This list may seem intimidating, but keep in mind that a lot of these items are things you are probably already good at if you are an effective school psychologist. To simplify things a bit, just remember to be ... *A TEACHER*.

Aware

One of your most critical responsibilities as a supervisor, particularly if you are working with supervisees who are not credentialed to practice independently, is to protect the welfare of any and all clients seen by your supervisee. In order to do this, you need to be well informed about what is happening in each of your supervisee's cases. You also need to stay aware of your supervisee's general functioning—including factors like stress and anxiety—and monitor for problems of professional competence (see Chapter 6).

Tolerant

"Lousy" supervisors have been described as expecting their supervisees to do things just as they do, stifling attempts to use new techniques or approach problems in an innovative way (Magnuson, Wilcoxon, & Norem, 2000). Remember that supervisors sometimes have much to learn from supervisees, particularly when the supervisor may be many years out of graduate school. Don't be afraid to try new ideas! Being tolerant also includes respecting diversity and modeling culturally responsive practice, key considerations that are addressed in Chapter 7.

Ethical

As a supervisor you must model ethical practice for your supervisees and actively teach ethical knowledge and principles when necessary (see Chapter 8 for a more detailed discussion of ethics and supervision). It is important to recognize that less experienced school psychologists often lack the flexibility and automaticity in problem-solving that veterans develop through years of practice (Harvey & Struzziero, 2008). Thus, when addressing an ethical dilemma, talking through your thought process (using a "think aloud" procedure) can be quite enlightening and educational for a supervisee to observe.

TABLE 1.4 Supervisor and Supervisee Roles and Responsibilities

Be…	Supervisor Responsibilities	Be…	Supervisee Responsibilities
AWARE	• Protect the welfare of supervisee's clients (students, teachers, parents) • Stay well informed about all cases • Monitor supervisee anxiety, stress, and self-care behaviors	ACTIVE	• Ask how to get involved, rather than waiting to be given things to do • Seek out new and challenging learning opportunities • Look for cases with a diverse range of clients • Share ideas and suggestions
TOLERANT	• Let supervisees try new ideas, methods, and techniques • Be patient • Answer questions • Model culturally responsive practice and respect for diversity	LISTENING	• Observe how supervisor conducts job responsibilities • Observe classrooms, meetings, and all aspects of the school environment • Improve active listening skills to enhance counseling, consultation, interviewing and leadership skills • Be open to supervisor feedback
ETHICAL	• Know and consult the NASP and APA ethics codes • Model ethical practice • Discuss your ethical decision-making process • Supervise only in your areas of competence	ETHICAL	• Learn and consult the NASP and APA ethics codes • Be open and honest with supervisor about all cases, particularly when mistakes occur • Ask questions when unsure
AVAILABLE	• Schedule regular (i.e., weekly) supervision meetings and protect the time • Identify a backup supervisor for times when you are not available	ACCOUNTABLE	• Follow through on tasks • Develop systems to stay organized • Observe due dates and complete cases in a timely manner

- Ensure that supervisees know how to contact you in crisis situations
- Maintain limits and boundaries

COMPETENT
- Only supervise in areas of competence
- Know theories and techniques of quality supervision
- Engage in ongoing professional development
- Seek meta-supervision

HONEST
- Provide frequent, specific, constructive feedback
- Balance criticism with specific praise
- Evaluate both domain-based knowledge and skills as well as professional work characteristics

ENGAGED
- Refrain from texting, emailing, or taking phone calls during supervision
- Be prepared for supervision
- Organize supervision sessions around short- and long-term goals for supervisee growth

ROLE MODEL
- Model ethical practice
- Model culturally responsive practice
- Model lifelong learning and a commitment to professional development
- Model good self-care behaviors

- Anticipate scheduling conflicts; plan ahead to complete tasks on time
- Arrive on time and inform supervisor of any scheduling conflicts

READY
- Complete all training requirements
- Know areas of strength and weakness
- Come to work prepared and sufficiently rested
- Be ready for supervision with questions, notes, and data

NETWORKING
- Seek out opportunities to collaborate with a variety of education and mental health professionals
- Participate in regional, state, and national school psychology associations
- Attend workshops and conferences

ENGAGED
- Limit personal communications during the school day (texting, email, phone calls)
- Restrict social media use to work-relevant purposes

REFLECTIVE
- View mistakes as opportunities for growth
- Think about what went well and what could be done differently in the future
- Keep notes or a journal to document growth over time
- Reflect on cultural considerations

Available

Make supervision a priority by scheduling a regular set time for face-to-face meetings and do all you can to protect that appointment. In between scheduled sessions, be sure you are available when supervisees need you, and have plans in place that detail who will provide backup supervision—particularly in a crisis situation—if you are out of the building or can't be reached. That being said, it is also important to set and maintain boundaries, so be clear with supervisees about when and how it is appropriate to reach you outside of school hours. You don't have to be on the clock 24 hours a day, and explaining that to a supervisee can be a useful means of modeling self-care and work-life balance.

Competent

As a supervisor you must be knowledgeable about all areas you are supervising. The NASP (2010b) *Principles for Professional Ethics* require that "school psychologists engage only in practices for which they are qualified and competent" (p. 6). With this in mind, you certainly should not supervise any practices that you yourself are not sufficiently trained to provide. Furthermore, you must be competent in supervision to be a competent supervisor. Engaging in ongoing professional development (including accessing resources like this book!) and seeking out meta-supervision are excellent strategies for maintaining competence. I've experienced this personally upon transitioning into the role of supervisor myself: the opportunity to learn from expert colleagues when working on tricky cases has helped me to gain greater knowledge of theories and techniques, and has also promoted valuable reflection on complex issues.

Honest

This includes providing constructive feedback. Though my students are frequently hesitant about the prospect of delivering criticism to their supervisees, research has shown that specific, constructive feedback is appreciated by trainees (e.g., Ladany, Mori, & Mehr, 2013). In fact, the "lousy" supervisors mentioned earlier were described as providing vague, abstract feedback (Magnuson et al., 2000). I encourage my students and the field supervisors who work with my interns to remember that "feedback is a gift." Without specific, timely, frequent, useful, and balanced feedback, supervisees cannot learn and supervision is basically a waste of time. This responsibility is so important that it is addressed in detail in Chapter 4.

Engaged

Give your supervisee your complete attention during supervision. Avoid texting, emailing, or answering your phone (even if this is easier said than done for a busy school psychologist!). Supervisees have highlighted these kinds of behaviors as hallmarks of some of their "worst" supervisors (Ladany et al., 2013). It is also important to be prepared for supervision: have a plan for each session, identify short- and long-term goals you are working towards, and keep brief notes to consult to recall action items that need following up.

A Role Model

Particularly when working with relatively inexperienced supervisees, as a supervisor you have the potential to be a very powerful influence on the formation of a school psychologist's values and theoretical orientation. Even for more advanced school psychologists, examples set by experienced supervisors can serve to help refine beliefs and extend knowledge and skills. Modeling ethical and culturally responsive practice and proactive self-care skills are all important responsibilities (culturally responsive supervision will be addressed in more detail in Chapter 7, Chapter 8 is dedicated to ethics, and self-care is the focus of Chapter 9).

Supervisee Responsibilities: Be ... A LEARNER

Some of the supervisee's responsibilities are similar to the supervisor's, while others are quite different. Table 1.4 lists the kinds of behaviors we should expect of our supervisees. You may have your own ideas about additional supervisee behaviors or responsibilities that are important; whatever your expectations are, clearly communicating them to your supervisees is essential to establishing an effective supervision relationship (more on that in the next chapter). One way to summarize these expectations is to remind each supervisee to be ... A LEARNER.

Active

Some of the most common compliments I hear from the field supervisors of my successful interns are that they are "proactive." I often hear, "she really takes initiative," or "he's self-directed." Successful supervisees make a point of participating in a wide array of learning opportunities and ask how they can get involved instead of waiting to be told what to do. I always encourage my supervisees to seek out experiences that broaden their exposure. These have included everything from attending school board and PTA meetings, to advising student organizations, to presenting at school-wide assemblies or parent meetings. It should also include pursuing opportunities to work with a diverse range of clients. As a supervisor it's reasonable for you to expect your supervisees to seek out learning opportunities and function with increasing independence, particularly supervisees with more experience and more advanced skills. Sharing these expectations with your supervisees from the very beginning can help to avoid confusion and frustration.

Listening

Because so much of learning comes from observation, it is essential that supervisees listen and watch as much as they actively engage in school psychology activities. This is particularly true for less advanced supervisees or for more experienced supervisees who find themselves in unfamiliar situations (even veterans can revert to being novices when faced with new responsibilities or new populations). Because strong active listening skills are also essential for many of a school psychologist's primary responsibilities (including counseling, consultation, interviewing, conflict resolution, and leadership), supervisees at all levels of experience can continually work to improve in this area. It is also reasonable to expect supervisees to be open to hearing both positive and critical feedback, provided it is delivered in a sensitive manner.

Ethical

Both supervisors and supervisees share the critical responsibility of engaging in ethical school psychology practice. Supervisees may vary widely in the knowledge of ethics codes, training in ethical problem-solving, and exposure to real-world ethical dilemmas. One of the most essential ethical imperatives that supervisees must observe is the requirement to alert supervisors to any and all situations in which clients might be at risk for harm, or instances in which supervisee may have made mistakes that could impact client welfare. Ethics should be a regular topic for consideration during supervision sessions.

Accountable

Supervisees should be expected to follow through on responsibilities and complete tasks in a timely manner. I have repeatedly encountered challenges with supervisees who struggle with organization, time management, and even consistent attendance at the supervision site. Clearly articulated expectations for factors like work hours, as well as due dates and timelines for long-term projects can help to prevent difficulties. When problems persist with such professional work characteristics, remediation efforts need to be undertaken and carefully documented (see Chapter 6).

Ready

Being ready refers to the expectation that supervisees have completed the necessary training and milestones to be prepared for the supervision experience, whether it is a domain-specific practicum, a capstone internship, or a job as a credentialed professional. It also means that they should be aware of their areas of strength and those in which they need further development to build competency. Finally, supervisees should be prepared on a day-to-day basis and arrive at school ready to do great work to support children and families, and they should come to supervision sessions prepared with questions, updates, and case data.

Networking

Professional networks are as essential to career success in school psychology as in any other field. Establishing a network has been recommended as best practice for early-career school psychologists (Silva, Newman, & Guiney, 2014) and actively maintaining such connections should be a goal for supervisees across the career trajectory. For novice school psychologists, practicum and internship experiences present some of the earliest opportunities to network with experienced clinicians from a variety of education- and mental health-related fields. Networking with fellow school psychologists begins on the first day of graduate school and can continue throughout one's career through participation in professional associations at the regional, state, and national level. Supervisees should actively seek out opportunities to connect with and learn from others.

Engaged

There's no denying that we live in a constantly connected world. Many of us have become used to texting friends and loved ones for instant responses and using the internet to answer almost any question in a fraction of a second. There are certainly advantages to these technological realities, but they can also present some challenging distractions. Being an engaged supervisee means staying focused on the responsibilities at hand during the school day and limiting things like social media use, texting, and personal phone calls (as a university-based supervisor I've been called upon to help address such behaviors on multiple occasions).

Reflective

Encouraging reflection is one of my top priorities, whether I am working with my school psychology interns or teaching supervisors-in-training. As supervisors we can encourage reflective practice through supervision discussions or even written reflective exercises, like journaling. These efforts are particularly important after challenging experiences or times when supervisees make mistakes. A supervisee with a growth mindset views mistakes as opportunities to learn and grow; reflecting on what went well, what did not, and what could be done differently the next time a similar challenge arises can be a powerful learning tool for supervisees at all levels of training, from novices to veterans (Wade & Jones, 2015). It is also important for supervisees to reflect on the role of cultural factors in their work, including personal experiences and biases. It can be extremely helpful to make it clear from early on that cultural considerations will be openly discussed in supervision.

Supervisor's Summary

- School psychology supervision involves a long-term, well-planned working relationship designed to promote growth.
- Because supervisors are responsible for the work of their supervisees and evaluate their competence, the relationship is a hierarchical one with an imbalance of power.
- Supervision is a distinct area of competency in school psychology and supervisors should engage in supervision-specific training.
- Quality supervision takes into account the supervisee's level of development and needs for growth.
- A relationship based on trust is essential for effective supervision.
- Following a model of supervision helps organize and guide the process; the DEP model is specific to school psychology and accounts for developmental, ecological, and problem-solving factors unique to the field.
- Effective supervisors are role models who stay informed about their supervisees' cases, are flexible about trying new ideas, model and teach ethical practice, are available and engaged when needed, have competence in supervision itself and the area(s) being supervised, and provide honest constructive feedback.
- Supervisees can be expected to be proactive, prepared, observant, and open to constructive feedback; to follow through on assignments and meet deadlines; to be attentive and engaged in their work; and to reflect on experiences to learn and grow.

Final Reflections

If you asked my students, they might describe me as obsessed with reflection. My classes require reflective logs, reflection papers, in-class reflection exercises, and large- and small-group discussions designed to encourage reflection. This is all for good reason: thoughtful reflection involves analyzing what we did well and what we could do better—what more could we as supervisors want to teach our supervisees? Effective supervisors model reflective practice and help supervisees to become reflective professionals and lifelong learners.

To encourage *you* to become a more reflective supervisor, each chapter will present a final reflection exercise. I would encourage you to actually record your reactions to these questions and to revisit them periodically as a means of progress monitoring your own development as a supervisor. You may be surprised by how much your reactions change over time!

FINAL REFLECTIONS

Whether you're embarking upon your first experience as a supervisor or you have supervised before but are looking to strengthen your approach, consider the following questions as you prepare to proceed:

- What are your priorities as a supervisor?
- What strengths do you currently bring to a supervisory relationship?
- What skills or knowledge do you think you need to develop further to be an effective supervisor?

References

American Psychological Association. (2014). Guidelines for clinical supervision in health service psychology. Retrieved from http://apa.org/about/policy/guidelines-supervision.

Bernard, J. M., & Goodyear, R. K. (2014). *Fundamentals of clinical supervision* (5th ed.). Upper Saddle River, NJ: Pearson.

Falender, C. A., Cornish, J. A. E., Goodyear, R., Hatcher, R., Kaslow, N. J., Leventhal, G., … Grus, C. (2004). Defining competencies in psychology supervision: A consensus statement. *Journal of Clinical Psychology, 60*(7), 771–785. doi:10.1002/jclp.20013.

Harvey, V. S., & Struzziero, J. A. (Eds.). (2008). *Professional development and supervision of school psychologists: From intern to expert* (2nd ed.). Bethesda, MD: National Association of School Psychologists.

Ladany, N., Hill, C. E., Corbett, M. M., & Nutt, E. A. (1996). Nature, extent, and importance of what psychotherapy trainees do not disclose to their supervisors. *Journal of Counseling Psychology, 43*(1), 10–24.

Ladany, N., Mori, Y., & Mehr, K. E. (2013). Effective and ineffective supervision. *The Counseling Psychologist, 41*(1), 28–47. doi:10.1177/0011000012442648.

Magnuson, S., Wilcoxon, S. A., & Norem, K. (2000). A profile of lousy supervision: Experienced counselors' perspectives. *Counselor Education and Supervision, 39*(3), 189–202. doi:10.1002/j.1556-6978.2000.tb01231.x.

McIntosh, D. E., & Phelps, L. (2000). Supervision in school psychology: Where will the future take us? *Psychology in the Schools, 37*(1), 33–38. doi:10.1002/(SICI)1520-6807 (200001)37:1<33::AID-PITS4>3.0.CO;2-F.

National Association of School Psychologists. (2010a). *Model for comprehensive and integrated school psychological services.* Bethesda, MD: Author.

National Association of School Psychologists. (2010b). *Principles for professional ethics.* Bethesda, MD: Author.

National Association of School Psychologists. (2016). *Guidance for postgraduate mentorship and professional support.* Bethesda, MD: Author

National Association of School Psychologists. (2018). *Supervision in school psychology* [Position statement]. Bethesda, MD: Author.

Rønnestad, M. H., & Skovholt, T. M. (2003). The journey of the counselor and therapist: Research findings and perspectives on professional development. *Journal of Career Development, 30*(1), 5–44.

Silva, A., Newman, D. S., & Guiney, M. C. (2014). Best practices in early career school psychology transitions. In A. Thomas & P. Harrison (Eds.), *Best practices in school psychology: Foundations* (pp. 553–566). Bethesda, MD: National Association of School Psychologists.

Simon, D. J., & Swerdlik, M. E. (2017). *Supervision in school psychology: The developmental, ecological, problem-solving model.* New York: Routledge.

Wade, J. C., & Jones, J. E. (2015). *Strength-based clinical supervision: A positive psychology approach to clinical training.* New York: Springer.

2

ESTABLISHING A STRONG SUPERVISION RELATIONSHIP

Chapter 1 proposed that one of the most important ideas in supervision is that *supervision is a relationship*. Research has supported this contention that the supervisory relationship is central to effective supervision (Ladany, Mori, & Mehr, 2013). In fact, one study concluded that the quality of the supervision relationship was "the most pivotal and crucial component of good supervision experiences" (Worthen & McNeill, 1996, p. 29). The relationship is so central to supervision that it is delineated as a specific area of competency in the APA (2014) *Guidelines for Supervision in Health Service Psychology*.

Like any working relationship, supervision can present both challenges and rewards for everyone involved. The goal of this chapter is to provide you with information and strategies for establishing a strong foundation that will help you weather any difficulties that arise. In particular, supervision contracts will be presented as a powerful tool for organizing and navigating the supervision relationship.

Managing Multiple Relationships and Respecting Boundaries

Boundaries are an important topic for both supervisors and supervisees. Awareness of and respect for boundaries is essential to navigating supervision interactions, particularly when multiple relationships arise.

Multiple Relationships

Codes of ethics for psychology and other helping professions address the complications that can arise from multiple relationships. The APA's (2017) *Ethical Principles of Psychologists and Code of Conduct* describes a multiple relationship as follows:

... when a psychologist is in a professional role with a person and (1) at the same time is in another role with the same person, (2) at the same time is in a relationship with a person closely associated with or related to the person with whom the psychologist has the professional relationship, or (3) promises to enter into another relationship in the future with the person or a person closely associated with or related to the person.

(p. 6)

Multiple relationships in and of themselves are not necessarily bad; in fact, they can be beneficial (Gottlieb, Robinson, & Younggren, 2007). For example, I have repeatedly had the experience of providing clinical supervision of therapy cases to doctoral students who are taking my supervision class. These multiple relationships can actually be great learning experiences, as students are able to see the supervision theory they are studying carried out in practice. Multiple relationships become problematic when they put us at risk of compromising service delivery or client or supervisee welfare (for example, due to conflicted interests). Issues often arise as a result of the inherent power dynamic that comes from the need for the supervisor to formally evaluate supervisee performance. Box 2.1 describes a real situation that I encountered as a university-based internship supervisor that required careful consideration of multiple relationships and boundaries. Consider the accompanying questions; as a supervisor, how would you proceed in such a case?

BOX 2.1 MULTIPLE RELATIONSHIPS

Supervision in the Real World

Michael was approaching his final year of school psychology training and needed to secure a site for his upcoming internship. He had been successful in his program, meeting all competency benchmarks and receiving consistently positive feedback from faculty and practicum supervisors. Throughout graduate school he had been working part-time with a special education program in the Hillcrest School District. He grew up in Hillcrest and had graduated from Hillcrest High School less than a decade earlier. He was acquainted with the Director of Special Education and several of the school psychologists in Hillcrest from his work with the district, and also because his mother worked as the administrative assistant to the department. Michael's training program had placed interns at Hillcrest High School for years and had a strong working relationship with the district. Not surprisingly, the Director offered Michael the opportunity to complete his internship in Hillcrest.

Questions to Consider:

- What multiple relationships would exist if Michael completed his internship in Hillcrest?
- Would you be comfortable acting as Michael's supervisor while his mother worked as the administrative assistant to your department?
- What potential benefits might there be (for Michael, for the district, and for you as a supervisor) to accept an intern who is highly familiar with the school, the district, and the community?
- What potential risks might there be? What, if anything, could you do to prevent them?

Boundaries

As essential as it is to form close working relationships with supervisees, ensuring that those relationships are perceived as positive requires that supervisors maintain appropriate personal and professional boundaries (Gottlieb et al., 2007). But striking this balance of close-yet-bounded poses challenges: being too rigid about boundaries might stifle the development of a strong supervision relationship, but the opposite extreme can present significant risks. Although much of the research literature on boundaries focuses on therapist–patient relationships, these concepts are also applicable to supervision. A particular distinction to consider is the difference between *boundary crossings* and *boundary violations* (see Gutheil & Gabbard, 1998).

Boundary Crossings

Boundary crossings are instances in which behavior deviates from the norm, possibly involving closer personal contact than is typical. These variations are not harmful and often represent normal human responses to unexpected circumstances. Personally, I have had supervisees experience a variety of significant crises and losses, from deaths of close loved ones to very serious medical complications. In such instances supervision has included discussions of sensitive family matters that I would never address otherwise. To resist doing so might have left a supervisee feeling unsupported and could have damaged the supervision relationship. Such conversations are also necessary to confirm that the supervisee is effectively coping with challenges and able to provide appropriate client- and self-care. However, I strive to respect supervisees' privacy in such instances by doing more listening and supporting than questioning or probing. I follow their lead and let them share what is comfortable.

Boundary Violations

Unlike boundary crossings, boundary violations are harmful to supervisees. These include behaviors such as sexual harassment or any other actions that might cause a supervisee to feel threatened or uncomfortable. Boundary violations involve "exploitation of the supervisee, a supervisor's loss of objectivity, disruptions of the supervisory relationship, or the reasonable foreseeability of harm" (Gottlieb et al., 2007, p. 242). Boundary violations are never acceptable.

Standard III.4.3 of NASP's (2010) *Principles for Professional Ethics* states, "school psychologists do not exploit clients, supervisees, or graduate students through professional relationships or condone these actions by their colleagues" (p. 11). This standard goes on to address the fact that supervisors should not engage in sexual relationships with supervisees. Any supervisor with the responsibility of evaluating supervisee performance—particularly those in a position to contribute to decisions regarding whether or not a supervisee will be approved for further training, independent practice, or professional milestones such as tenure or promotion—is in a position of significant power over the supervisee. This means that you need to think carefully about any situations in which your position of authority might make the supervisee feel pressured to do something or otherwise affect his or her ability to make an objective, independent decision. Supervisors are advised to consider decisions from the perspective of the supervisee (Gottlieb et al., 2007).

Specific Boundary Considerations

Both supervisors and supervisees have responsibilities when it comes to setting and observing boundaries. Doing so can help to establish and maintain a strong supervisory relationship. The following issues warrant careful attention.

Communication

It's important to think about boundaries in terms of setting limits. As a supervisor you should consider the kinds of boundaries you are comfortable having when it comes to communication outside of school hours. For example, are you willing to read emails, take phone calls, or receive texts from your supervisees when you are at home, or would you prefer to limit such interactions to emergencies only? It is your prerogative to opt for either of these approaches, but you are well advised to clearly explain your choice to supervisees at the outset of the supervision relationship.

Text messages seem to be a particularly challenging consideration in the modern world. Although quite convenient for quick communication, they can quickly become informal and personal. They also take communications off of district-issued channels and blend work life with personal life. I have had supervisors tell me they wished they had never started texting with supervisees, particularly when messages began arriving with emojis and abbreviations that reflected a lack of professionalism. One compromise seems to be to clearly discuss when texting is an acceptable means of communication (e.g., a brief message to say someone is running late to a meeting) and when it would not be (e.g., to ask a question about how to approach a case). Such guidelines may need to be reviewed and revisited periodically as the supervision relationship evolves.

Boundaries with Clients

Novice supervisees, or even veteran supervisees in need of professional development regarding ethics, may struggle to maintain appropriate boundaries with clients. In fact, a study by Fly, van Bark, Weinman, Kitchener, and Lang (1997) found that boundary violations were the second most common type of ethical transgression committed by psychology trainees (failure to maintain confidentiality was first). These concerns may be particularly salient in school psychology, where multiple relationships are common and practitioners and their student-clients can sometimes be fairly close in age. For example, my interns may be in their early to mid-twenties and less than a decade out of high school. When such trainees are assigned to secondary-level sites, there can be a relatively small age gap between interns and clients. This can be helpful for building rapport and demonstrating genuine empathy for the adolescent experience, but it requires close monitoring for boundary violations. Sexual relationships in schools might seem hard to imagine, but if you have a 24-year-old intern working with 17- or 18-year-old students, the two may seem more like peers than counselor and client.

It is advisable to have explicit (and sometimes repeated) discussions in supervision about maintaining appropriate boundaries. Keeping in mind that supervisees may be hesitant to disclose mistakes, particularly lapses in ethical judgment, it is essential to encourage open communication (Gabbard & Crisp-Han, 2010). Even if it seems like an uncomfortable discussion to have up front, it will be a lot less uncomfortable than the ones you'll need to have if a supervisee commits a serious boundary violation.

> If there is ever anything at all that you feel like concealing from me, that is probably the most important thing to discuss.
>
> *(Gabbard & Crisp-Han, 2010, p. 371)*

The Line between Supervision and Counseling

Supervisees navigating shifting roles and new work settings can be subject to significant stress and anxiety (Lamb & Swerdlik, 2003). As noted above, supervisees may also experience challenges in their personal lives that cannot be ignored. As supervisors we must navigate how to be supportive without crossing the line into serving as therapist. Supervision does share some elements with counseling, and it can absolutely be appropriate and productive to address emotional content in the context of the supervisory relationship. But as Bernard and Goodyear (2014) noted, "therapeutic interventions with supervisees should be made only in the service of helping them become more effective with clients" (p. 11). If you find yourself struggling to identify a link between your supportive interventions and ensuring quality service delivery on the part of your supervisee, or if personal circumstances are becoming a significant focus of supervision time, it is likely time to provide a referral for formal mental health support.

Changes in Professional Relationships

Often as supervisors we are meeting supervisees for the first time at the start of the supervision relationship, but this is not always the case. Relationships can change somewhat suddenly in school-based practice, particularly when administrative decisions result in new roles and responsibilities. For example, in some districts it is common for interns to be hired into open positions at the conclusion of their training. In such scenarios, supervisees can become professional colleagues overnight. As an administrative supervisor or clinical supervisor for a more advanced psychologist, you could see your relationship suddenly change if you take on a new role or get promoted—you could go from being someone's peer to becoming their boss in the course of a single school board meeting. Like multiple relationships, these changes are not inherently bad and they may even have potential positive benefits. However, they warrant examination and open discussion to prevent confusion and conflicts.

Your Most Powerful Tool: The Supervision Contract

> I definitely appreciated the importance of having the contract because it can be difficult to remember all of the details that were discussed conversationally, but having it written serves as a permanent reminder.
>
> *(E.T., first-time supervisor)*

> Using a contract is a crucial step in developing and agreeing to standards, expectations, and timelines.
>
> *(A.M., first-time supervisor)*

Why Use a Supervision Contract?

If you've never used a contract as a supervisor or been presented one as a supervisee, you're far from alone: a recent survey of early career school psychologists found that of those who had access to supervision, 76% did not have a written contract with their supervisors (Silva, Newman, Guiney, Valley-Gray, & Barrett, 2016). Personally, as a supervisee I never had any formal agreements with my supervisors and to be completely honest, it didn't really cause any problems. I have been fortunate to have a variety of wonderful supervision experiences, but since assuming a role as a university-based internship supervisor I have witnessed supervision relationships that were not so successful. In many instances, a good supervision contract likely could have prevented a range of difficulties, from confusion over roles and responsibilities to frustration about evaluation. I've become so convinced of the importance of supervision contracts that I now routinely use them when I enter into long-term supervision relationships. There are several reasons why supervision contracts are an essential tool for establishing successful supervision relationships.

Contracts Establish Clear Expectations

Anyone with experience writing behavior intervention plans understands the importance of having crystal-clear behavior expectations. We recognize that children and adolescents benefit from knowing exactly how they're expected to behave and what the consequences will be if they fail to do so; this is why a fundamental question to ask when troubleshooting classroom behavior problems is, "Are classroom rules posted?" (Witt, VanDerHeyden, & Gilbertson, 2004, p. 382). Having a supervision contract is a little bit like posting classroom rules; it helps everyone involved to know what they're expected to do. It clarifies what the supervisor is responsible for, what is expected of the supervisee, and the joint responsibilities of both members of the supervisory dyad. This is so essential that the *APA Guidelines for Clinical Supervision* specify outright, "supervisors seek to specify the responsibilities and expectations of both parties in the supervisory relationship" (APA, 2014, Domain C).

Contracts Get You Organized and Provide Structure

As Bernard and Goodyear (2014) astutely observed, "it is very difficult later in a supervisory relationship to recover from a disorganized beginning" (p. 146). As a profession in which one must be borderline obsessed with organization to be successful, school psychology should embrace the organizational potential of supervision contracts more than any other discipline! Having a supervision contract will help to keep everyone on track throughout a hectic school year, as it is a written document that you can refer back to periodically as the supervision relationship progresses. Contracts are also great for less experienced supervisors who may feel a bit unsure about how to structure an initial meeting with a new supervisee, as they provide a step-by-step agenda for what to cover (Osborn, Paez, & Carrabine, 2007).

Contracts Facilitate Informed Consent

An essential principle in the NASP (2010) *Principles for Professional Ethics* requires school psychologists to respect the autonomy and self-determination of all persons. We are taught to seek informed consent before providing services such as counseling and consultation; why should it be any different for supervision? Thomas (2007) provides a helpful overview of how the contracting process can facilitate informed consent and prevent potential problems in the supervisory relationship. See Box 2.2 for examples I have encountered in which clear contracting and informed consent could have prevented difficulties. Presenting and reviewing a supervision contract is an ideal way to ensure that supervisees understand what the supervision experience will (and will not) entail, including essential details such as how they will be evaluated, what kinds of supervision methods will be used, what to do in crisis situations, and even basic logistics like how frequently supervision will occur and how long it will last. Clarity regarding such factors is a key building block to a successfully supervisory relationship.

BOX 2.2 PREVENTING PROBLEMS THROUGH CONTRACTING

Supervision in the Real World

The following examples reflect issues that I have been confronted with in my years as a university-based internship supervisor. How might clear contracting at the start of the experience have helped to prevent them?

- Sarah regularly arrived late, left before the end of the school day, or failed to come to school at all without notifying the supervisor about the absence.
- Henry made personal phone calls throughout the school day, spending considerable time speaking to his wife and parents.
- Lisa complained about a lack of opportunity to engage in challenging learning experiences early on in the internship year.
- In the weeks following the 2016 election, Kate found herself spending considerable time on news websites during the school day.
- Supervisor Smith expressed frustration about an intern seeking guidance from other members of the psychological services team, rather than speaking to her first.

Contracts Help Build Trust and Reduce Anxiety

Perhaps the most overarching reason to use a supervision contract is that by laying an organized foundation built on well-defined and transparent expectations, you are establishing an atmosphere of trust. As was addressed in Chapter 1, trust is essential to ensure that supervisees are open to attempting challenging tasks in order to learn, willing to disclose concerns and mistakes, and secure enough to discuss sensitive topics in supervision.

Contracts can help to build trust by providing information about the supervisor's qualifications and experience, which can help a supervisee to feel comfortable that the supervisor is sufficiently competent to provide supervision and facilitate learning. A professional disclosure statement (PDS), a more one-size-fits-all rundown of training and experience that is mandated for mental health providers in some states (Bernard & Goodyear, 2014), can also serve this function. This is an additional option for supervisors to use in conjunction with a contract that is personalized to the specific conditions of a given supervision relationship. Appendix B provides an example of a PDS that I would share with a supervisee during the contracting process. A contract and/or PDS should help a supervisee realize, "This supervisor knows his or her stuff. I'm in good hands here and I will be able to learn from this person."

Trust also comes from clarity about details such as who to turn to with questions if the supervisor isn't available and what to do in crisis situations. Such details should be explicitly addressed at the beginning of the supervision relationship. Contracts can also normalize things that have the potential to cause supervisees anxiety, such as the use of different supervision methods, including live observation. If a supervisee does not realize that it's routine for a supervisor to sit in on sessions, such behavior may be interpreted as a sign of poor performance. Contracting allows the school psychology supervisor to essentially say, "I may show up now and then to observe your sessions; this is a good thing and an opportunity for quality feedback—it doesn't mean you're doing something wrong." Finally, a contract should preview what to expect regarding evaluation procedures. Clarity on these factors can reduce anticipatory anxiety about when and how to expect feedback and what will occur in the event that intervention or remediation is required. See Chapter 5 for more on supervisee evaluation.

Contracts Can Protect You

A final reason that supervisors are well advised to use contracts is as a means of risk management. Thomas (2007) presents examples of supervision relationships gone wrong, highlighting how a stronger contracting process might have prevented conflict or even avoided a lawsuit. If you have a clear, specific supervision contract, and document that you reviewed it in detail with your supervisee at the outset of the supervision relationship and periodically thereafter, ideally you will avoid major problems. However, if you do end up in a troubling situation with a supervisee, you are in a position to defend your actions if you can establish that you took steps to clarify expectations and obligations. Remember that as a supervisor you are ultimately responsible for your supervisees' actions and the welfare of the clients they see; the contracting process should make this known to the supervisee. It should also include a clear discussion of the expectation that supervisees will both adhere to the codes of ethics that govern school psychology practice and apprise you of all important facts related to their casework. Contracts can also address the kinds of procedures and policies that will apply in the event of serious difficulties or problems of professional competence (PPC). Chapter 6 will address PPC in greater detail.

What Should Be in a Supervision Contract?

Supervision contracts can get very detailed (and very long) very quickly. For a school psychology supervisor, finding a way to strike a balance between a document that is comprehensive and sufficiently detailed to be effective, yet short enough to be realistically applied can be a bit of a challenge. Maybe this is why so few school psychology supervisees reported having a contract with their supervisors (Silva et al., 2016)! Still, it is important to find a way to develop a reasonable school psychology supervision contract. Appendix C provides a sample contract that I use for supervision of doctoral students; it could be adapted to reflect the specific considerations of any particular school psychology learning experience. It also includes an accompanying handout that reviews key points for supervisees. This has been my way of navigating the line between too much and too little information; every supervisor must find what works and is comfortable.

There are several resources that address suggested components for supervision contracts and provide sample documents, but the majority of these come from the literature of other mental health fields (e.g., Bernard & Goodyear, 2014; Osborn & Davis, 1996; Sutter, McPherson, & Geeseman, 2002; Thomas, 2007). Harvey and Struzziero (2008) provide a comprehensive list of suggested contract elements that are more tailored to school psychology practice, and Simon and Swerdlik (2017) address contracting in detail as part of the Developmental component of the DEP model of school psychology supervision. I would highly recommend reviewing these sources to support the development of your own personalized supervision contract. Also, Kelly and Davis (2017) provide a sample agreement that is specific to the supervision of practicum students. But in the event that you don't quite have the time to do that research right now, the following is an overview of the kinds of details that could be included in a contract for school psychology supervision.

Logistics

Who's making this agreement? When is it in place? For how long? What is/are the goal(s) for supervision? Where will supervision occur? How often and for how long? How will it be documented? Will anyone be paid? Will telesupervision (i.e., phone or videoconference) be used at all? Some portion of the contract should address these "nuts and bolts" considerations to lay the foundation for an organized and mutually agreeable supervision experience.

Joint Responsibilities

In addition to mutually agreeing on the logistical details of the supervision relationship, both parties should concur regarding important factors like how and when to contact one another, how technology will be used, supervision methods that can be anticipated, and practicing in accordance with relevant ethics codes.

Supervisor Responsibilities

A contract should address factors such as availability outside of school hours, the limits of confidentiality of supervision sessions, and vicarious liability for client welfare. It can also be helpful to specifically state that the supervisor will seek feedback regarding the supervision experience and will be open to hearing both positive and critical comments.

Supervisee Responsibilities

Typical supervisee responsibilities include: attending supervision promptly and regularly, arriving prepared for sessions, completing tasks assigned by the supervisor to facilitate learning, keeping the supervisor apprised of all assigned cases, providing feedback to the supervisor about supervision, sharing any concerns about the supervision relationship, and—most importantly—informing the supervisor about any circumstances in which clients might be at risk of harm or any other crisis situations.

Feedback and Evaluation

The contract itself may not need to say a tremendous amount about evaluation, but the process of contracting should address this factor in detail. If you are supervising an intern, the university training program will likely present you with an evaluation form to complete at the end of each semester. Administrative supervisors also may have district-developed evaluation forms or methods they are required to use. Whatever the requirements, discussing them at the start of the supervision relationship will help to alleviate any confusion or uncertainty a supervisee might feel about how they will be assessed. Evaluation will be discussed in more detail in Chapter 5. Your contracting discussion should also address the role of feedback in supervision, such as your approach to providing feedback and the fact that it's a normal and expected part of the process that is designed to promote growth, not to highlight mistakes or weaknesses. See Chapter 4 for an example of how you could structure such a conversation.

Presenting the Supervision Contract

> To my surprise, my supervisee did not seem as uncomfortable as I thought she would (or I did) ... We read through the contract together

and talked about the different portions, changing it as we went. She often provided good ideas in terms of what we should add or change.

(L.S., intern supervisor)

Developing and having a supervision contract are very important, but the *presentation* of the contract may be the most critical part of laying the foundation for a strong supervision relationship. It might seem awkward, stilted or overly formal, but my supervision students say again and again that they're glad they did it, or, when things don't go so smoothly, that looking back they regret not engaging in a more formalized contracting process. Remember that this is similar to an informed consent discussion, so you probably already have many of the skills you need to facilitate this important conversation. But if like me you learn well by example, Box 2.3 illustrates how you might get started.

BOX 2.3 CONTRACTING CONVERSATION

Supervision in the Real World

One of the very first things I want us to work on together is talking through the fundamental details of this supervision relationship to make sure we're both clear on who is responsible for what. This contract for supervision includes a lot of important information. Some of it may seem obvious, but by laying it all out like this, we can both be sure that we understand what will be required and involved in this experience. I want us to have a chance to go through each point, step by step, so that we can make sure we agree to these terms and so that you can ask any questions you have about anything that is in here. We can also make changes or add things in if we think of them along the way. If we both agree we will sign the contract and then I will give you a copy for your files. Does that sound ok? Great. So first . . .

Getting to Know You: Taking Time to Get Started

I wish that I had more time to develop a relationship with [the supervisee] in the beginning of the experience because I think [she] would have been less anxious about expressing her perceived weaknesses and may have been more forthcoming in sharing her anxieties if she had been more comfortable with me. I think that lack of time was the biggest challenge within the context of the relationship.

(Anonymous supervision student)

As important as it is to set and observe boundaries and to lay an organized foundation by using documents like contracts and PDSs, we should not lose sight of the fact that supervision is a relationship, and relationships take time to develop. Just like a therapy or counseling relationship, a supervision relationship will likely proceed through some predictable phases as you and your supervisee become acquainted, particularly if you have never met one another before. And like therapy clients, different supervisees will bring different personalities and levels of extroversion to supervision; this process may move quickly or slowly depending on such factors and your own personality and style as a supervisor. No matter how these variables present themselves, taking time to get to know one another, including some professionally appropriate self-disclosure about personal interests and basic background, is an essential part of getting the supervision relationship off to a strong start. Remember to find time for those conversations early on and be careful not to launch into work from the first moment.

Also remember that for a supervisee who is new to a building or a district, there are many logistics to understand. It may sound obvious, but your supervisee may need a lot of basic information from you about how to navigate the site. Be sure to discuss factors like where to park (and where *not* to park!), how to obtain appropriate identification, building sign-in procedures, expected arrival time, which bathrooms to use or not use, how to work the copy machine, and any other details that might help a new team member feel comfortable. Introduce your supervisee to as many teachers, administrators, and staff members as possible—particularly the front office staff and related service providers. Giving your supervisee documents like a faculty and staff list, a building map, and a copy of the master schedule is always a good idea. And don't forget the student, parent, and faculty handbooks! By meeting some of these most basic of your supervisee's needs you will help to establish a sense of security and likely relieve some of the anxiety that comes with the transition to a new site and role.

My supervision students have told me time and again that, looking back on their experiences as first-time supervisors, they wish they had slowed things down and taken more time at the outset to just get to know their supervisees. It can be hard in the busy world of schools, even at the start of the year, to scale back the pace and relax, but it can be a worthwhile investment. The next chapter will address supervision planning, and the importance of understanding a supervisee's areas of strength and weakness in order to do so effectively. By taking time to get comfortable, you may find yourself better able to understand your supervisee's needs and therefore be ready to plan a high-quality supervision experience.

Supervisor's Summary

- A strong and trusting working relationship is central to effective supervision.
- Being attuned to potential multiple relationships and ensuring that they don't compromise objectivity or present conflicts of interest is a key ethical obligation for supervisors.

- Supervisors must respect boundaries and the inherent power imbalance in the supervision relationship and never put a supervisee in a position to feel pressured, exploited, or otherwise uncomfortable.
- It is appropriate to set your own boundaries as a supervisor; just be sure to communicate them clearly to supervisees.
- Contracts are a key tool for organizing the supervision experience and should be used to establish clear expectations, facilitate informed consent, and reduce supervisee anxiety. Use of a contract can also protect you as a supervisor if problems arise.
- Supervision contracts should address the "nuts and bolts" of how supervision will happen, along with the respective responsibilities of supervisors and supervisees. How feedback will be provided and how performance will be evaluated are additional key components of a supervision contract.
- Investing time in getting to know a supervisee at the start of the experience is worthwhile for building trust and informing subsequent planning and goal setting.

FINAL REFLECTIONS

Here are some questions to think about as you prepare to embark upon your next supervision relationship:

- How have your previous experiences as a supervisee (and as a supervisor, if applicable) affected your views regarding supervision relationships?
- How will you set limits and boundaries as a supervisor? What, if anything, might be challenging about doing so?
- What do you see as the most important factors to discuss during the initial stages of the supervision relationship? Why?

References

American Psychological Association. (2014). *Guidelines for clinical supervision in health service psychology*. Washington, DC: Author. Retrieved from http://apa.org/about/policy/guidelines-supervision.

American Psychological Association. (2017). *Ethical principles of psychologists and code of conduct*. Washington, DC: Author. Retrieved from www.apa.org/ethics/code/ethics-code-2017.pdf.

Bernard, J. M., & Goodyear, R. K. (2014). *Fundamentals of clinical supervision* (5th ed.). Upper Saddle River, NJ: Pearson.

Fly, B. J., van Bark, W. P., Weinman, L., Kitchener, K. S., & Lang, P. R. (1997). Ethical transgressions of psychology graduate students: Critical incidents with implications for training. *Professional Psychology: Research and Practice, 28*(5), 492–495. doi:10.1037/0735-7028.28.5.492.

Gabbard, G. O., & Crisp-Han, H. (2010). Teaching professional boundaries to psychiatric residents. *Academic Psychiatry, 34*(5), 369–372. doi:10.1176/appi.ap.34.5.369.

Gottlieb, M. C., Robinson, K., & Younggren, J. N. (2007). Multiple relationships in supervision: Guidance for administrators, supervisors, and students. *Professional Psychology: Research and Practice, 38*(3), 241–247. doi:10.1037/0735-7028.38.3.241.

Gutheil, T. G., & Gabbard, G. O. (1998). Misuses and misunderstandings of boundary theory in clinical and regulatory settings. *American Journal of Psychiatry, 155*(3), 409–414. doi:10.1176/foc.1.4.415.

Harvey, V. S., & Struzziero, J. A. (Eds.). (2008). *Professional development and supervision of school psychologists: From intern to expert* (2nd ed.). Bethesda, MD: National Association of School Psychologists.

Kelly, K. K., & Davis, S. D. (2017). *Supervising the school psychology practicum: A guide for field and university supervisors.* New York: Springer.

Ladany, N., Mori, Y., & Mehr, K. E. (2013). Effective and ineffective supervision. *The Counseling Psychologist, 41*(1), 28–47. doi:10.1177/0011000012442648.

Lamb, D. H., & Swerdlik, M. E. (2003). Identifying and responding to problematic school psychology supervisees: The evaluation process and issues of impairment. *The Clinical Supervisor, 22*(1), 87–110.

National Association of School Psychologists. (2010). *Principles for professional ethics.* Bethesda, MD: Author.

Osborn, C. J., & Davis, T. E. (1996). The supervision contract. Making it perfectly clear. *Clinical Supervisor, 14*, 121–134.

Osborn, C. J., Paez, S. B., & Carrabine, C. L. (2007). Reflections on shared practices in a supervisory lineage. *The Clinical Supervisor, 26*(1–2), 119–139. doi:10.1300/J001v26n01_09.

Silva, A. E., Newman, D. S., Guiney, M. C., Valley-Gray, S., & Barrett, C. A. (2016). Supervision and mentoring for early career school psychologists: Availability, access, structure, and implications. *Psychology in the Schools, 53*(5), 502–516. doi:10.1002/pits.21921.

Simon, D. J., & Swerdlik, M. E. (2017). *Supervision in school psychology: The developmental, ecological, problem-solving model.* New York: Routledge.

Sutter, E., McPherson, R. H., & Geeseman, R. (2002). Contracting for supervision. *Professional Psychology: Research and Practice, 33*, 495–498. doi:10.1037//0735-7028.33.5.495.

Thomas, J. T. (2007). Informed consent through contracting for supervision: Minimizing risks, enhancing benefits. *Professional Psychology: Research and Practice, 38*(3), 221–231. doi:10.1037/0735-7028.38.3.221.

Witt, J., VanDerHeyden, A., & Gilbertson, D. (2004). Troubleshooting behavioral interventions: A systematic process for finding and eliminating problems. *School Psychology Review, 33*(3), 363–383.

Worthen, V., & McNeill, B. W. (1996). A phenomenological investigation of "good" supervision events. *Journal of Counseling Psychology, 43*(1), 25–34.

3

SUPERVISION PLANNING

I think that pre-planning ... and making your expectations of the supervisee clear are essential components of a smooth and productive learning experience for both members in the supervision partnership.

(N.T., first-time supervisor)

An error that I made was overlooking a discussion about goals early on in the supervision relationship. I asked about goals eventually, but realized that I should have addressed goals during one of the first meetings. If I had done this, we could have incorporated goal attainment into our conversations each time we met.

(A.B., first-time supervisor)

If you are adept at writing individualized education plans (IEPs), good news: you will probably be great at supervision planning! This chapter will focus on how you and your supervisees can use supervision plans to organize and monitor the overall supervision experience. As with contracts, there are helpful resources out there that address supervision planning in greater detail than there is room or time for here. One outstanding one, particularly if you are supervising school psychology interns, is Daniel Newman's (2013) *Demystifying the School Psychology Internship: A Dynamic Guide for Interns and Supervisors*, which has an entire chapter devoted to this subject. Simon and Swerdlik's (2017) *Supervision in School Psychology: The Developmental, Ecological, Problem-solving Model* also includes a sample supervision plan as an appendix.

This chapter will explain what a supervision plan is and why it can be helpful to use one. It will also explain how to use assessment to help set the goals included in the supervision plan (a sample self-assessment is provided as Appendix D) and discuss the importance of reviewing the plan regularly to monitor progress and lay the foundation for evaluation of supervisee performance. Examples of supervision plans are included in the Appendices, including one that could be used for the supervision of interns (Appendix E) and one for credentialed school psychologists (Appendix F).

What Is a Supervision Plan?

A supervision plan is a document that identifies training goals and specifies experiences that the supervisee will engage in to achieve them. Newman (2013) stated that effective supervision plans are developed collaboratively by the supervisor and supervisee, include plans for both formative (ongoing) and summative (end-of-experience) evaluation, designate a breadth of training experiences designed to build school psychology knowledge and skills, and identify one or more areas of professional interest to build depth of specialized knowledge. As opposed to a plan for an individual supervision session, what we're talking about here is an overarching document that helps to direct the entire supervision experience. It's a big-picture document that should be reviewed regularly and revised as things proceed.

Why Use a Supervision Plan?

If the supervision contract is your most powerful tool for establishing a strong supervision relationship, then the supervision plan is your most powerful tool for keeping it focused and productive. Let's examine why using a supervision plan will help you be a more effective supervisor.

A Plan Helps Clarify Expectations

Supervisees report that failure to clarify expectations is a characteristic of "lousy" supervision (Magnuson, Wilcoxon, & Norem, 2000). Much like the supervision contract, the supervision plan promotes open communication about what can be expected of the supervision experience. With a plan, supervisors know what kinds of training experiences supervisees need and want and supervisees know what they can expect to get out of the training or professional development experience. A plan is also very helpful when things get busy; consulting the plan can get things back on track if the school year is flying by and needed or desired training experiences aren't happening.

A Plan Helps Prioritize Needs

Particularly for less-experienced supervisees, there is likely to be a wide range of goals and requirements to be addressed during a year-long or semester-long training experience. Areas of need will also vary based on individual supervisee differences and variability across training programs; supervisees will arrive with strengths and weaknesses in different areas, and a supervision plan should be specifically designed to address these factors. For example, a supervisee with a background in counseling may need to focus more on developing knowledge of school functioning and academic interventions than skills in school-based mental health, whereas a school psychologist with prior teaching experience may have advanced knowledge of classroom management and instruction but lack experience with crisis prevention and intervention.

Whether you're supervising a first-year practicum student or a veteran school psychologist looking to hone skills, agreeing upon a plan that lays out a small number of top priorities can help to focus supervision and make it productive. Newman (2013) recommends identifying three broad goals that are revisited and revised throughout the training experience to reflect the changes in needs and priorities that come with supervisee development.

A Plan Sets the Stage for Feedback and Evaluation

One of your most important responsibilities as a supervisor is to evaluate supervisee performance (see Chapter 5 for more on this). Effective evaluation is based on clear goals paired with regular feedback (Lehrman-Waterman & Ladany, 2001). By working collaboratively with supervisees to develop supervision plans supervisors identify areas in need of further development and preview the domains and behaviors that will be assessed during the supervision experience. With this supervisees can better anticipate how they will be evaluated, which can alleviate anxiety and prevent confusion.

For my students, their supervision plans are tied directly to the 10 domains of school psychology practice identified in the NASP (2010a) Practice Model, as are their summative evaluations at the end of each semester of internship. With knowledge of the summative evaluation tool, supervisees and their supervisors can say,

> Ok, by the end of the year you need to demonstrate competence in all these areas; what specific activities do you need to engage in and what kind of resources do you need access to in order to make them happen?

Where to Begin? Using Assessment to Inform Goal Setting

Supervisees have identified the failure to assess initial skill levels as a hallmark of poor supervisors (Magnuson et al., 2000). Beginning with assessment eliminates the possibility of over or underestimating a supervisee's level of knowledge or skill, either of which could lead to anxiety, frustration, and other problems. One of the first tasks my supervisees undertake is a self-assessment. The format and extent of this evaluation vary depending on the nature of the experience; students embarking upon their year-long internships conduct a broader and more detailed reflection (see Appendix D) than my supervisees who are completing a targeted counseling or assessment practicum. But either way, it helps me organize my approach as a supervisor when I am armed with a sense of my supervisee's areas of strength and weakness.

What to Assess

School psychologists at all levels of experience need to have *knowledge* of content and concepts across the domains of school psychology practice, as well as the *skills* to put this information to work supporting children, families, and schools. They also need to possess strong *professional work characteristics*, or the types of behaviors that foster effective work in schools. As a supervisor, gathering data about each of these three domains can be extremely helpful for supervision planning.

Knowledge

Particularly if you supervise school psychologists with a range of levels of experience, you may find substantial variability in how much your supervisees know about everything: from what a school psychologist really does, to theories or models that guide practice. For example, each year I require our first-year graduate students to interview a practicing school psychologist. They routinely report learning a tremendous amount about the role of a school psychologist that they had not been aware of previously. On the other hand, I also teach advanced doctoral students who are practicing school psychologists with a much more extensive understanding of the field, but even their knowledge can vary widely. Some have jobs that consist entirely of counseling; they know a tremendous amount about topics such as child and adolescent mental health or cognitive behavioral therapy, but not as much about assessment. Others are well trained in bilingual assessment but have limited awareness of models of school-based consultation. Whether due to prior experience, variation in training program approaches, or simple individual differences in learning, no two supervisees will know all the same things. Assessing knowledge is the first step in planning a supervision experience that will build on existing expertise and fill gaps.

Skills

Just as supervisee knowledge can vary tremendously, the ability to apply knowledge to deliver quality school psychology services is also likely to be different for each individual you supervise. Like knowledge, variation here can result from differences in previous opportunities to build and practice skills, training program variability, or even individual differences in personality. Take, for example, rapport building. Some supervisees seem naturally able to make students of all ages feel comfortable from the moment they enter the office. Others might do very well with preschool students but struggle to connect with adolescents (or vice versa). Even those who are great with kids may have less well-developed skills when it comes to collaborating with teachers or parents. There's really no one-size-fits-all when it comes to the wide range of skills that are needed to be an effective school psychologist.

Knowing models and theories is necessary but not sufficient for a successful career as a school psychologist: high-quality supervision is planned in such a way that supervisees get many opportunities to practice and improve upon the skills needed to apply knowledge. What to assess will vary depending on the nature of the supervision experience: for an intern you may need to understand supervisee skills across the 10 domains of the NASP (2010a) Practice Model; for a student completing a targeted practicum (e.g., assessment, consultation, counseling) or a more advanced supervisee seeking to strengthen performance in a specific domain, your assessment will focus primarily on skills related to the domain(s) being supervised.

Professional Work Characteristics

The NASP (2010b, 2010c) *Standards* delineate a number of personal qualities and behaviors that are expected of school psychologists. They include respect for diversity and social justice, communication skills, effective interpersonal skills, responsibility, adaptability, initiative, dependability, ethical responsibility, and skills for using technology. It is as important to assess in these domains as it is to evaluate supervisees' knowledge and skills and to incorporate development of professional work characteristics into a strong supervision plan. The self-assessment tool presented in Appendix D includes a variety of items related to these factors that a supervisor could use to collect both baseline and ongoing progress-monitoring data regarding these important behaviors.

Gathering Data

Now you know what to assess as you begin to plan your supervision experience, but the better question may be, "*how* can I assess knowledge, skills, and professional work characteristics?" As school psychologists we are great data gatherers, so you likely already possess a strong skill set to help you with this process. For example, you may use the RIOT approach (review records, interview, observe, test) to organize your approach to assessment. Let's consider how RIOT might apply to planning supervision see Table 3.1 for a summary).

Review of Records

If you were evaluating a student you would probably start by looking at past report cards, test scores, work samples, or other existing materials that provide background information about knowledge and skills. Depending on the nature of the supervision experience (e.g., an internship with a competitive application process), you may have access to records such as graduate school transcripts and results from standardized tests of knowledge, like the Praxis exam. However, at a minimum you can start by

TABLE 3.1 Using RIOT to Plan Supervision

Review	• Request to see or hear summaries of previous supervisors' evaluations
	• Review work samples such as evaluation reports, FBAs, and BIPs
	• For interns and practicum students, consult university-based supervisor or other graduate school faculty
Interview	• Ask about previous feedback the supervisee has received
	• Talk to prior supervisors
	• Discuss goals
Observe	• Role play scenarios
	• Have supervisee administer assessments to you
	• Watch interactions with teachers, administrators and parents
	• Sit in on sessions with clients
Test	• Use supervisee self-assessment of knowledge, skills, and professional work characteristics to gather baseline data

requesting copies of summative evaluation forms completed by previous supervisors, as this information could be very helpful for understanding prior supervision experiences and planning current ones. Work samples such as reports of psychological or behavioral assessments can also provide insight into a supervisee's level of skill and experience and help set the stage for planning and goal setting.

Interview

An essential step in the supervision planning process is talking with your supervisee about perceived areas of strength and weakness, prior experiences, and goals for development. Handout 3.1 at the end of this chapter provides ideas for structuring such a conversation.

A formalized self-assessment process can be extremely valuable for supervision planning; this is discussed in more detail below. But starting out with a conversation about perceived strengths and weaknesses and goals for development can get the ball rolling. Of course, like all self-reports, what supervisees share with you is subjective. This does not always mean they overemphasize strengths and minimize weaknesses; in fact, sometimes strong supervisees are blind to areas of strength because they seem to come naturally and without much noticeable effort (Wade & Jones, 2015). With this in mind, it can be helpful to speak with previous supervisors and/or training program faculty (with the supervisee's permission, of course) to get additional perspectives on areas of strength and weakness to guide supervision planning. When possible, gathering data from recipients of the supervisee's services (e.g., ratings from consultees or counseling clients) can also be informative (Newman, 2013), though these still come with the risk of subjectivity, particularly when consultees or clients know they are providing feedback that supervisors are likely to use to evaluate supervisee performance.

Observe

Observation is a great way to assess supervisee skills and professional work characteristics as you work on planning the supervision experience. For example, many field-based internship supervisors who work with my students start the year by watching supervisees administer cognitive assessment measures (e.g., they have the supervisee "test" the supervisor). This provides insight into administration skills that can inform first steps in assessment experiences for the year. For more advanced supervisees looking to hone existing skills, an experienced supervisor might sit in on a counseling or consultation session to get a sense of the supervisee's level of competence. Observation is an invaluable technique throughout the supervision experience, as it provides opportunities for objective feedback based on actual things that the supervisee said or did. Beginning the supervision experience with live observations sets a tone that observation is a normal and expected part of supervision that will occur regularly.

Test: Supervisee Self-Assessment

The testing component of RIOT may not be the most applicable to supervision planning, but it has its place. There is plenty of evaluation incorporated into effective supervision (this will be discussed in more detail in Chapter 5), but the initial stages of the supervision are about using planning to lay the foundation for eventual evaluation.

Newman (2013) provides several helpful suggestions for promoting self-reflection as part of the supervision planning process for interns. This approach lays the groundwork for self-reflection and professional development planning throughout the school psychologist's career. Newman recommends that supervisees reflect on their perceived competence across the NASP (2010c) domains of graduate education before identifying a short list of broad goals for the supervision experience. To mitigate the inherent subjectivity of self-evaluations, Newman suggests that supervisees strive to incorporate feedback provided by faculty, previous supervisors, peers, and recipients of school psychology services as part of the self-assessment process. Again, there is a copy of a self-assessment document I use with my interns in Appendix D.

For credentialed practitioners, Williams and Monahon (2014) present a five-step self-evaluation process that encourages school psychologists to (a) complete a comprehensive assessment of knowledge, skills, and professional work characteristics based on the ten domains of the NASP (2010a) Practice Model, (b) reflect upon and incorporate student outcome data and feedback from previous supervisor evaluations, (c) set objectives for improved performance, (d) engage in professional development to target identified areas of need, and (e) re-assess using the same framework to measure progress. Their chapter includes a comprehensive framework for self-assessment that could be helpful for planning and guiding supervision for supervisees at all levels of development.

A specific tool that has the potential to guide self-assessment for both school psychology trainees and practitioners is the NASP (n.d.) Self-Assessment Checklist for School Psychologists (available at http://apps.nasponline.org/standards-and-certification/survey/Survey_Page.aspx?app=10781&page=1). This online survey is organized around the ten domains of the NASP (2010a) Practice Model and asks respondents to evaluate both how much specific activities that reflect Practice Model domains describe their current work, and how important they perceive each activity to be for their overall effectiveness. Interestingly, the tool can be customized to guide self-assessments for school psychology supervisors and administrators, and even graduate educators.

What Should Be in a Supervision Plan?

Not unlike a good IEP, a solid supervision plan should revolve around long-term goals for growth and short-term objectives that can be used to monitor and document progress. There are a variety of ways to organize supervision plans with different degrees of detail. Personally, I have tried to keep the plan format relatively simple for my students (see Appendix E), and this has generally been successful. Even with just three or four primary goals and a limited number of objectives for each of the 10 domains of the NASP (2010a) Practice Model, these training plans can become overwhelming pretty quickly for my more detail-oriented or overachieving interns. When they are overly burdensome neither supervisees nor supervisors can realistically address every item, which might increase the likelihood that the plan is set aside and left unused. So, like supervision contracts, the key to crafting a useful plan is finding a balance between being sufficiently detailed to be meaningful but not so oversimplified as to be pointless.

Goals and Objectives

The most fundamental component of a good supervision plan is a set of goals and objectives that stem directly from the assessment data you collected. As a school psychologist you probably have a lot of experience with goal setting; this will be very helpful to your work as a supervisor! For example, you may already know about working with teachers or service providers to craft "SMART" goals for students. There are a variety of similar words used for the components of SMART goals, but they generally refer to goals that are *specific, measurable, attainable, realistic,* and *time-bound* (Harvey, Struzziero, & Desai, 2014).

SMART goals can help keep you and your supervisee accountable. Because they are usually quite clear and leave little room for interpretation, they serve as a good way to check on whether your supervisee is making progress. As you work with your supervisee to develop a supervision plan with specific, measurable goals, you might even discuss how setting SMART goals for students is often an important part of the work of a school psychologist. Table 3.2 provides some examples and non-examples of SMART goals to give an idea of how this idea might be applied to supervision planning.

There's no requirement that supervision goals be SMART goals. However, the idea of making goals specific rather than generic does have support in the supervision literature. Lehrman-Waterman and Ladany (2001) summarized recommendations for effective goal setting, highlighting that goals should be:

- Specific
- Clearly worded
- Attainable (in terms of ability, opportunity, and available resources)
- Modifiable
- Measurable
- Mutually agreed upon

Personally, I tend to let my supervisees stick to fairly broad and sometimes generic goals, but I expect to see specific objectives that we can attack to make progress towards them. Whether you call them goals, objectives, targets, or anything else you like, it's important to *specify* the things you and the supervisee are going to do and be responsible for, to ensure there are sufficient opportunities to make progress and gather data to provide meaningful feedback. A goal like, "I will improve my counseling skills" is going to be more difficult to evaluate than, "I will effectively apply cognitive behavioral therapy techniques in at least one counseling case."

TABLE 3.2 SMART Goal Examples

Not-So-SMART Goal	SMART Goal
I will improve my assessment skills.	By November 1st I will hand-score a WISC–V protocol without making errors.
I will be more organized.	By the last school day of each month I will complete a spreadsheet listing all upcoming cases and due dates for reports within the following two months.
I will engage in ethical practice.	Before the end of December I will apply (in writing) an ethical problem-solving model to make a challenging decision.
I will collaborate more frequently with parents.	By April 1st I will present a workshop for parents on strategies for supporting homework completion.

University/State/District Requirements

In addition to specific, measurable, attainable goals and objectives, a good supervision plan must account of any required experiences or components that are necessary to meet training program guidelines, state credentialing or licensure mandates, or school district policies related to tenure or promotion. If you are supervising an intern from a state- or NASP-approved training program you might be provided with a training plan template to complete with your supervisee (as is the case with field supervisors for my interns). In contrast, if you are supervising certified school psychologists completing post-doctorate licensure hours, they should be familiar with licensure requirements for all states in which they plan to pursue licensure so you can plan training experiences that will foster a successful application. For example, if candidates are expected to complete a high number of direct client contact hours in a particular state, it is important to craft a supervision plan that provides for a sufficient amount of such experience (Dittmann, 2004).

Utilizing the Supervision Plan

Review Regularly

Another way a supervision plan is like an IEP is that it should be consulted frequently to guide learning activities and monitor progress towards goals. The greatest supervision plan in the world is of no use to anyone if it is shoved in a drawer in September and only dusted off in June just in time for a final performance evaluation. Newman (2013) calls this "internship plan hibernation" (p. 20). Ideally, consulting the supervision plan should be a regular feature of supervision. The plan should be a "living document" (Newman, 2013, p. 23), that is updated periodically to reflect changes in supervisee skills and emerging training needs.

Collaborate with Colleagues

In Chapter 1 we established the importance of being competent as a supervisor, including having sufficient competence in a particular area of practice to be able to effectively supervise in that domain. As school psychologists we have a wide range of roles and responsibilities and we are all more skilled in some domains than others. If you encounter a supervisee who needs or desires supervision in an area that is not one of extensive expertise for you, don't hesitate to call upon additional resources to support implementation of the plan. For example, if you have a supervisee looking to gain experience with bilingual assessment and you have a bilingual psychologist in your district, why not arrange for the supervisee to observe your colleague and possibly even complete a case under his or her supervision? Or perhaps your school counselor runs a group with a focus of interest to your supervisee and would be willing to work with your supervisee as a co-leader. The point is: although you as the identified supervisor retain ultimate responsibility for your supervisee and the clients he or she serves, you are not barred from collaborating with others at your school site to provide the experiences needed to meet the goals set forth in the supervision plan.

Supervisor's Summary

- A supervision plan lays out goals for the supervision experience along with the learning activities that need to occur in order to progress towards achieving them.
- A supervision plan sets the stage for evaluation.
- Supervisees and supervisors work together collaboratively to develop the supervision plan.
- Planning should begin with assessment of supervisee knowledge and skills across the domains of school psychology practice that are the focus of the supervision experience. Professional work characteristics should be assessed as well.
- Assessment can involve review of records, interviews with the supervisee and previous supervisors, observation of supervisee skills, and supervisee self-assessment.
- The supervision plan should account for any experiences that are required for training program completion, state or national certification or licensure, or tenure/promotion.
- Collaborate with colleagues to provide training experiences that you are not able to offer.
- The supervision plan should be reviewed and revised regularly.

FINAL REFLECTIONS

- How important do you think it is to use a supervision plan? Do you like the idea of having a structure to follow, or would you prefer to let the supervision experience unfold more organically?
- What level of detail in a plan feels right for you?
- Knowing how busy a school year gets, what will you do to ensure that you and your supervisee find time to regularly review your supervision plan?
- Thinking about your strengths, experience, and skill set, who might you need to collaborate with to provide a well-rounded supervision experience?

References

Dittmann, M. (2004). What you need to know to get licensed: Experts offer a lesson on how to become a licensed psychologist. *gradPSYCH Magazine*, *2*(1). Retrieved from www.apa.org/gradpsych/2004/01/get-licensed.aspx.

Harvey, V. S., Struzziero, J. A., & Desai, S. (2014). Best practices in supervision and mentoring of school psychologists. In: P. L. Harrison & A. Thomas. (Eds.), *Best practices in school psychology: Foundations* (pp. 567–580). Bethesda, MD: National Association of School Psychologists.

Lehrman-Waterman, D., & Ladany, N. (2001). Development and validation of the evaluation process within supervision inventory. *Journal of Counseling Psychology*, *48*(2), pp. 168–177. doi: 10.1037//0022-0167.48.2.168.

Magnuson, S., Wilcoxon, S. A., & Norem, K. (2000). A profile of lousy supervision: Experienced counselors' perspectives. *Counselor Education and Supervision, 39*, pp. 189–202.

National Association of School Psychologists. (2010a). *Model for comprehensive and integrated school psychological services*. Bethesda, MD: Author.

National Association of School Psychologists. (2010b). *Standards for credentialing of school psychologists*. Bethesda, MD: Author.

National Association of School Psychologists. (2010c). *Standards for graduate preparation of school psychologists*. Bethesda, MD: Author.

Newman, D. S. (2013). *Demystifying the school psychology internship: A dynamic guide for interns and supervisors*. New York: Routledge.

Simon, D. J., & Swerdlik, M. E. (2017). *Supervision in school psychology: The developmental, ecological, problem-solving model*. New York: Routledge.

Wade, J. C., & Jones, J. E. (2015). *Strength-based clinical supervision: A positive psychology approach to clinical training*. New York: Springer.

Williams, B., & Monahon, L. W. (2014). Best practices in school psychologists' self-evaluation and documenting effectiveness. In: P. L. Harrison & A. Thomas. (Eds.), *Best practices in school psychology: Foundations* (pp. 581–598). Bethesda, MD: National Association of School Psychologists.

HANDOUT 3.1 SUPERVISION PLANNING INTERVIEW

As we work together to plan out a supervision experience that is going to help you really learn and grow, it would be helpful to me to learn more about your strengths, needs, and goals. So tell me . . .

What do you see as your areas of greatest strength as a school psychologist or school psychologist in training? What do you feel most comfortable doing?

What areas are most in need of development? What aspects of the job challenge you the most?

Tell me about the feedback you've received from previous supervisors and/or program faculty. What have they said you do well? What has been recommended for further development?

Have you ever been provided with any kind of remediation plans or assignments to address specific areas of difficulty? If so, was the experience helpful? Why or why not?

How would you rate your organization and time management skills?

Do you think you have strong communication skills? How confident do you feel about presenting your work to others (e.g., parents)?

An important part of the work of a school psychologist, and something we'll address regularly in supervision, is culturally responsive practice. How much experience have you had working with a diverse range of clients and families? What would help you enhance your skills in this area?

Based on prior feedback and your perceptions of your strengths and weaknesses, what do you think are the most important areas to focus on during this supervision experience?

Navigating the Supervision Experience

4

COMMUNICATING FEEDBACK

This chapter will address the importance of providing effective feedback to supervisees and presents some strategies for doing so. It should be helpful to both clinical and administrative supervisors, given that providing feedback to support supervisee skill development is an essential feature of both types of supervision.

What's the Difference between *Feedback* and *Evaluation*?

The terms *feedback* and *evaluation* are sometimes used interchangeably, but they're actually two different concepts. Evaluation involves the process of assessing long-term performance based on set external criteria, while feedback is about giving supervisees information that will help them improve their skills compared to their current level of performance (Wade & Jones, 2015). Hoffman, Hill, Holmes, and Freitas (2005) defined feedback as, "information that supervisors communicate to their supervisees about aspects of their skills, attitudes, behavior, and appearance that may influence their performance with clients or affect the supervisory relationship" (p. 3). So we're talking about the kind of constructive criticism, corrections, and encouragement that effective supervisors give supervisees on a regular basis to support learning and the ongoing improvement of skills.

The Importance of Feedback

Feedback is essential to promoting learning and growth (Wade & Jones, 2015). It can also differentiate effective from ineffective supervisors: Magnuson, Wilcoxon, and Norem (2000) found that supervisees cited vague, global, and abstract feedback as characteristic of poor supervision, and trainees have repeatedly endorsed that effective supervisors provide frequent and balanced feedback

(Chur-Hansen & McLean, 2006; Ladany, Mori, & Mehr, 2013). One study found that 83% of supervisees felt feedback from field supervisors had a positive effect on their learning (Abbott & Lyter, 1998). As Ende (1983) observed, "without feedback, mistakes go uncorrected, good performance is not reinforced, and clinical competence is achieved empirically or not at all" (p. 778).

Providing feedback is also an important part of maintaining a positive supervision relationship. For one thing, supervisees can interpret a lack of supervisor feedback as a lack of caring (Wade & Jones, 2015). As Bernard and Goodyear (2014) point out, "you cannot *not* communicate" (p. 234) so if you fail to give feedback supervisees will make meaning from your silence. They may think you're not willing to take the time to share feedback, or assume that they're doing fine. You might think supervisees would prefer not to hear negative feedback, but research has shown that, particularly for relatively novice supervisees, clear structure and direction are preferred (Lazar & Eisikovits, 1997). Similarly, Lehrman-Waterman and Ladany (2001) found that goal setting and feedback strengthen supervisory relationships. But providing feedback is about more than just preserving a strong working relationship; it is also an ethical imperative. The APA (2017) code of ethics specifically states, "psychologists establish a timely and specific process for providing feedback to students and supervisees" (p. 10). So like it or not, as a supervisor you need to be ready to provide frequent feedback.

How Do You Feel about Giving Feedback?

> At first, I was extremely hesitant to give her constructive feedback. I was nervous it would ruin our relationship. Since then, I have grown and understand the importance of moving through the feedback process, as well as, how [the supervisee] takes my feedback and uses it to better her practices.
>
> *(S. G., practicum supervisor)*

It's clear that providing quality feedback is an important responsibility for supervisors. Unfortunately, it is not uncommon for supervisors to avoid giving feedback: one study found that 98% of supervisors surveyed acknowledged withholding feedback from supervisees (Ladany & Melincoff, 1999). Why would supervisors refrain from sharing information that might help supervisees improve their skills? For one thing, unpleasant past personal experiences giving or receiving feedback might make a supervisor uncomfortable with this aspect of their role (Ende, 1983). Other reasons include feeling that it's not the supervisor's place to give the feedback, reluctance to appear critical of the supervisee, concern that the feedback might damage the supervision relationship, fear of potential litigation, and a simple lack of time to provide feedback (Chur-Hansen & McLean, 2006). Supervisors have also reported withholding feedback from supervisees due to concerns about a negative reaction (Ladany & Melincoff, 1999). But ironically, failing to provide criticism can actually breed anxiety in supervisees, as it can force them to try and derive their own feedback from available cues. As Ende (1983) put it, "a raised eyebrow then implies, 'I'm not performing up to standards'" (p. 778).

There may be legitimate reasons to not share your every impression with a supervisee, such as respect for the boundary between supervision and therapy or an expectation that as training progresses, the supervisee will soon independently discover what you are observing (Ladany & Melincoff, 1999). For example, you may find that a supervisee is overly focused on small details in a counseling case, but realize that with time it will become easier to focus on the big picture. Pointing this out may not be essential. But when you find yourself biting your tongue, you need to honestly assess whether you're holding back for a legitimate training reason or to avoid a potentially uncomfortable situation.

It's important to consider your own feelings about feedback as you work to use it effectively to support your supervisees. Simon and Swerdlik (2017) offer a process activity to help build self-awareness; it encourages supervisors to reflect on their own experiences receiving both positive and negative feedback and the factors that affected how each type of feedback was received. The "Final Reflections" section of this chapter also presents some questions to consider regarding your approach to providing feedback.

Characteristics of Effective Feedback

Several factors come up time and again in the literature on feedback. For example, psychology supervisees have characterized quality feedback as balanced, accurate, immediate, frequent, clear, specific, based on direct observation, and accompanied by suggestions for improvement (Heckman-Stone, 2003). And medical students have expressed similar preferences, indicating that their "good" supervisors were those who provided frequent, balanced feedback (Chur-Hansen & McLean, 2006).

This means you should aim to provide feedback that is:

- **Balanced**: highlight positive behaviors and provide constructive criticism.
- **Immediate**: feedback should occur as soon as possible after observation.
- **Goal-oriented**: link feedback to goals and provide suggestions for improvement.
- **Frequent**: feedback should be a regular feature of supervision.
- **Objective**: stick to observed behaviors and avoid subjective judgments.
- **Reciprocal**: the supervisee should provide you with feedback too!

Box 4.1 provides an example of how real-world feedback could incorporate some of these features. Imagine that your supervisee, Fiona, just presented evaluation results to members of the multidisciplinary team at a special education eligibility meeting. This is only the second time Fiona has done this; the first time she was quite nervous, particularly about discussing cognitive and academic weaknesses with a group that included the child's parents. This time she seemed more relaxed, but still stumbled over some of her words and used several psychological terms without explaining what they meant. How could you encourage Fiona, but also help her continue to improve?

BOX 4.1 SAMPLE OF EFFECTIVE FEEDBACK

Supervision in the Real World

"Ok, Fiona, let's talk about this morning's meeting. First things first, I want to hear *your* impressions about how it went . . ."

"Overall, you definitely seemed more comfortable today than you did the last time you presented at a meeting, which is great! I noticed several things that you did really well: you made regular eye contact with both of the parents and you highlighted positive behaviors you observed while you were working with Charlie. This seemed to make his parents feel a little more relaxed. I know one of your goals this year is to become more comfortable presenting with parents, so you should definitely keep approaching future meetings this way. To continue working towards that goal, I have a few things for you to focus on. First, you were talking pretty quickly, and I noticed that you stumbled over your words at a few points. It's important to speak slowly and clearly, so I recommend you practice presenting your results out loud and maybe even recording yourself to listen to the pace of your speech. The second thing to remember is the importance of presenting results in language that everyone at the meeting can understand. I heard you tell Charlie's parents that he demonstrated a weakness in 'perceptual-motor skills.' This is accurate, based on the testing results, but it might be more helpful to say, 'Charlie had difficulty copying designs,' because that describes behavior that listeners can relate to. Do these observations sound accurate to you? What do you think you will do next based on hearing this feedback?"

Communicating Feedback

Even with a good relationship, giving constructive feedback in a way that accomplishes the task of teaching skills without making the supervisee feel bad is definitely a challenge.

(J. A., first time supervisor)

School psychologists must have strong communication skills for virtually all aspects of their work. As a supervisor you're a powerful model, so seeing and hearing how you communicate feedback can be a learning experience in and of itself for your supervisee. How can you set a good example even when you have to deliver a difficult message? Here are some guidelines and specific techniques that can help.

General Guidelines

As you prepare to deliver feedback, keep the following ideas in mind (Ende, 1983):

- **Link feedback to goals** you and your supervisee develop together. Each supervision session should start with a review of progress towards goals and should end with a plan for things to be done to move towards the next level of improved skill (Bernard & Goodyear, 2014).
- Ask the supervisee to **self-evaluate** before providing your feedback (e.g., "What do you think went well in that session? What could have gone better?").
- Be thoughtful about where and when you provide feedback; try to **ensure the supervisee knows that feedback is coming**, especially if it is negative.
- Provide a **limited amount** of feedback at a time; don't overwhelm the supervisee.
- Limit feedback to behaviors that can be changed.
- Use **descriptive, non-evaluative language** and **focus on specific behaviors**, not generalizations; use examples of observed behaviors (e.g., "When Jack's mom questioned the accuracy of your results, you started speaking before she was finished and your voice was louder than it had been before.").
- When including subjective judgments, label them as such (e.g., "My impression after watching your counseling session was that you came across as somewhat distracted.").
- Be supportive, but don't go overboard with praise; when you provide it, make it specific, not global or personal.

Handout 4.1 at the end of this chapter provides a quick-reference resource to help you provide feedback effectively.

Technique: The Feedback Sandwich

What Is It?

One classic method of sharing constructive criticism is the sandwich method, or as James (2015) called it, "the Sh*t Sandwich" (p. 762). This approach "sandwiches" a negative comment between two positive ones. It sounds simple enough, but using it well requires more than just saying two nice things and one critical thing. All three parts of the sandwich (the opening, middle, and closing statements) need to focus on the same general area or skill and need to be related to one another (James, 2015). So don't compliment the supervisee's great consultation abilities when you're critiquing her test scoring. Also, the statements must be specific to be of any use to the supervisee. Saying, "I like how you interacted with the student" is less enlightening than, "It was great that you asked questions about his interests before you began testing because it helped to build some rapport and make him feel more at ease."

To use the feedback sandwich effectively a supervisor can't shy away from the "meat" of the sandwich: the critique (Cantillon & Sargeant, 2008). Doing so may leave a supervisee with an inaccurately positive impression. However, a sandwich mistake some supervisors make when they do share the negative feedback is to over rely on the word "but" in the middle of the sandwich (Cantillon & Sargeant, 2008). Supervisees may learn to wait for the "but" before they start listening and ignore the opening praise statement and they may become anxious while they wait. Finding a variety of ways to present constructive criticism is an important part of delivering feedback. Box 4.2 provides one example of how the feedback sandwich can be used in supervision.

BOX 4.2 THE FEEDBACK SANDWICH

Example: The Feedback Sandwich

"I could see that you were referring to the manual regularly throughout the testing session, which suggests you were making a great effort to follow standardized administration practices. At the same time, I noticed that you didn't make a lot of eye contact with the student while the two of you were working together, because you were often looking at the manual or the testing protocol. This can make you miss behavioral observations that are important for understanding the child. That being said, you did a great job writing down the student's complete responses."

Strengths and Weaknesses of This Technique

The feedback sandwich can help ease the discomfort that comes with delivering bad news, because it allows you to end on a high note with a positive comment. However, by sandwiching the important constructive criticism in the middle, you run the risk of the supervisee missing the point, particularly if the message is too subtle (James, 2015). The "open-faced sandwich" is an alternative that includes just one positive comment instead of two. This approach could reduce the potential for the critical feedback to be buried between two things the supervisee is happier to hear. However, some research suggests that both types of sandwiches have no observable effect on supervisee performance, even though students *think* that their work improved after receiving sandwiched feedback (Parker, Abercrombie, & McCarty, 2013).

Technique: The Pendleton Method

What Is It?

Pendleton (1984) presented an alternative to the feedback sandwich that encourages supervisee self-reflection. First, the supervisee identifies things he or she feels went well, and then as the supervisor you confirm and extend upon areas in which you agree the supervisee was successful. The same approach is then used to reflect upon areas in need of further development: the supervisee states what could have gone better before the supervisor shares his or her own impressions of things that need improvement. See Box 4.3 for an example of the Pendleton Method.

BOX 4.3 THE PENDLETON METHOD

Example: The Pendleton Method

SUPERVISOR: "What do you think you did well during that testing session?"

SUPERVISEE: "Well, I tried really hard to follow the manual and read all of the subtest directions exactly as written. I also wrote down all of the student's responses to the verbal questions—last time I only jotted down a few words for each item."

SUPERVISOR: "I noticed the same things. I could see that you were referring to the manual regularly throughout the testing session, which suggests you were making a great effort to follow standardized administration practices. And you did a nice job writing down the student's complete responses. We saw the importance of this when we were reviewing those answers that required deciding between a one- or two-point response; it was really helpful to be able to go back to precisely what the student had said."

SUPERVISOR: "Now, what do you think you could have done better in this session?"

SUPERVISEE: "I still feel like it's hard to follow all the standardized instructions correctly without it making the testing take forever. I felt like I had my face buried in the manual the whole time and I didn't look at the student enough. I don't think I did a very good job building rapport with him."

SUPERVISOR: "I would agree with you on some of that. I noticed that you didn't make a lot of eye contact with the student while the two of you were working together, because you *were* often looking at the manual or the testing protocol. This is not unusual at your level; it takes time and lots of practice to become fluid and efficient at testing. For now, as you're still becoming familiar with the tests, one thing you can do is to take a minute in between subtests to attend to the student, make casual conversation, and work on that rapport. You can also spend time before you start the standardized portion of testing to chat and ask questions and make sure the student feels comfortable."

Strengths and Weaknesses of This Technique

The strengths of this approach are that it fosters a collaborative approach to feedback and promotes the development of self-evaluation skills in supervisees. However, it's not a technique that always works well in the moment, particularly if a supervisor needs to provide a correction in the presence of a client (e.g., during observation of a testing or counseling session); it's better suited to a conversation after the fact. Using the Pendleton Method also runs the risk of missing opportunities to address your supervisory concerns if they do not match the weaknesses that are identified by the supervisee (Cantillon & Sargeant, 2008). So it's great when a reflective supervisee is cognizant of his or her areas of weakness, but may not be the right choice when you need to address a deficit that the supervisee isn't able or willing to self-identify when reflecting on what needs improvement.

Technique: A Motivational Interviewing Approach to Feedback

What Is It?

Motivational interviewing (MI; see Miller & Rollnick, 2013) has its origins as a treatment for substance abuse. The approach is designed to decrease resistance and increase motivation to change problematic behavior. It has been suggested as a potentially effective approach for addressing supervisee resistance, particularly when resistant behaviors are an expression of supervisee anxiety (Wahesh, 2016). MI even has applicability in school-based consultation, as it employs an empathic and non-confrontational style and specific communication skills designed to help others convince themselves of the need to change (Blom-Hoffman & Rose, 2007). With respect to supervision, an MI approach encourages supervisees to really collaborate in the feedback discussion and promotes openness through a non-confrontational, non-judgmental, empathic approach (Wade & Jones, 2015). See Box 4.4 for examples of questions that might be used in an MI-based supervision session.

BOX 4.4 AN MI APPROACH TO FEEDBACK

Example: MI Approach to Feedback

"I've reviewed your tape and self-critique. Why don't you tell me about what you heard when you listened to the session recording?"

"It sounds like you were trying to reflect the student's feelings at that moment. You struggled to do this earlier in the year. How were you able to do that this time?"

"Next time you encounter a similar situation, how might you phrase things differently?"

"What other things might you do differently?"

"What can we work on to help you move to the next level?"

Note: see Sobell et al. (2008)

Strengths and Weaknesses of This Technique

As a therapeutic intervention, MI has a strong and growing evidence base (Miller, 2004). Its approach is consistent with several desired features of supervision, such as establishing a safe environment for disclosures, encouraging respect and empathy, and promoting supervisee responsibility for professional development and active involvement in supervision (Sobell et al., 2008). However, employing an MI-based approach to feedback may be time consuming for both supervisees and supervisors, particularly when sessions need to be recorded, transcribed and reviewed. That being said, supervisees reported that the self-critique process was very helpful, particularly for improving clinical skills, and they universally endorsed that they would use such a method when they themselves were providing supervision in the future (Sobell et al., 2008).

Setting Up for Success: Preparing Supervisees to Expect Feedback

I realized that at the beginning of the school year, I [provided my supervisee] with more positive feedback, as I understood that she was just starting and was anxious. However, as the year progressed and our relationship developed, I felt that it was sufficient (and a time-saving practice) to minimize feedback that I felt was not necessary and focus on the aspects that [she] needed to improve upon. Nevertheless, I missed one very important point: I never focused on how this shift might have made my supervisee feel.

(L. S., second-time supervisor)

Even if you perfect the use of these feedback delivery strategies, your constructive criticism is unlikely to be well received if your supervisee is not open to hearing what you have to say. Hoffman et al. (2005) found that supervisee openness was a factor that made it easy to deliver needed feedback, while a lack of openness hindered feedback delivery. Thus, the process and expectations for sharing feedback should be discussed at the start of the supervision relationship (Kelly & Davis, 2017).

As the quote presented above suggests, you might leave your supervisee feeling confused if you don't articulate the rationale behind your approach to feedback. Early discussions about feedback and the supervision experience should address factors such as when, how, and how often feedback will be provided, the purpose of providing feedback, and the fact that both supervisor and supervisee will be expected to engage together in the sharing of feedback. As Cantillon and Sargeant (2008) noted, "feedback should ideally be a 'conversation about performance' rather than a one-way transmission of information" (p. 1,293).

A discussion that addresses the importance of feedback as a tool for learning should emphasize that feedback is a good thing, not a sign of weakness or poor performance. Bernard and Goodyear (2014) even suggest that supervisors should spend time teaching supervisees how to receive corrective feedback by helping them to examine past defensive reactions and relationships with authority figures. It can also be helpful to connect a discussion about feedback to the role of evaluation in supervision. In fact, sitting together to review any summative evaluation forms that will be completed at the end of the supervision experience is an excellent way to ensure that you and your supervisee are clear on the long-term outcomes you are working towards. Linking your ongoing feedback to the goals set forth in the supervision plan and criteria for summative evaluation will help to ensure that everyone is on the right track and minimize the likelihood of the supervisee being surprised by anything in the final evaluation. This may sound like a lot to cover, but it can be done! See Box 4.5 for an example of how a supervisor could introduce the role of feedback in supervision.

BOX 4.5 DELIVERING FEEDBACK

Supervision in the Real Word

"One key aspect of supervision will be providing you with regular feedback on your work. Supervisees are sometimes anxious about getting feedback because they think it reflects weaknesses or things they are doing wrong. I couldn't see it more differently: I often say, 'feedback is a gift,' because it's such an important means of supporting growth as you work towards the goals outlined in our supervision plan. I will aim to provide you with some feedback each time we meet. I will strive to make it as specific and as objective as possible. As much as I can, I will try to observe your work directly so I can give you feedback on exactly what you are doing well and what I think you can do differently to build your skills. Feedback typically focuses on school psychology skills, but can also address professional issues related to things like organization and time management, or communication and interpersonal interactions. These are all things that are included in the summative evaluation I will complete at the end of this supervision experience, so I want to be sure you know where you stand in these different areas. I also want you to know that I'll be asking you for *your* feedback: I'd like to hear from you about how you feel the supervision relationship is working and what is helpful and not helpful about my approach as a supervisor. I'll periodically ask you about this, but you should never hesitate to share your impressions at any time, whether I've asked for them or not. How does all this sound to you? What questions do you have?"

Supervisor's Summary

- Feedback includes the kinds of constructive criticism and positive reinforcement supervisors provide to supervisees on a regular basis to support the ongoing improvement of skills.
- Even though some supervisors feel uncomfortable giving critical feedback, research suggests that supervisees look favorably on supervisors who provide regular, balanced feedback.
- Failure to provide feedback can have a potentially negative effect on the supervision relationship.
- Effective feedback is balanced, immediate, goal-oriented, frequent, objective, and reciprocal.
- As much as possible, feedback should be linked to goals developed collaboratively by supervisor and supervisee.
- Supervisee self-evaluation should be incorporated into the provision of feedback. Both the Pendleton Method and the MI approach encourage supervisee self-reflection.
- The supervision contracting process should include a discussion about when, how, and how often feedback will be provided and establish that feedback is a positive feature of supervision.

FINAL REFLECTIONS

- What have your experiences receiving feedback been like?
- How do you feel about getting feedback? Do you like it? Does it make you anxious?
- Think of a time when you've gotten helpful feedback. What made it helpful? How did getting that feedback affect your learning and/or professional performance?
- Think of a time you received feedback that was not helpful. Why was it unhelpful? How did it make you feel?
- How would you feel if you had to give a supervisee critical feedback about performance of a school psychology skill in need of development? About professional work characteristics? About a personality characteristic that was problematic?
- How do you feel about the idea of asking your supervisees for feedback about your performance?

References

Abbott, A. A., & Lyter, S. C. (1998). The use of constructive criticism in field supervision. *The Clinical Supervisor, 17*(2), 43–57. doi:10.1300/J001v17n02_02.

American Psychological Association. (2017). *Ethical principles of psychologists and code of conduct.* Washington, DC: Author. Retrieved from www.apa.org/ethics/code/ethics-code-2017.pdf.

Bernard, J. M., & Goodyear, R. K. (2014). *Fundamentals of clinical supervision* (5th ed.). Upper Saddle River, NJ: Pearson.

Blom-Hoffman, J., & Rose, G. (2007). Applying motivational interviewing to school-based consultation: A commentary on "Has consultation achieved its primary prevention potential?" an article by Joseph E. Zins. *Journal of Educational and Psychological Consultation, 17*(1–2), 151–156. doi:10.1080/10474410701346451.

Cantillon, P., & Sargeant, J. (2008). Giving feedback in clinical settings. *British Medical Journal, 337*, 1292–1294. doi:10/1136/bmj.a1961.

Chur-Hansen, A., & McLean, S. (2006). On being a supervisor: The importance of feedback and how to give it. *Australasian Psychiatry, 14*, 67–71. doi:10.1080/j.1440-1665.2006.02248.x.

Ende, J. (1983). Feedback in clinical medical education. *Journal of the American Medical Association, 250*(6), 777–781. doi:10.1001/jama.1983.03340060055026.

Heckman-Stone, C. (2003). Trainee preferences for feedback and evaluation in clinical supervision. *The Clinical Supervisor, 22*(1), 21–33.

Hoffman, M. A., Hill, C. E., Holmes, S. E., & Freitas, G. F. (2005). Supervisor perspective on the process and outcome of giving easy, difficult, or no feedback to supervisees. *Journal of Counseling Psychology, 52*(1), 3–13. doi:10.1037/0022-0167.52.1.3.

James, I. A. (2015). The rightful demise of the sh*t sandwich: Providing effective feedback. *Behavioural and Cognitive Psychotherapy, 43*, 759–766. doi:10.1017/S1352465814000113.

Kelly, K. K., & Davis, S. D. (2017). *Supervising the school psychology practicum: A guide for field and university supervisors.* New York: Springer.

Ladany, N., & Melincoff, D. S. (1999). The nature of counselor supervisor nondisclosure. *Counselor Education and Supervision, 38*(3), 161–176. doi:10.1002/j.1556-6978.1999. tb00568.

Ladany, N., Mori, Y., & Mehr, K. E. (2013). Effective and ineffective supervision. *The Counseling Psychologist, 41*(1), 28–47. doi:10.1177/0011000012442648.

Lazar, A., & Eisikovits, Z. (1997). Social work students' preferences regarding supervisory styles and supervisor's behavior. *Clinical Supervisor, 16*, 25–37. doi:10.1300/ J001v16n01_02.

Lehrman-Waterman, D., & Ladany, N. (2001). Development and validation of the Evaluation Process within Supervision Inventory. *Journal of Counseling Psychology, 48* (2), 168–177. doi:10.1037//0022-0167.48.2.168.

Magnuson, S., Wilcoxon, S. A., & Norem, K. (2000). A profile of lousy supervision: Experienced counselors' perspectives. *Counselor Education and Supervision, 39*, 189–202.

Miller, W. R. (2004). Motivational interviewing in service to health promotion. *American Journal of Health Promotion, 18*(3), A1–A10.

Miller, W. R., & Rollnick, S. (2013). *Motivational interviewing: Helping people change.* New York: Guilford Press.

Parker, J., Abercrombie, S., & McCarty, T. (2013). Feedback sandwiches affect perceptions but not performance. *Advances in Health Science Education, 18*, 397–407. doi:10.1007/s10459-012-9377-9.

Pendleton, D. (1984). *The consultation: An approach to learning and teaching.* Oxford: Oxford University Press.

Simon, D. J., & Swerdlik, M. E. (2017). *Supervision in school psychology: The developmental, ecological, problem-solving model.* New York: Routledge.

Sobell, L. C., Manor, H. L., Sobell, M. B., & Dum, M. (2008). Self-critiques of audiotaped therapy sessions: A motivational procedure for facilitating feedback during supervision. *Training and Education in Professional Psychology, 2*(3), 151–155.

Wade, J. C., & Jones, J. E. (2015). *Strength-based clinical supervision: A positive psychology approach to clinical training.* New York: Springer.

Wahesh, E. (2016). Utilizing motivational interviewing to address resistant behaviors in clinical supervision. *Counselor Education & Supervision, 55*, 46–59. doi:10/1002/ceas.12032.

HANDOUT 4.1 TIPS FOR PROVIDING FEEDBACK

- **Make feedback a normal part of supervision.** Discuss your approach to feedback during the contracting phase at the start of the supervision relationship and ask supervisees how they feel about receiving feedback.
- **Ask supervisees to self-evaluate.** Before you launch into your feedback, ask your supervisee to share impressions about what went well and what could have gone better or should have been done differently.
- **Tie feedback to goals and evaluation.** Set goals collaboratively with your supervisees and give feedback that highlights how supervisees can do things that will narrow the gap between current performance and desired/required performance. Make sure supervisees understand how they will be evaluated at the end of the supervision experience and link your ongoing feedback to those ultimate outcomes.
- **Be specific.** Broad, global statements like "You did a great job in that meeting!" don't give supervisees information about what they did well or how they could do better. And when you have to address problems and it feels uncomfortable, fight the urge to be vague. Dancing around the issue will leave your supervisee confused or unaware of what needs to change.
- **Base your feedback on direct observations.** Even though you can't sit in on every testing or counseling session or every consultation with a teacher, try as much as you can to directly observe your supervisee in action so you can use objective language and specific examples when you provide feedback. One strategy for doing this efficiently is to co-lead groups or co-administer testing; your work gets done *and* you can see your supervisee in action. Even better: your supervisee learns by watching you!
- **Provide feedback regularly.** Feedback should be a part of set (e.g., weekly) supervision meetings, but should also occur in the moment whenever possible to provide immediate reinforcement or correction (that's why those observations of supervisees are so important!).
- **Be thoughtful about where and when you provide feedback.** A hallway drive-by conversation is not the way to provide feedback. Particularly if you have to deliver significant criticism, make a point of scheduling a time to sit down in a quiet spot for a private discussion.
- **Limit the amount of feedback you give at a time.** Don't overwhelm supervisees with long lists of things they're doing wrong. Supervisees are

more likely to be open to hearing what you have to say and motivated to work towards improving performance if you focus on just a few specific behaviors and how to change them. If you have multiple issues to address, try spreading out your feedback over several meetings.

- **Be positive and supportive, but don't overdo it with praise.** Too much global praise without constructive criticism can lead supervisees to question the accuracy of supervisors' feedback. Plus it does little to support learning as it doesn't highlight exactly what the supervisee is doing so well and should keep doing.

5

EVALUATING SUPERVISEES

The aim of this chapter is to help you navigate the sometimes intimidating prospect of formally evaluating supervisee performance. This is a critical feature of both clinical and administrative supervision, though how evaluation proceeds may be different for these two types of supervisors. The evaluation of preservice school psychologists (i.e., interns) will be addressed, along with considerations for administrative and clinical supervisors tasked with evaluating school psychologists.

Evaluation Defined

As was indicated in Chapter 4, evaluation, also known as *summative assessment*, refers to a review of performance that emphasizes final conclusions and gate-keeping at the end of a supervised experience (Harvey, Struzziero, & Desai, 2014). It has higher stakes than feedback, given that evaluation is often tied to outcomes such as successful completion of mandated training experiences, obtaining certification or licensure, or earning tenure or promotion. Evaluation is also closely linked with efforts to remediate problems of professional competence (PPC), when needed (see Chapter 6 for more on addressing PPC). So, unlike feedback, which is provided throughout the supervision experience to promote learning and support ongoing improvements in performance, evaluation can be more like a pass/fail final exam.

Foundations of Effective Evaluation

Supervisee evaluation may be viewed as a stressful or unpleasant responsibility for supervisors, but it doesn't have to be. As Harvey and Struzziero (2008) suggest, "supervisors should consider it an *opportunity* to provide information and professional development—with the ultimate goals of both protecting students and helping supervisees improve" (p. 408).

Goals and Feedback

> Providing specific, formative feedback makes life easier at the end, if done throughout the supervision experience.
>
> *(Anonymous supervisor)*

In previous chapters we've examined the underpinnings of effective evaluation: goal setting and feedback (Lehrman-Waterman & Ladany, 2001). By identifying goals at the start of the supervision relationship and regularly assessing and collaboratively discussing progress towards them, supervisors and supervisees set the stage for a productive and positive evaluation experience. Nothing in the final evaluation should come as any surprise to the supervisee if you've consistently been providing frequent feedback on progress toward goals along the way (Chur-Hansen & McLean, 2006; Wade & Jones, 2015).

Setting Up for Successful Evaluation

Bernard and Goodyear (2014) identified "favorable conditions for evaluation" (pp. 226–229) that can help make the process productive and considerate of the needs of supervisees. To facilitate effective supervisee evaluations, supervisors are advised to:

1. Remember that supervision is a hierarchical relationship in which supervisees have less power than supervisors.
2. Clarify expectations (e.g., through thoughtful contracting). Who will evaluate? Who will have access to evaluation results? What gatekeeping decisions will be based on evaluation results? Who will make those decisions?
3. Openly address supervisee defensiveness.
4. Discuss individual cultural differences that may affect evaluation (see Chapter 7 for more on culturally responsive supervision).
5. Actively involve supervisees in setting goals for supervision and provide continuous formative feedback.
6. Consider the administrative structure in which feedback is provided (e.g., school, district, clinic, training program). Supervisors and supervisees should understand due process procedures for appealing evaluations.

7. Don't evaluate too early. Take time to develop evaluations based on data, not first impressions.
8. Model a professional growth mindset by soliciting feedback from supervisees. Discuss your continuing education efforts with supervisees to model the need for growth throughout the professional lifespan.
9. Maintain a professional relationship that is neither too close nor too distant. Make supervisees feel safe and supported, but be sure you can stay objective.
10. Don't supervise if you don't want to. Evaluation can be tough even for supervisors who enjoy the role; those who don't may do a serious disservice to supervisees.

Evaluation for Preservice School Psychologists

Evaluation may hold the highest stakes for interns and practicum students, who are not yet certified to practice independently. Summative evaluations for these trainees often inform whether or not they can continue with training or obtain the necessary credentials for practice. What follows is an overview of methods of evaluation you may choose or be asked to use as a field-based supervisor of a typically performing school psychology trainee.

University-Provided Forms

If you are supervising a school psychology intern you will likely be asked to complete evaluation forms provided by the intern's training program (see Appendix G for a copy of the form used by Fairleigh Dickinson University; The Illinois School Psychology Internship Consortium Internship Plan is available as an appendix in Simon and Swerdlik's (2017) book on the DEP model of school psychology supervision). This paperwork is often required at the end of each semester of the year-long internship experience. NASP-approved training programs are expected to promote and evaluate competence across the 10 domains of the NASP Practice Model (NASP, 2010a), so forms will likely ask you to assess performance over this broad array of school psychology skills and knowledge (NASP, 2010b). Reviewing these forms with supervisees at the *start* of the supervision relationship as well as periodically throughout each semester is a great way to structure formative feedback and proactively set the stage for a successful summative evaluation experience. It also ensures that you are familiar with the behaviors and criteria you will ultimately be expected to rate, so you can attend to relevant examples of performance throughout the evaluation period. So don't wait until the end of the semester to pull out that form; it should be one of the first things you and your intern do together at the start of the year.

Supplementing with Additional Measures

Of course, even if your intern's training program provides you with evaluation paperwork, you remain free to use additional tools to complete more comprehensive assessments of skill development. This might be particularly valuable for cases in which supervisees are struggling to attain competence in certain domains of practice or to demonstrate appropriate professional work characteristics. For example, the Supervision Utilization Rating Form (Vespia, Heckman-Stone, & Delworth, 2002) is a 52-item scale designed to assess qualities thought to characterize successful counseling supervisees. It assesses domains such as compliance with expectations, responsibility, initiative and independent thinking, openness, self-insight, relationship/interpersonal skills, risk-taking behaviors, and positive personal characteristics. For supervisees who struggle to maintain successful work-life balance, Simon and Swerdlik (2017) present a Healthy Lifestyle Assessment (see Chapter 9 for more on self-care and preventing burnout). The point is: don't feel limited to the items on the university training program's rating form if your supervisee needs attention in additional domains.

Portfolio Evaluations

An additional method of evaluation commonly used by school psychology graduate programs is the internship portfolio. Training programs may require interns to submit a compilation of work products that document growth and positive impact on stakeholders. As a field-based internship supervisor you can support your interns in identifying appropriate cases and experiences that will highlight skill development and effective service delivery. Field supervisors should also communicate with university-based supervisors to understand expectations and navigate situations in which the training program requires activities that are not within the scope of the field supervisor's practice. Collaboration with colleagues at the internship site can often be helpful for addressing such discrepancies. Be sure to review portfolio requirements with your intern and the university-based supervisor early in the supervision experience, and plan ahead to avoid last-minute stress and problems with summative evaluation.

Communicating Evaluation Results

No matter what forms or format you use to document your summative feedback, you need to share your impressions with your supervisee. Harvey et al. (2014) provide recommendations for communicating evaluation results. See Handout 5.1 at the end of this chapter for a list of tips to help with such discussions.

Evaluation for Credentialed School Psychologists

When supervising professional school psychologists you may have more work to do when it comes to providing meaningful evaluations, because no university training program is going to hand you an evaluation form to complete at the end of the semester. Depending on whether you are providing administrative or clinical supervision (or both) to a practicing school psychologist, "evaluation" will mean different things and possibly have different goals. However, both types of supervisors should seek to provide meaningful evaluations that can inform professional development planning for credentialed school psychologists.

Administrative Supervisors and Evaluation

As an administrative supervisor you are typically tasked with managing the operations and "nuts and bolts" of service delivery, including personnel evaluation. Such evaluation is likely required by the school district and may be a key component of high-stakes decisions such as whether or not to grant tenure or renew an employment contract. Some districts have evaluation tools designed specifically for evaluating the performance of school psychologists: Washoe County, NV evaluates school psychologists on four domains from the NASP Practice Model (NASP, 2010a), and some portions of the Washington, DC school personnel evaluation system are school-psychology specific and based on NASP standards (Skalski & Myers, 2014). However, many school psychologists are evaluated using forms and tools designed to assess the effectiveness of classroom teachers (Harvey et al., 2014). Given the importance of some of the decisions made based on such evaluation data, it would be helpful for school psychologists to be evaluated based on criteria relevant to their role.

A complete treatment of the literature on designing effective personnel evaluations is beyond the scope of this book. If you are tasked with creating a valid and reliable school psychologist evaluation tool I strongly recommend Harvey and Struzziero's (2008) *Professional Development and Supervision of School Psychologists: From Intern to Expert* (2nd Ed.), which has an entire chapter devoted to performance evaluations and professional development, accompanied by illustrative vignettes and samples of school psychologist evaluation tools. NASP's *Best Practices in School Psychology* series also includes several resources on this topic, including chapters by Skalski and Myers (2014) and Harvey et al. (2014). To hit the highlights, common themes that emerge from this literature on personnel evaluation are presented in Box 5.1.

BOX 5.1 FUNDAMENTALS OF EFFECTIVE SCHOOL PSYCHOLOGY PERSONNEL EVALUATIONS

- Personnel evaluations should be fair and reliable, have a well-defined purpose, and result in actionable feedback that supervisees can use to improve practice.
- Evaluation processes should be meaningful and acceptable to supervisees and must protect their due process rights.
- Performance expectations and criteria for evaluation should be clearly communicated to new supervisees and reviewed periodically to ensure understanding.
- The NASP Practice Model provides a helpful organizing framework to guide the evaluation of school psychologists' performance.
- School psychologists should be involved in the process of designing the evaluation systems that will be used to assess their performance.
- Evaluation processes should include data from multiple sources (e.g., peers, teachers, parents, fellow related services providers, and self-evaluations).
- Evaluation tools can include Likert rating scales, behaviorally anchored rating scales, critical incident records, and portfolios.
- The personnel evaluation process itself should be reviewed periodically and modified as necessary to be as effective and productive as possible.

Clinical Supervisors and Evaluation

A well-designed personnel evaluation process should include data from multiple raters. Although administrative supervisors (e.g., principals or special services directors) may be required to directly observe school psychologists' performance, if they do not have a background in school psychology they may lack familiarity with best practices and be unaware of behaviors that provide evidence of effective service delivery (Harvey & Struzziero, 2008). A clinical supervisor, who by definition has knowledge of school psychology, is in an excellent position to contribute to the evaluation process by communicating with an administrative supervisor (of course, the supervision contracting process should address confidentiality and clarify with whom, if anyone, the professional supervisor will share such information). Furthermore, a clinical supervisor can play a key role in helping supervisees at all levels identify areas of strength to be maintained, as well as areas in need of ongoing professional development.

Using Evaluation to Inform Professional Growth Plans

The current half-life of knowledge for school psychology (i.e., the amount of time it takes for 50% of "facts" in our field to become obsolete) is just under 10 years and continues to decrease (Neimeyer, Taylor, Rozensky, & Cox, 2014). This means that school psychologists need to be engaged in ongoing professional development to remain abreast of current research and skilled at best practices. To this end, the NASP Practice Model (NASP, 2010a) specifically states, "school psychologists engage in lifelong learning and formulate personal plans for ongoing professional growth" (p. 9). For credentialed school psychologists, supervisor evaluations can play an important role in informing professional growth plans. As Skalski and Myers (2014) put it, "an effective evaluation system will help school psychologists evaluate their individual needs and seek out professional development specifically designed to improve their skills and practice" (p. 606).

Armistead (2014) presents best practices for designing a program of continuing professional development, noting that most school psychologists receive no formal instruction in how to do so. This makes the supervisor's modeling and experience with professional growth planning particularly valuable to supervisees. Armistead emphasizes the importance of considering the school psychologist's role and context of practice when prioritizing professional growth needs, while also assessing existing competencies across the 10 domains of the NASP Practice Model (NASP, 2010a). Supervisors of credentialed school psychologists can support supervisee self-reflection by encouraging use of NASP's Self-Assessment for School Psychologists (available through the NASP website). They can also provide insight into areas of strength and those in need of development. See Box 5.2 for an example of how this might work for an early-career school psychologist receiving professional supervision from a more experienced colleague.

BOX 5.2 USING EVALUATION TO INFORM PROFESSIONAL GROWTH PLANNING

Supervision in the Real World

"Ok Lilah, we are meeting today to work on updating your professional growth plan. I've reviewed your self-assessment and see that you rated your need for professional development as 'high' for Domain 4: Interventions and Mental Health Services to Develop Social and Life Skills. Given that we recently learned your role next year will involve working with our new special class for students with emotional disabilities, I agree that this is a domain you should focus on. From our supervision meetings this year I know you've had success implementing the Coping Cat curriculum, because we saw that post-intervention ratings of participating students' anxiety were lower than the pre-intervention scores. So you have experience and emerging effectiveness with group counseling and evidence-based interventions, which is great! Let's think about how you can transfer these competencies to working with children who might exhibit challenging behaviors, and what knowledge and skills you will need to build to work effectively with these students and their teachers. Then we can set specific goals for professional growth and identify resources you can study, workshops you can attend, and things we can do with our supervision time to help you make progress towards your goals."

Reciprocal Evaluation

As important as it is to evaluate supervisees, supervisor evaluation is just as critical to effective supervision. As Harvey et al. (2014) observed, evaluation of supervisors can result in improved performance, as it has the potential to inform professional development efforts, document effectiveness, identify programs or procedures in need of improvement, and even provide professional recognition. Any discomfort that comes with asking supervisees to provide feedback on supervisor performance should help foster empathy for supervisees who are so often on the receiving end of such evaluations. More importantly, it models a positive approach to professional development and demonstrates openness to career-long growth and improvement.

Although supervisors should ask supervisees for informal feedback on a regular basis (e.g., "How helpful was today's supervision session for you?"), there are tools available to help collect more structured evaluation information. The most comprehensive school-psychology specific tool is Simon and Swerdlik's (2017) DEP Supervisor Self-reflection and Supervisor Feedback Survey (DEP-SSFS). The DEP-SSFS, available in its entirety as an appendix to Simon and Swerdlik's book, asks supervisees to rate a variety of supervisor behaviors and qualities that characterize effective supervisors across the developmental, ecological, and problem-solving domains of the DEP supervision model. It's an excellent tool for school-based school psychology supervisors at all levels of experience.

Supervisor's Summary

- Evaluation differs from feedback because it reflects a final, summative judgment of performance that often influences high-stakes outcomes like completion of training requirements, attaining certification or licensure, or earning promotion or tenure.
- Supervisors can set the stage for effective evaluation through thoughtful contracting, collaborative goal setting, and the provision of frequent feedback.
- When supervising interns and practicum students, review university-provided evaluation forms together at the *start* of the internship experience to clarify expectations and prompt a discussion about how evaluation will be

conducted. Review the forms periodically to structure your formative feedback. This will prevent unpleasant surprises when the time comes for summative evaluations.

- Personnel evaluation by administrative supervisors should be valid, reliable, based on data from multiple sources, and used to inform professional growth plans.
- Professional supervisors of credentialed school psychologists do not typically serve as gatekeepers in the way they do for interns or practicum students, but they can contribute to personnel evaluations and provide data to be used for the development of professional growth plans.
- Reciprocal evaluation processes should be used to promote the evaluation of supervisors by supervisees.

FINAL REFLECTIONS

- How do you feel about evaluating supervisees? Do you see it as an exciting opportunity, or does the prospect fill you with dread? Perhaps you feel somewhere in between?
- What do you recall about how you were evaluated as an intern? Was the process helpful? Anxiety provoking? Why or why not? What would you do similarly or differently from what your supervisor did when evaluating you?
- Think about your current personnel evaluation process. How helpful is it to your own practice? How helpful is it to you as a supervisor of school psychologists? What are the strengths and weaknesses of the current process? What could be changed to make it more effective?
- What information would be most helpful or most important to collect to support your evaluation of supervisees? How will you go about gathering that information?

References

Armistead, L. D. (2014). Best practices in continuing professional development for school psychologists. In A. Thomas & P. Harrison (Eds.), *Best practices in school psychology: Foundations* (pp. 611–626). Bethesda, MD: National Association of School Psychologists.

Bernard, J. M., & Goodyear, R. K. (2014). *Fundamentals of clinical supervision* (5th ed.). Upper Saddle River, NJ: Pearson.

Chur-Hansen, A., & McLean, S. (2006). On being a supervisor: The importance of feedback and how to give it. *Australasian Psychiatry, 14*, 67–71. doi:10.1080/j.1440-1665.2006.02248.x.

Harvey, V. S., & Struzziero, J. A. (2008). *Professional development and supervision of school psychologists: From intern to expert* (2nd ed.). Bethesda, MD: National Association of School Psychologists.

Harvey, V. S., Struzziero, J. A., & Desai, S. (2014). Best practices in supervision and mentoring of school psychologists. In P. L. Harrison & A. Thomas (Eds.), *Best practices in school psychology: Foundations* (pp. 567–580). Bethesda, MD: National Association of School Psychologists.

Lehrman-Waterman, D., & Ladany, N. (2001). Development and validation of the evaluation process within supervision inventory. *Journal of Counseling Psychology, 48*(2), 168–177. doi:10.1037//0022-0167.48.2.168.

National Association of School Psychologists. (2010a). *Model for comprehensive and integrated school psychological services.* Bethesda, MD: Author.

National Association of School Psychologists. (2010b). *Standards for graduate preparation of school psychologists.* Bethesda, MD: Author.

Neimeyer, G. J., Taylor, J. M., Rozensky, R. H., & Cox, D. R. (2014). The diminishing durability of knowledge in professional psychology: A second look at specializations. *Professional Psychology: Research and Practice, 45,* 92–98. doi:10.1037/a0036176.

Simon, D. J., & Swerdlik, M. E. (2017). *Supervision in school psychology: The developmental, ecological, problem-solving model.* New York: Routledge.

Skalski, A. K., & Myers, M. A. (2014). Best practices in the professional evaluation of school psychologists using the NASP practice model. In P. L. Harrison & A. Thomas (Eds.), *Best practices in school psychology: Foundations* (pp. 599–609). Bethesda, MD: National Association of School Psychologists.

Vespia, K. M., Heckman-Stone, C., & Delworth, U. (2002). Describing and facilitating effective supervision behavior in counseling trainees. *Psychotherapy: Theory/Research/Practice/Training, 39*(1), 56–65. doi:10.1037/0033-3204.39.1.56.

Wade, J. C., & Jones, J. E. (2015). *Strength-based clinical supervision: A positive psychology approach to clinical training.* New York: Springer.

HANDOUT 5.1 TIPS FOR COMMUNICATING SUPERVISEE EVALUATIONS

- Have supervisee complete and submit written self-assessment before the evaluation meeting
- Hold the meeting in private and without interruptions
- Remain honest, straightforward, and kind at all times
- Begin by reviewing strengths and positive behaviors
- Address deficits clearly and succinctly
- Present examples of areas that need to change
- Provide specific suggestions for improvement
- Ask supervisee to share honest reactions to evaluation results
- Solicit feedback from supervisee about what you can do better or differently to help support his or her improvement
- Protect the supervisee's due process rights (e.g., know training program guidelines or school district policies)
- Summarize the session
- Follow up with written summary of evaluation; for supervisees demonstrating significant problem behaviors or difficulties, include timelines and specific criteria for measuring improvement.

Note: see Harvey et al. (2014)

6

ADDRESSING PROBLEMS OF PROFESSIONAL COMPETENCE

Whether you're a first-time supervisor or you've been supporting the development of school psychologists for decades, working with a supervisee who is struggling is likely to be stressful, anxiety-provoking, and time consuming. These supervisees are usually the exception, not the norm, but prevalence rates suggest that most supervisors will encounter them during their careers. Although some research suggests that between 4–10% of psychology trainees exhibit competence problems (Veilleux, January, VanderVeen, Reddy, & Klonoff, 2012), one survey of psychology trainees found that 44% of students could identify a peer who exhibited problems of professional competence (PPC; Shen-Miller et al., 2011). Other research has reported rates as high as 95% (Mearns & Allen, 1991).

Addressing PPC is a distinct domain of the *Guidelines for Supervision in Health Service Psychology* (APA, 2014) and a key responsibility for field- and university-based supervisors of school psychology trainees. But credentialed practitioners can exhibit PPC too, so clinical and administrative supervisors should be prepared to address these problems when they arise. Unfortunately, difficult supervisees may be passed along from one setting to another without intervention to address problematic behaviors in what Johnson et al. (2008) refer to as a "hot potato game" (p. 590). Supervisors have an ethical and legal obligation to address PPC, given their role as gatekeepers for the profession of school psychology and the vicarious liability held by supervisors of non-credentialed trainees. In other words, as a supervisor you are charged with ensuring that only qualified individuals provide school psychology services, and if someone you are supervising fails to do so, you may find yourself on the hook for their mistakes.

This chapter will define PPC and present an approach to addressing it that uses the four-step problem-solving model. It will also provide guidance on what to do when efforts to remediate PPC don't work. Finally, because addressing PPC requires straightforward communication, the chapter concludes by presenting specific strategies for conducting difficult conversations.

What *Is* PPC?

We use the term *problems of professional competence* to describe, simply stated, "performance or behavior [that] does not meet professional and ethical standards" (Jacob et al., 2011, p. 177). This may include actions that violate professional codes of ethics and/or levels of skill or knowledge that fall noticeably below what could be reasonably expected for the supervisee's phase of development. These difficulties can take a wide range of forms, such as consistently repeating mistakes, failing to respond to feedback, lacking self-awareness, engaging in unethical or unprofessional behavior, or experiencing personal problems that affect professional functioning (Kaslow et al., 2007). PPC is about more than just difficulty in learning concepts or exhibiting skills; it describes supervisees who are experiencing significant interference in their ability to function at the expected level. See Box 6.1 for some hypothetical examples of PPC.

BOX 6.1 EXAMPLES OF SUPERVISEES EXHIBITING PPC

- Arnold, a veteran school psychologist assigned to multiple buildings, often arrives late and/or leaves early from the site he is assigned to for a given day. Some weeks he hardly visits one of his sites at all.
- Despite passing several courses in assessment and receiving detailed feedback from her site supervisor on her first three evaluations of the year, Belinda continues to make fundamental administration errors when testing students.
- Cathy was known for using a "direct" personal style that many consultee teachers found off-putting.
- Dennis struggled with noticeable anxiety throughout his school psychology coursework, but passed his classes. As an intern, he repeated questions multiple times but did not take notes when they were answered. He requested assistance from office staff so frequently that they soon complained to the supervisor about the excessive interruptions.
- Ellen felt extremely overwhelmed by the demands of her position as a first-year school psychologist while her mother was undergoing cancer treatment. She often seemed distracted and spent a good deal of time on the phone during the school day. When her director asked for an

---

update on a sensitive counseling case, Ellen broke down crying and admitted that she had not seen the student in several weeks.
- Francine changed scores in an electronic copy of a report from an independent evaluator in order to make a student appear more severely impaired and increase the likelihood that he would be found eligible for special education services.

Using a Systematic Problem-Solving Process to Address PPC

Working systematically facilitates thoughtful, organized, and goal-directed efforts to remediate difficulties, as opposed to a reactive and frustrating approach of "putting out fires." The four components of a sound problem-solving model include (1) problem identification, (2) problem analysis, (3) intervention, and (4) evaluation (Pluymert, 2014). This approach is best practice for addressing many problems in schools; thus, you probably already have many tools in your toolkit that you can put to work in these challenging supervision situations.

Respect Due Process

First and foremost, it is essential to ensure that the supervisee's due process rights are respected. For interns or practicum students, this means working closely with university-based supervisors and faculty to observe program policies and procedures. Credentialed supervisees may have rights afforded by union membership, employment contracts, or guidelines developed by the district or school board. As a supervisor, it is important to be aware of and protect all rights afforded to supervisees.

Step 1: Problem Identification (What Is the Problem Here?)

When it seems a supervisee is exhibiting PPC, the first step is to define the behavior(s) of concern. As best as possible, the language used to describe the problem should frame the situation in a way that helps all parties. For example, "Harry is having difficulty communicating" is not as clear as, "Members of the team have expressed that they feel Harry has addressed them in a disrespectful manner."

The importance of identifying a problem in specific terms is highlighted by Jacob et al. (2011), who note that when supervisors "can understand, describe, and talk about the problem in specific terms, it may be less emotionally arousing and facilitate a more specific conversation with a trainee exhibiting PPC about what change is needed" (p. 177). At the problem identification stage a good operational definition of the target behaviors in need of change can be extremely helpful. Box 6.2 presents some examples of how the problems exhibited by the hypothetical supervisees from earlier in this chapter could be operationally defined.

BOX 6.2 EXAMPLES OF OPERATIONAL DEFINITIONS FOR PPC BEHAVIORS

- Arnold is exhibiting *inconsistent attendance*. Over the past two weeks of school he has arrived on site after 9:00am five times, has left school before 3:30pm four times, and has not visited Memorial School.
- Belinda is demonstrating *difficulty meeting standardization requirements for testing*. During the most recent administration of the WJ-IV, she made two errors establishing basals and one error establishing a ceiling, provided an incorrect amount of time for the Sentence Reading Fluency test, and did not provide required corrective feedback on the Visual-Auditory Learning test.
- Cathy is displaying *inconsiderate communication*. During a pre-referral intervention team meeting Cathy told a teacher, "it's clear you haven't tried hard enough to solve this issue yourself" and "next time come to this meeting prepared with data so you don't waste our time."
- Dennis is *asking questions without noting the answers*. During the past week, on three occasions he asked a question of his supervisor without taking any notes regarding the answer and then asked the same question at least one additional time. Dennis has also exhibited this same behavior with at least two other members of the Special Services Office team.
- Ellen is *making personal phone calls during work hours* and is *not completing mandated counseling sessions*. Over the past two weeks Ellen has been observed talking on her cell phone multiple times per day for as long as 30 minutes at a time. During that time she has not conducted mandated counseling sessions for at least one student on her assigned caseload.
- Francine *altered the work of another psychologist* and *falsified student records* by changing test scores.

Step 2: Problem Analysis (Why Is this Problem Happening?)

Understanding why PPC is happening is essential to addressing it, just like understanding the function of a child's behavior is critical to developing an effective BIP. It can sometimes be challenging to figure this out. Kaslow et al. (2007) provide an extensive discussion of processes for identifying, evaluating, and addressing PPC that informed the development of Handout 6.1, provided at the end of this chapter. Handout 6.1 provides a variety of questions supervisors can consider while working to better understand the factors that might be causing and/or maintaining a supervisee's PPC.

Self-Assessment

One important point Kaslow et al. (2007) stress is the value of self-assessment. As part of the problem analysis process, supervisors are encouraged to have supervisees self-evaluate their performance and any sources of difficulty. Not only might this process yield valuable information regarding causes of PPC (e.g., a supervisee might share that she has been experiencing previously undisclosed sources of stress in her personal life), but observing that a supervisee struggles with self-assessment can be quite informative in and of itself: as Kaslow et al. note, "lacking the capacity to self-assess is tantamount to failing to attain professionalism, lacking the skill of thinking like a psychologist, and being insulated against self-corrective behavior" (p. 483). These authors note that remediation of difficulties may not be possible for supervisees who lack insight into their own functioning.

Handout 6.2 provides one example of a self-assessment tool that could be used to investigate the source of PPC. Another option would be to have supervisees complete the very summative evaluation forms that supervisors are required to submit to university training programs or administrators within a school district. In my experience, this process has been helpful for identifying deficits in knowledge or skills that could be targeted for remediation through structured learning experiences.

Can't-Do or Won't-Do Problem?

As a school psychologist approached about a struggling student, one of the first questions you may ask is whether the source of the child's difficulties is a lack of ability or a lack of motivation. This distinction is as key to effective intervention with supervisees as it is with children and adolescents. A supervisee may be driven to succeed, but struggles due to a lack of foundational knowledge or insufficient previous training opportunities. On the other hand, a supervisee may demonstrate adequate content knowledge and skill but still fail to meet expectations. These two scenarios require very different types of remediation.

Can't-Do Analysis: What Is Lacking?

When working from a mental health consultation perspective (Caplan, 1963) we often examine the "lacks" a consultee may be experiencing: is the difficulty due to a lack of understanding/knowledge, a lack of skill, a lack of objectivity about the case, or a lack of confidence? This framework provides a helpful way to assess the source(s) of supervisees' difficulties as well. For example, supervisees may lack awareness about things that experienced supervisors take for granted as common knowledge. Training programs vary widely in approaches and course requirements and are never able to teach all that school psychologists need to know in the typical 60 or 90 credits of coursework that specialist- or doctoral-level graduate students complete. Thus, an assessment of foundational knowledge is a good place to start when a supervisee is exhibiting PPC (see Chapter 3 for more on assessing supervisees' knowledge and skills at the start of the supervision relationship). For interns or practicum students, it can be helpful to talk with the university-based supervisor for details about course requirements and content to get a better understanding of what your supervisee is likely to know.

A supervisee can have all the required knowledge to be successful but still struggle to be effective at a developmentally appropriate level (e.g., they can tell you all about the standardization process and factor structure of the WISC-V but still fail to query correctly or observe mandated time limits). If the knowledge is there but problems persist, a lack of opportunities to practice and receive quality feedback may be at issue. Another problem can be excessive anxiety. Although it is not unusual for supervisees to be apprehensive about their performance, when nerves make it difficult to do the job intervention is necessary. Sorting out whether PPC is due to a lack of knowledge, skill, or anxiety can begin through a conversation with your supervisee. Table 6.1 presents some questions that could facilitate such discussions.

TABLE 6.1 Suggested Questions for Exploring Can't-Do Problems

Is it a lack of . . .?	Try asking the supervisee . . .
Knowledge	• What did your graduate program teach you about this topic? • Have you had other professional development in this area, like conferences or workshops? • What readings have you done about this topic? • Overall, how much would you say you know about this topic?
Skill	• How much practice have you had with this activity? • Have you ever done this before? How many times? • Has anyone ever observed you doing this before? • If you've been observed, what kind of feedback did you get afterwards?
Confidence	• How do you feel when you need to engage in this activity? • How nervous would you say you are about doing this? • Have you experienced significant anxiety in the past? What was that like? How did it affect you? What did you do about it? • Do you feel like you avoid doing things that make you nervous?

The answers to such questions can also be helpful for guiding plans for intervention. Figure 6.1 provides a decision tree to assist with assessment of can't-do problems and suggestions for remediation.

Won't-Do Analysis: Resistance

If you are able to establish that a supervisee possesses the requisite knowledge, skills, and confidence to be successful, yet PPC persists, the supervisee may be engaging in resistant behavior. This could include things like resisting the supervisor's influence by withholding or distorting information or engaging in power struggles, resisting supervision itself by skipping or coming late to sessions, noncompliance with supervisory tasks (e.g., failing to bring recordings to supervision), or noncompliance with implementation of interventions (Bernard & Goodyear, 2014). These forms of resistance could occur concurrently with, and as a reaction to, a lack of knowledge, skill, or confidence that needs to be addressed through intervention and increased support. But if resistance

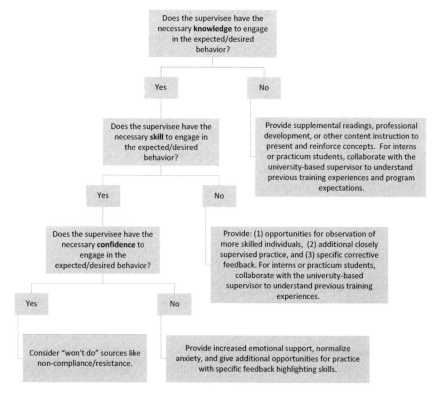

FIGURE 6.1   A Decision Tree to Guide Assessment of Potential "Can't-Do" Problems

itself seems to be the sole source of PPC, it can be worth considering the questions presented in Table 6.2.

Step 3: Intervention (What Can We Do About this Problem?)

With an understanding of the reasons behind a supervisee's PPC, a *remediation plan* can be developed to clearly delineate what needs to occur to try and address the problem. Much like a BIP, a remediation plan should objectively define the behaviors of concern and their frequency, intensity, and/or duration of occurrence, while also specifying replacement behaviors that will reflect growth and progress. Clear objectives, plans for evaluation, and timelines for review of performance should be included to keep all parties involved accountable for the success of the remediation plan. A remediation plan template is included as a Handout 6.3 at the end of this chapter and a sample remediation plan is available in Appendix H. Figure 6.2 highlights some strategies to consider depending on the nature of the PPC your supervisee is exhibiting.

Step 4: Evaluation (Is the Remediation Plan Working?)

A strong remediation plan includes a clear description of how progress will be monitored and evaluated. It should address things like who will be responsible for tracking change and what all parties involved need to see in order to feel confident that the PPC has abated. It should also explicitly state what the supervisee can expect to happen if the problem behavior(s) do not sufficiently improve, including whether this might result in termination from a training program or employment. The clearer all this is, the better, particularly when you are dealing with a supervisee who is at risk of serious consequences. Just like a good BIP, the remediation plan should be reviewed regularly by all parties involved. Confirming that the plan is being implemented as stated is essential, particularly if there is a chance that a supervisee might experience significant consequences due to failure to show improvement.

What If Remediation Doesn't Work?

Ideally the process of identifying, analyzing, and planning to remediate PPC helps a supervisor and supervisee to collaboratively make changes that result in improved performance. I've seen this happen for my own supervisees: the experience of sitting down and talking explicitly about areas of difficulty and systematically providing needed supports can be just what is needed to move a struggling supervisee forward to attain competence. Sometimes the initial conversation itself is enough to spark change, such as when a discussion about attendance problems reveals that a supervisee needs to cut back on responsibilities

TABLE 6.2 Considerations for Exploring Resistance

Factor	Questions to Consider
Trust	• Does your supervisee trust you? • Have you spent enough time building a solid working relationship? • Have there been experiences that may have threatened the supervisee's ability to trust you?
Communication	• Do you feel there is open communication between you and the supervisee? Do you find yourself holding back from sharing things with the supervisee? • How would you describe your communication style? Your supervisee's communication style? How well matched are they? • Do you feel your supervisee accurately perceives and understands the things you say?
Agreement on goals	• Are there clear and mutually agreed-upon goals for the supervision experience? • Are they realistic and attainable? • Does the supervisee feel there have been sufficient opportunities to work towards set goals and objectives?
Supervisee's level of development	• Could the supervisee be reacting to feeling that you are providing too much support? Not enough support? • (For moderately experienced supervisees) Is the supervisee trying to assert his or her independence?
Supervisor style or traits	• How directive/nondirective are you as a supervisor? Is it a good match for the supervisee's style, needs, and level of development? • How willing/able are you to explain the rationale for things you ask (or tell) the supervisee to do? • How do you use self-disclosure in supervision?
Supervisee style or traits	• Is the supervisee highly sensitive to criticism or constraints? • Does the supervisee seem to react negatively to individuals in positions of authority? • Are aspects of the supervisee's communication skills or interpersonal style affecting performance? • Is the supervisee experiencing problems or circumstances in his or her personal life that are causing PPC?

Note: Adapted from Bernard & Goodyear (2014)

outside the school day in order to meet the obligations of professional practice. In other instances a supervisee was truly not aware of the extent of the problem, having little previous experience with the norms and expectations of school-based practice.

Category	Interventions
Lack of Knowledge	• Provide readings • Suggest/assign attendance at conference sessions, webinars, or other professional development opportunities
Lack of Skill	• Provide additional opportunities for practice (e.g., role play) • Allow supervisee to observe supervisor performance • Observe performance and provide frequent feedback (i.e., coaching)
Lack of Confidence	• Highlight specific areas of strength • Explore sources of insecurity (e.g., fear of failure, fixed mindset, perfectionistic tendencies) • Encourage risk taking and provide supportive feedback
Organization, Time Management, and Initiative	• Use your knowledge of evidence-based executive functioning interventions for students; have supervisee research effective interventions • Model time management and organization strategies; share what works for you
Interpersonal Skill Difficulties	• Specify behaviors that contribute to interpersonal challenges • Use your knowledge of social skills training; model and rehearse prosocial replacement behaviors, provide feedback • Monitor progress and provide frequent feedback; seek input from clients and colleagues
Communication Difficulties	• Model strong communication skills; find frequent opportunities for supervisee to observe you communicating effectively • Check for understanding; have supervisee summarize what you communicated in own words • Follow up in-person communications with written documentation (e.g., email)
Unethical Practice	• Refer regularly to professional codes of ethics to highlight specific standards and how they apply to practice • Provide paper/electronic copies of ethics codes for reference • Model ethical problem solving: use "think aloud" approach to explain to supervisee how and why you decided to act
Respecting Diversity	• Encourage self-reflection, self-examination of personal experiences and biases • Assign readings, videos • Raise issues related to culturally responsive practice in supervision
Engagement in Supervision	• Use behavioral strategies to address attendance, preparation for supervision • Examine the supervision relationship and working alliance—does the supervisee feel supported? Comfortable? • Solicit feedback from supervisee about your supervision style and effectiveness
Difficulties in Personal Life	• Be supportive, but maintain appropriate boundaries (remember, supervision is not therapy) • Suggest personal counseling/therapy

FIGURE 6.2 Potential Interventions to Consider for Remediation Plans, Based on the Suspected Source(s) of PPC

Unfortunately, even the best remediation plans are sometimes not enough to address PPC. Particularly when the source of the problem is not a lack of knowledge or confidence, but rather a significant lack of skill or professionalism, it can be necessary to counsel a supervisee out of the field. As Ende (1983) noted, "if behaviors are observed that are not within the trainee's power to change … the trainee should alter his or her goals, not the process by which he or she attempts to meet a goal" (p. 780). As difficult as such conversations can be, in my experience this is not a universally negative outcome, particularly when the source of PPC is a poor fit between the supervisee's career goals or personality and the demands of a career as a school psychologist. Some supervisees recognize, even after several years of training and reaching the point of internship, that school psychology is not the career for them. A supervisee who lacks a commitment to a career in school psychology will be better served pursuing a different path.

Conducting Difficult Conversations

Addressing PPC is a necessary part of the supervisory role, but one that many supervisors may not be properly prepared to tackle. Jacob et al. (2011) highlight how barriers such as a lack of skill or training for engaging in difficult conversations, as well as avoidant tendencies, resentment of having to have the conversation at all, and fear of legal retribution, can hinder supervisors' ability or willingness to engage in the discussions that are required for tackling PPC. Even well-intentioned empathy for struggling supervisees can stand in the way of doing what's needed if a supervisor looks the other way regarding PPC because they do not want to engage a supervisee in an upsetting conversation.

Like it or not, supervisors need to take steps to ready themselves for what Patterson, Grenny, McMillan, and Switzler (2012) call "crucial conversations." These are discussions in which opinions differ, emotions run strong, and the stakes are high. Becoming truly skilled at such discussions takes experience and practice, just as it does to become an effective consultant or counselor. But busy supervisors may find it helpful to keep the following suggestions in mind (they are based in part on guidance aimed at program faculty by Jacob et al., 2011) in advance of a conversation to address PPC:

- Be prepared. This may seem obvious, but be sure you've done your homework before sitting down for the conversation. What *exactly* are the issues you plan to address? How do the areas of difficulty relate to the knowledge, skills, and professional work characteristics school psychologists need to possess and exhibit? What documentation do you need to have on hand to refer to (e.g., evaluation forms, job descriptions, handbooks)? Once when I was preparing for a meeting in which I had to discuss unethical behavior with a supervisee, I printed out the NASP *Principles of Professional Ethics* and literally highlighted the specific ethical standards that the supervisee had violated. Even though I never had to bring this document out during the meeting, the process helped me to feel organized, prepared, and confident in my conviction that the discussion needed to happen.

- Consider communication styles. Individuals communicate differently due to interpersonal differences, cultural backgrounds, and cognitive or behavioral style. As part of preparing for a difficult conversation, give thought to how your communication style and that of your supervisee might differ. Are you comfortable speaking directly, or do you tend to speak in more vague or coded terms? Is your supervisee of a cultural background that depends more on nonverbal communication or values deference to authority more than your own? Thinking through these factors in advance will help you communicate more effectively in the moment.

- Establish ground rules. For high-stakes conversations, it can be helpful to devote a moment or two to setting up agreed-upon parameters before anyone gets going. For example, all parties involved should agree to listen without interrupting, speak respectfully, and engage in the discussion openly and honestly.

- Engage in problem-solving. School psychologists solve problems. It's what we do day in and day out. Applying the same approach you would use to work with a parent, teacher, or struggling student may be helpful as you discuss PPC with your supervisee. What is anticipated to be a difficult conversation can be reframed as a productive opportunity to identify goals and discuss options for achieving them. This integrates well with remediation planning; through discussion you can actively involve the supervisee in crafting a remediation plan to support development and change. Of course, this assumes that all involved believe that change is possible. Part of the conversation should elicit the supervisee's perspective on what would need to change to achieve a minimum level of required competence, and whether those changes are feasible, or even things the supervisee is willing to do.

- Focus on behaviors. If you've clearly defined and identified the behaviors of concern in the lead up to your conversation, you should be well prepared for the discussion. As much as possible, stick to the specific behaviors that need to change (e.g., "Your last three reports have been submitted after their due dates"). This can be hard when PPC is related to interpersonal difficulties or cultural differences. In such instances, I have found it helpful to focus on the behaviors that are required for success as a school psychologist. "Being able to listen carefully and consider the consultee's perspective is essential to being an effective school-based consultant" is more digestible than "teachers have been complaining that you are rude and condescending." Practicing this kind of reframing in advance of your PPC conversation can be extremely helpful.

- Stay alert. Throughout the discussion, be sure to stay attuned your own emotional and psychological reactions as well as the supervisee's verbal and nonverbal behavior. In particular, it is important to attend to signs of shame (as opposed to guilt) in the supervisee. As Jacob et al. (2011) highlight, guilt is a normal reaction to a tough conversation about a failure to meet standards, while shame is a self-attacking and potentially damaging response. An ashamed supervisee may also feel defensive, which can make it difficult to process your feedback in the moment.
- Follow up. As challenging as the initial PPC conversation may be, it's unlikely to be a one-time event. Subsequent discussions will likely be needed to follow up on next steps and monitor the supervisee's response to a difficult discussion. It may feel appropriate to schedule a next meeting during the first one, but if not it can be sufficient to simply inform the supervisee that you will be getting in touch to set up another conversation.

Don't Go It Alone

Supervision is incredibly rewarding, but can be extremely challenging. This is never more true than when a supervisee is struggling with PPC. As a supervising school psychologist you are probably extremely busy, and addressing PPC may require time that is already in short supply. This can lead to feelings of resentment, or even anger towards your supervisee. You might feel anxious about the responsibility you bear for your supervisee's errors or lapses in judgment. Perhaps you feel overwhelmed by the need to address a problem that is different from anything you have encountered before. Or you may be devastated about the prospect of having to tell a supervisee you care about that a career in school psychology may not become a reality. All of these feelings, and a host of others, are normal and understandable reactions when confronting PPC. Acknowledging them and managing them, with the help of trusted colleagues or even your own former supervisors, is an important aspect of self-care, a topic that will be addressed in more detail in Chapter 9. When struggling with any aspect of supervision, seeking support, consultation, and guidance should be a top priority.

Supervisor's Summary

- PPC is evident when supervisees engage in behavior that is not consistent with ethical standards or when they exhibit levels of skill or knowledge that fall noticeably below what could be reasonably expected for the supervisee's level of development.

- Supervisors must be sure to respect supervisees' due process rights by collaborating with university training programs or district administrators to address PPC in a manner that conforms to all applicable policies and procedures.
- A systematic problem-solving process to address PPC includes four components: problem identification, problem analysis, intervention, and evaluation.
- Problem identification involves defining the problem behavior(s) in specific objective terms that present the issue in language that all parties involved can understand in the same way.
- Problem analysis may involve differentiating between whether the PPC is a *can't-do* problem resulting from a lack of knowledge, skill, or confidence; or a *won't-do* problem reflecting supervisee resistance. How you address the PPC will depend on which of these factors is likely to be causing it.
- Intervention to address PPC involves the development of a remediation plan that identifies the supports needed to help a supervisee improve, who will provide them and how, and specifies exactly how progress towards goals will be monitored and ultimately evaluated.
- When evaluation indicates that a well-implemented remediation plan did not effectively address PPC, it may be necessary to counsel a supervisee out of the field of school psychology.
- Planning ahead, setting ground rules, focusing on behaviors and problem-solving, attending to emotional reactions, and following up are key to navigating difficult conversations.
- When working to address PPC, supervisors should seek support from trusted colleagues.

FINAL REFLECTIONS

- Research shows that psychology students often observe PPC but feel that faculty and supervisors do little to address issues. Have you observed PPC in a colleague or trainee? If so, what did you do about it? Looking back, how do you feel about your decision to act or not act?
- Where do you draw the line between normal struggles to learn and develop and PPC?
- How would you rate your communication skills for conducting "crucial conversations?" Where could they improve?
- What steps can you take as a supervisor to *prevent* PPC?

Notes

1 Based in part on Kaslow et al.'s (2007) discussion of identifying, evaluating, and addressing PPC.
2 See Rodolfa et al. (2005) for a description of the Cube Model for Competency Development for professional psychology.

References

American Psychological Association. (2014). Guidelines for clinical supervision in health service psychology. Retrieved from http://apa.org/about/policy/guidelines-supervision.

Bernard, J. M., & Goodyear, R. K. (2014). *Fundamentals of clinical supervision* (5th Ed). Upper Saddle River, NJ: Pearson.

Caplan, G. (1963). Types of mental health consultation. *American Journal of Orthopsychiatry*, *33*(3), 407–481. doi:10.1111/j.1939-0025.1963.tb00381.x.

Ende, J. (1983). Feedback in clinical medical education. *Journal of the American Medical Association*, *250*(6), 777–781. doi:10.1001/jama.1983.03340060055026.

Jacob, S. C., Huprich, S. K., Cage, E., Elman, N. S., Forrest, L., Grus, C. L., . . . Kaslow, N. J. (2011). Trainees with competence problems: Difficult but necessary conversations. *Training and Education in Professional Psychology*, *5*, 175–184. doi:10.1037/tep0000072.

Johnson, W. B., Elman, N. S., Forrest, L., Robiner, W. N., Rodolfa, E., & Schaffer, J. B. (2008). Addressing professional competence problems in trainees: Some ethical considerations. *Professional Psychology: Research and Practice*, *39*, 589–599. doi:10.1037/a0014264.

Kaslow, N. J., Rubin, N. J., Forrest, L., Elman, N. S., Van Horne, B. A., Jacob, S. C., . . . Thorn, B. E. (2007). Recognizing, assessing and intervening with problems of professional competence. *Professional Psychology: Research and Practice*, *38*, 479–492. doi:10.1037/0735-7028.38.5.479.

Mearns, J., & Allen, G. J. (1991). Graduate students' experiences in dealing with impaired peers, compared with faculty predictions: An exploratory study. *Ethics & Behavior*, *1*, 191–202. doi:10.1207/s15327019eb0103_3.

Patterson, K., Grenny, J., McMillan, R., & Switzler, A. (2012). *Crucial conversations: Tools for talking when stakes are high*. New York: McGraw Hill.

Pluymert, K. (2014). Problem-solving foundations for school psychological services. In P. Harrison & A. Thomas (Eds.), *Best practices in school psychology: Data-based and collaborative decision making* (pp. 25–39). Bethesda, MD: National Association of School Psychologists.

Rodolfa, E., Bent, R., Eisman, E., Nelson, P., Rehm, L., & Ritchie, P. (2005). A cube model for competency development: Implications for psychology educators and regulators. *Professional Psychology: Research and Practice*, *36*(4), 347.

Shen-Miller, D. S., Grus, C., Van Sickle, K., Schwartz-Mette, R., Cage, E., Elman, N. S., . . . Kaslow, N. J. (2011). Trainees' experiences with peers having competence problems: A national survey. *Training and Education in Professional Psychology*, *5*, 112–121. doi:10.1037/a0023824.

Veilleux, J. C., January, A. M., VanderVeen, J. W., Reddy, L. F., & Klonoff, E. A. (2012). Differentiating amongst characteristics associated with problems of professional competence: Perceptions of graduate student peers. *Training and Education in Professional Psychology*, *6*, 113–121. doi:10.1037/a0028337.

HANDOUT 6.1 QUESTIONS TO CONSIDER FOR ADDRESSING PPC[1]

1. What is the problem? Provide a clear and objective description of the specific observable behaviors of concern.

   _____

   _____

   _____

2. Is the PPC manifesting itself in any of the following foundational and/ or functional competency areas[2]?

Foundational	Functional
☐ Reflective practice/self-assessment	☐ Assessment
☐ Scientific knowledge and methods	☐ Intervention
☐ Interpersonal relationships	☐ Consultation
☐ Ethical and legal standards	☐ Research/evaluation
☐ Individual and cultural diversity	☐ Supervision/teaching
☐ Involvement with colleagues and peers	☐ Management of services

3. This problem reflects
   - ☐ a chronic/ongoing pattern of behavior
   - ☐ a specific critical incident of PPC

4. What seems to be the source(s) of the problem?
   - ☐ Lack of knowledge needed for adequate performance
   - ☐ Lack of skill that could be reasonably expected for supervisee's level of training
   - ☐ Lack of professionalism
   - ☐ Lack of self-awareness
   - ☐ Lack of cultural awareness or sensitivity
   - ☐ Failure to respond to feedback
   - ☐ Personal characteristics affecting professional functioning

     - ○ Communication style
     - ○ Mental health difficulties
     - ○ Personality
     - ○ Physical health problems
     - ○ Substance use
     - ○ Stress in personal life

   - ☐ Other: _____

5. How severe is the problem? Is it reasonable to expect it could be resolved with an appropriate remediation plan?

6. If the problem reflects a lack of knowledge or skill, has the supervisee had sufficient training opportunities, experiences, and exposure to reasonably be expected to possess such knowledge or skill?

7. How frequently and consistently has supervision been provided? Is the amount of supervision sufficient for a supervisee at this level?

8. What, if any, is the risk of harm to clients based on the supervisee's PPC?

9. What, if any, immediate steps need to be taken to protect client welfare?

10. What strengths does the supervisee exhibit that can be enhanced and built upon to facilitate remediation of the present difficulties?

HANDOUT 6.2 SELF-ASSESSMENT OF COMPETENCE

1. In your own words, what problem or problems are you experiencing in your work as a school psychologist? Can you provide a clear and objective description of specific observable behaviors of concern?

_____

_____

_____

2. In which of the following areas are you having difficulty demonstrating a level of competence that is reasonable for someone at your level of training?

Knowledge (I don't sufficiently understand . . .)	Skill (I'm not sufficiently able to conduct . . .)	Professional work characteristics
☐ Cognitive assessment	☐ Cognitive assessment	☐ Respect for diversity and social justice
☐ Academic assessment	☐ Academic assessment	☐ Communication skills
☐ Behavior assessment	☐ Behavior assessment	☐ Interpersonal skills
☐ Social-emotional assessment	☐ Social-emotional assessment	☐ Time management
☐ Consultation and collaboration with teachers	☐ Consultation and collaboration with teachers	☐ Organization of materials
☐ Consultation and collaboration with parents	☐ Consultation and collaboration with parents	☐ Adaptability/ flexibility
☐ Academic intervention	☐ Academic intervention	☐ Initiative
☐ Behavior intervention	☐ Behavior intervention	☐ Dependability/ accountability
☐ Mental health intervention	☐ Mental health intervention	☐ Ethical responsibility
☐ Systems-level intervention	☐ Systems-level intervention	☐ Legal practice
☐ Crisis intervention	☐ Crisis intervention	☐ Use of technology
☐ Culturally responsive practice	☐ Culturally responsive practice	☐ Other: _____
☐ Other: _____	☐ Other: _____	

3. To what extent do you feel the following factors are contributing to your current difficulties?

Factor	Not at all	A little bit	A fair amount	Quite a bit
My communication style				
My personality				
Aspects of my cultural background not well understood by others				
Stress in my personal life				
Mental health challenges I am experiencing (e.g., anxiety, depression)				
Physical health difficulties I am experiencing				
Substance use				
Other:				

4. In your opinion, how serious is this problem?

It's not a very serious problem	It's kind of a serious problem	It's a serious problem	It's a very serious problem

5. If the competence problem reflects a lack of knowledge or a lack of skill(s), do you feel you've had sufficient training opportunities and support to attain the knowledge or skill(s) by this point in your development as a school psychologist? ☐ Yes ☐ No

   If not, what experiences/exposure do you think you need to build the knowledge and/or skill(s) you currently lack?

6. What interventions and supports would be most helpful to you in addressing the problem(s) you are currently experiencing?

7. Please share any other thoughts, questions, or comments you have at this time:

HANDOUT 6.3 REMEDIATION PLAN TEMPLATE

SUPERVISEE NAME:
SUPERVISOR(S) NAME:
WORK/TRAINING SITE(S):
PLAN START DATE: PLAN END DATE:

TARGET BEHAVIOR(S)

Provide a clear and objective description of the specific observable behavior(s) of concern. The definition should be an unambiguous description of outwardly observable behavior(s) that can be reliably and consistently observed by multiple individuals.

PRESENT LEVELS OF TARGET BEHAVIOR

Describe the current frequency/intensity/duration of the target behavior. How serious is the PPC?

ACTIONS TAKEN TO DATE

What has been done previously to try to address the behavior(s) of concern? Describe, as specifically as possible, what has been communicated to the supervisee and any other supervisors and what supports have been provided to try to help the supervisee improve.

SUPERVISEE STRENGTHS

What strengths and resources does the supervisee have that can be used to help build up areas of weakness (e.g., interpersonal skills, content knowledge, motivation, resilience, creativity).

AREAS OF NEED

Does the supervisee lack knowledge or skills that can be reasonably expected for his or her level of development? Is there evidence of a lack of professionalism (including unethical behavior) that is typically demonstrated by school psychologists?

REQUIRED SUPPORTS

Based on your analysis of the problem, what does the supervisee need to be successful? Does the supervisee need specific instruction, training, or exposure to gain required knowledge? More opportunities for practice to build skills? More frequent feedback to build professional work characteristics?

PROVISION OF SUPPORTS

Describe exactly how the required supports will be provided. What steps will be taken? When? By whom? Be as specific as possible.

GOALS AND OBJECTIVES

What, specifically, will the supervisee need to do to demonstrate progress and success? What behavior will need to change? What will that need to look like?

PROGRESS MONITORING AND PLAN EVALUATION

How will progress towards short-term objectives and long-term goals be assessed? How will supervisor and supervisee know if the plan is working?

CONSEQUENCES FOR CONTINUING OCCURRENCES OF TARGET BEHAVIOR(S)

Spell out precisely what will happen if the remediation plan goals are not met. Remember the importance of respecting supervisees' due process rights: being crystal clear about what to expect is part of treating supervisees fairly.

7

PROVIDING CULTURALLY RESPONSIVE SUPERVISION

Arlene Silva

At its core, the profession of school psychology is about caring for others. The most fundamental way students, parents, teachers, and supervisees can be cared for is to be understood and accepted for who they are. The provision of culturally responsive supervision not only facilitates this basic need for supervisees, but ensures they in turn are able to provide it for those they serve.

Culturally Responsive Practice: Understanding the Basics

For the purposes of this chapter, the term *cultural responsiveness* is preferred over *cultural competence* to emphasize the lifelong vigilance required for success in this domain; one is never sufficiently "competent" in this domain to stop learning and improving.

> *One is never sufficiently "competent" to stop learning and improving when it comes to cultural factors and school psychology practice.*

Diverse Diversities

The APA's (2014) *Guidelines for Clinical Supervision in Health Service Psychology* indicate that competent supervision must consider "a broad range of diversity dimensions" (p. 36) as they relate to the supervisor, supervisee, and clients being served. While race and ethnicity are often at the top of the list of diversity considerations, the APA notes that the intersectionality of many elements—including age, gender, gender identity, sexual orientation, culture/acculturation, national origin, religion, disability, language, and socio-economic status—need to be considered as part of culturally responsive practice. Figure 7.1 highlights some of the types of diversity domains to consider for supervisors, supervisees, or clients when providing culturally responsive supervision.

Reflecting on Our Biases

A key consideration within culturally responsive practice is the idea that client experiences must be understood from client perspectives, rather than from our assumptions about the experiences of others. Part of a culturally responsive practitioner's work is to cultivate awareness and self-reflection about one's own biases, stereotypes, and inaccurate assumptions of others, recognizing that they inevitably occur. Seeking supervision may be necessary to ensure that these biases do not negatively influence one's practice. So as important as it is to encourage reflective practice in supervisees, as supervisors we too must regularly examine our beliefs and engage in ongoing professional development.

The Importance of Context

Individuals and their thoughts, feelings, and behaviors must also be understood within the context of the broader socio-political culture, while maintaining an awareness that, throughout history and continuing today, various groups have been disadvantaged, marginalized, and even oppressed. Historically in the United States, individuals who identify as white, male, native English speaking, able-bodied, middle or upper class, Christian, cis-gendered, and heterosexual have experienced greater power and privilege in society compared to those who identify differently in any one (or more) of these categories. Schools, as social and often public institutions, are continually shaped by the dominant cultures in society. Being a culturally responsive practitioner, then, includes advocating for

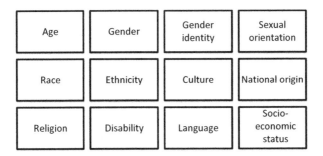

FIGURE 7.1 Competent Supervision Responds to a Broad Range of Diversity Dimensions and Requires Sensitivity to the Diversity Factors of all Three Members of the Supervisory Triad: Supervisee, Client, and Supervisor

equity and social justice in our schools, such that every student is not necessarily given the same resources and supports (i.e., equality), but rather the individual resources and supports they personally need to be as social-emotionally, behaviorally, and academically successful as their peers (i.e., equity; for more on this subject, refer to www.theinclusionsolution.me/equity-vs-equality-eliminating-opportunity-gaps-education).

The Dual Nature and Benefits of Culturally Responsive Supervision

Culturally responsive supervision involves both developing culturally responsive supervisees as well as providing supervision in a culturally responsive manner. So it simultaneously reflects the skills and knowledge you foster in supervisees to help them become culturally responsive school psychologists, and the extent to which you interact with supervisees in a culturally responsive manner. Specifically, this approach can be defined as one that "(a) provides a forum for examining how human diversity influences quality of life and (b) uses that knowledge to improve effectiveness of services, with the goal of ensuring a just and fair environment for clients" (Lopez & Rogers, 2010, p. 120).

It is important to note that the use of a culturally responsive supervision approach can lead to improved outcomes for clients, improved supervisee satisfaction, and increased supervisee confidence in serving diverse clients (e.g., Burkard et al., 2006; Lopez & Rogers, 2010; Sohelian, Inman, Klinger, Isenberg, & Kulp, 2014). Notably, when the supervisor and supervisee belong to different racial groups, supervisees of color are more likely to experience culturally unresponsive supervision compared to their European-American peers (Burkard et al., 2006).

What Can Supervisors Do?

The following guidelines—adapted from the literature on school, counseling, and clinical psychology—can assist school psychologists in providing culturally responsive supervision and modeling culturally responsive practice (APA, 2014; Eklund, Aros-O'Malley, & Murrieta, 2014; Falender & Shafranske, 2004; Soheilian, Inman, Klinger, Isenberg, & Kulp, 2014).

- **Establish a safe, respectful supervisory relationship and strong working alliance**. While establishing a good working relationship is important for all supervision activities, creating a sense of safety and trust is an essential precursor for a relationship in which diversity and difference will be routinely discussed. Supervisors should engage in active listening and show interest and support for their supervisees' perspectives and opinions. They should adopt a *growth mindset* approach, where mistakes and challenges are embraced as learning opportunities (Dweck, 2006). Supervisors should invite feedback on their supervision process, both from their supervisees and from other colleagues as appropriate. A simple "is there anything I can do differently to make supervision more effective for you?" can go a long way towards nurturing a supervisory relationship.

- **Invite the multiple identities of oneself and the supervisee into the supervision relationship**. Supervisors should encourage their supervisees to bring their own culture into the supervision relationship during the early stages of the relationship, and identify differences and similarities in areas such as communication and learning styles. Supervisors should remain open, respectful, and curious towards all aspects of diversity as they arise. One creative way to begin might be for both the supervisor and supervisee to develop an "I Am From" poem (for free templates and additional inspiration, visit http://freeology.com/worksheet-creator/poetry/i-am-from-poem and www.georgeellalyon.com/where.html). Incidentally, this activity can also be done with students of all ages to invite their cultures and identities into the classroom.
- **Explicitly define all interactions as multicultural, and initiate conversations about social justice, diversity and difference**. Supervisors should initiate and actively engage their supervisees in conversations about diversity when engaging in case conceptualization and problem-solving. Explicitly ask supervisees how cultural variables may be impacting their consultation, counseling, and assessment cases.
- **Understand power and privilege, identity development, social justice, and other key topics**. Supervisors can ramp up their own knowledge, as well as that of their supervisees, regarding key topics related to cultural responsiveness. Ted Talks, graphic novels, and documentaries can bring these issues to light in an authentic and engaging way (samples of possible learning resources are included in Table 7.1).
- **Maintain self-awareness, engaging in honest and continuous self-reflection to check assumptions/beliefs**. This is an essential component of culturally responsive practice, and by definition, culturally responsive supervision. All individuals have inherent biases and reactions to those who are different from them. The key is not being defensive about these reactions, but instead noticing when they occur and ensuring they do not negatively impact professional actions. To assist supervisees in their own discovery around their beliefs and assumptions, supervisors can use collaborative communication skills to point out when assumptions may be occurring. For instance, a supervisee may indicate they are frustrated they have been unable to meet with the parents of a student who is struggling. During supervision, the supervisee comments that the parents "must not care" about their child. The supervisor responds, "It can be frustrating

TABLE 7.1 Suggested Learning Resources

Cultural Concept	Title	URL
Power and privilege	*The Pencilsword: On a Plate*	http://thewireless.co.nz/articles/the-pencil sword-on-a-plate
Identity development	*Toolkit: Identity Development*	www.actforyouth.net/adolescence/toolkit/ identity.cfm
Understanding culture	*The Danger of a Single Story*	www.ted.com/talks/chimamanda_adi chie_the_danger_of_a_single_story? language=en
Immigrant perspectives	*Not in Our Town: New Immigrants Share Their Stories*	www.youtube.com/watch? v=33OINi3xVbc
Racism, power, and privilege	*Shades of Youth*	www.youtube.com/watch?v=STgtyvAjs-Q
Transgender youth	*Raising Ryland*	www.raisingryland.com/watch-index/ #watch
Disability	*I'm Not Your Inspiration, Thank You Very Much*	www.ted.com/talks/stella_young_i_m_not _your_inspiration_thank_you_very_much
Poverty	*The Story We Tell About Poverty Isn't True*	www.ted.com/talks/mia_birdsong_the_ story_we_tell_about_poverty_isn_t_true

when you are really concerned about a child and you are unable to connect with their parents. However, we have to be careful with our assumptions about this family. Many parents in our school have multiple jobs and do shift work, and don't have the flexibility to leave work and come to school during the day. Let's see if we can work with the family and our schedules to offer the parents viable meeting times, and consider doing a home visit if that would be helpful."

- **Pursue ongoing professional development in cultural responsiveness**. When a supervisor is unsure of how to proceed in a particular case, they should engage the supervisee in a conversation about how to gain knowledge and skills in relevant areas. For instance, a supervisor who has not had formal training or experience working with transgender students can model the importance of seeking resources and speaking with local experts on how best to support a newly arrived transgender student.

- **Jointly set goals with your supervisee relating to personal growth in cultural responsiveness**. Given that developing cultural responsiveness is a lifelong practice, supervisors can model the process of identifying and making progress towards goals in this area. Supervisors and supervisees can complete a personal goal-setting worksheet (see Appendix I) and check in around their respective progress during supervision. For instance, a supervisee who tends to jump into a parent meeting with lots of data might decide to work on building rapport with culturally diverse families by first asking parents for their perspective on how they understand what is going on for their child in school, and how this may contrast with what is seen at home.

- **Seek experiences that expand your knowledge of different cultures**. To better understand the experiences of those who may belong to marginalized racial or ethnic groups, supervisors who belong to majority cultures can seek out experiences where the tables are turned and they are in a position to "get sweaty" (S. Dowd, personal communication). A classic example is international travel to a country where the supervisor must function while not speaking the language and clearly standing out as a foreign visitor. However, opportunities for cross-cultural immersion also exist locally, particularly for those who live near major metropolitan centers. Supervisors are encouraged to go outside of their cultural comfort zones, and share their experiences and lessons learned with their supervisees. Supervisors should also ensure supervisees seek out learning opportunities with a range of diverse clients within their own work.
- **Encourage assessment of cultural responsiveness within the school setting**. Supervisors can help their supervisees engage in school culture and climate assessments to determine areas of cultural responsiveness that may need attention. Specific tools include the Self-assessment Checklist for Personnel Providing Services and Supports to Children and their Families (available at www.nasponline.org/resources-and-publications/resources/diversity/cultural-competence/self-assessment-checklist) and the School-wide Cultural Competence Observations Checklist (available at www.uwec.edu/RTI-CCP/upload/THE-SCHOOL-1.doc).
- **Promote social justice and organizational change efforts**. Based on data gathered as part of an assessment and problem-solving process, supervisors can support their supervisees in systems change efforts aimed at improving equity and culturally responsive practice. For instance, a non-Hispanic supervisee working within a predominately Latinx school district may notice that many of the children and families served introduce themselves as having two last names (the first from their father and the second from their mother). During supervision, the supervisee notes one of his counseling clients expressed deep sadness at "always having to pick just one name" on all his school paperwork, and the anxiety caused by having to "disrespect" the parent whose name was not chosen. The supervisor encourages the supervisee to work with the school administrators to review their school paperwork and student intake procedures, such that students are welcomed to use both of their last names throughout their time in the school. Supervisors can also model social justice efforts at the state and

federal levels by encouraging their supervisees to join them in advocating for legislation, policies, and funding aimed at improving the lives of children. The NASP Advocacy Action Center makes it easy to become an advocate (http://cqrcengage.com/naspweb/home).

• **Actively seek and respect the experiences of supervisees, who may have more personal experience in multicultural aspects than the supervisor**. Understanding the experiences of others includes the experiences of supervisees, particularly if there are any cultural variables that differ between the supervisor and supervisee. Supervisors should remain open to the possibility that their supervisees may have a deeper knowledge in certain diversity topics, based on their own experience. In addition, supervisors should consider their supervisees' behavior during supervision and while on the job within the context of culture and prior experiences with privilege and prejudice. For instance, a supervisee who identifies as a member of a racial or ethnic minority group might attribute a failed consultation case to a teacher's undue bias against her skill set (see Eklund et al., 2014). It is important to be open to understanding supervisee experiences from the supervisee's perspective, and taking such concerns about possible instances of bias seriously.

• **Help supervisees understand their clients' experience from their clients' perspective**. Of fundamental importance, supervisors can help supervisees understand their clients' experience from their clients' worldview, and remind them not to make assumptions about the experiences of others. Having a deep understanding of this principle can make a profound difference in school psychologists' interactions with those they serve. As an example, a female supervisee is counseling a male high school student who self-identifies as a white Latino. During a counseling session, the student indicates he feels constant anxiety about being a "person of color". The supervisee responds that she is surprised to hear this because he is obviously white, and therefore not a person of color. During supervision, the supervisor helps the supervisee process this interaction and understand that it is not appropriate to tell someone else how they should identify. The supervisor encourages the supervisee to listen to, learn from, and validate the student's experience from his perspective. During the next counseling session, the supervisee acknowledges that after reflecting on their previous session, she realized her comment might have felt dismissive or hurtful, and instead engages the student in a conversation about what his life has been like as a person of color.

Growing as a culturally responsive supervisor is no small task, and the journey will at times feel challenging. When missteps are made, supervisors can acknowledge them openly and have an honest conversation with their supervisees about lessons learned. Ultimately, supervisors who engage in the difficult work of culturally responsive practice will provide the best possible care to those they serve, including their supervisees.

Supervisor's Summary

- The term *culturally responsive* supervision (as opposed to *culturally competent*) reflects that we never stop learning when it comes to how diversity factors affect school psychology practice.
- Culturally responsive practice takes into account a wide range of diversity factors, including age, gender, gender identity, sexual orientation, culture/acculturation, national origin, religion, disability, language, and socio-economic status.
- Ongoing reflection regarding the inherent biases, stereotypes, and assumptions that we all have is essential to culturally responsive practice.
- Culturally responsive supervision involves understanding supervisees and clients from the context of societal culture.
- Culturally responsive supervision reflects two key responsibilities: (1) developing supervisees' ability to practice as culturally responsive school psychologists, and (2) providing supervision in a manner that considers and respects supervisees' unique cultural experiences.
- There are many ways supervisors can provide culturally responsive supervision. These include: establishing safe and respectful working relationships; incorporating cultural identities into supervision; defining all interactions as multicultural; understanding power, privilege, and social justice; engaging in reflective and self-aware practice, pursuing ongoing professional development regarding culturally responsive practice; jointly setting goals for growth with supervisees; engaging in experiences that expand knowledge of diverse cultures; assessing the cultural responsiveness of the school setting; modeling advocacy for social justice; respecting and incorporating supervisees' cultural experiences into supervision; and helping supervisees understand clients' experiences from clients' perspectives.

FINAL REFLECTIONS

- How important do you feel it is to provide culturally responsive supervision? Why?
- What experiences have contributed to your understanding of the role diversity factors in education generally and school psychology specifically?
- What inherent biases, assumptions, and stereotypes do you hold about cultural groups?
- What are your goals for professional development regarding culturally responsive practice? How can you use tools like the goal-setting worksheet provided in Appendix I to progress toward them?

References

American Psychological Association. (2014). Guidelines for clinical supervision in health service psychology. *American Psychologist*, *70*(1), 33–46. doi:10.1037/a0038112.

Burkard, A. W., Johnson, A. J., Madson, M. B., Pruitt, N. T., Contreras-Tadych, D. A., Kozlowski, J. M., & Hess, S. A. (2006). Supervisor cultural responsiveness and unresponsiveness in cross-cultural supervision. *Journal of Counseling Psychology*, *53*(3), 288–301. doi:10.1037/0022-0167.53.3.288.

Dweck, C. S. (2006). *Mindset: The new psychology of success*. New York: Ballantine Books.

Eklund, K., Aros-O'Malley, M., & Murrieta, I. (2014). Multicultural supervision: What difference does difference make? *Contemporary School Psychology*, *18*, 195–204. doi:10.1007/s40688-014-0024-8.

Falender, C. A., & Shafranske, E. P. (2004). *Clinical supervision: A competency-based approach*. Washington, DC: American Psychological Association.

Lopez, E. C., & Rogers, M. R. (2010). Multicultural competence and diversity: University and field collaboration. In J. Kaufman, T. L. Hughes, & C. A. Riccio (Eds.), *Handbook of education, training, and supervision of school psychologists in school and community* (Vol. II, pp. 111–128). New York: Routledge.

Soheilian, S. S., Inman, A. G., Klinger, R. S., Isenberg, D. S., & Kulp, L. E. (2014). Multicultural supervision: Supervisees' reflections on culturally competent supervision. *Counseling Psychology Quarterly*, *27*(4), 379–392. doi:10.1080/09515070.2014.961408

SECTION III

Professional Issues in Supervision

8

ETHICS AND SUPERVISION

Devoting a distinct chapter to ethics and supervision is somewhat challenging, because as Harvey and Struzziero (2008) put it so eloquently, "all ethical and legal issues pertinent to the practice of school psychology are also pertinent to the supervision of school psychologists" (p. 146). This underscores the need for supervisors of school psychologists to be knowledgeable about ethics codes and skillful at ethical problem-solving across all aspects of school psychology practice. Supervisors can serve as powerful role models to less-experienced school psychologists, so what your supervisee observes of you may have implications for future clients long after your supervisees move on to the next stages of their own careers (M. Swerdlik, personal communication). This chapter will address your responsibilities as an ethical role model, along with some specific ethical considerations related to supervision in school psychology. It will also review a structured ethical problem-solving model and consider some unique ethical issues that can arise within the context of the supervisory relationship.

Readers are strongly encouraged to consult chapters on ethics and supervision by Simon and Swerdlik (2017) and Harvey and Struzziero (2008). Simon and Swerdlik present a number of case studies with accompanying ethical problem-solving steps, and Harvey and Struzziero highlight ethics considerations related to all four themes of the NASP (2010) *Principles for Professional Ethics* (PPE) and provide accompanying handouts. Both resources are extremely informative and helpful.

Supervisors as Ethical Role Models

When I teach courses on supervision I ask my students to describe the supervisors they've had over the course of their training and careers. What they share tends to fall into one of two pretty diametrically opposed categories: they recall either pretty terrible supervisors who showed them what to avoid in practice, or wonderful and amazing supervisors they hoped to emulate in their own careers. This may be true of your own experiences as a supervisee—what about the way you practice today reflects how you saw your supervisors approach the job? It's clear that supervisors can have a powerful impact; nowhere is this more true than when it comes to ethical practice. The extent to which you model ethical practice may even factor into the working alliance with your supervisee: a study by Ladany, Lehrman-Waterman, Molinaro, and Wolgast (1999) found that 51% of therapists in training reported witnessing at least one ethical violation by their supervisors, and witnessing this unethical behavior was correlated with poorer supervisee perceptions of the relationship and less overall satisfaction with supervision.

Aside from practicing ethically whenever your supervisee is within earshot, there are some practical steps you can take to be a standout ethical role model for your supervisees. Box 8.1 highlights some strategies for consideration.

BOX 8.1 SUPPORTING ETHICAL DEVELOPMENT AS A ROLE MODEL

- **Highlight the ethical considerations in your work**. School psychologists at the competent, proficient, or expert level of development are able to approach complex situations with confidence and even automaticity (Harvey & Struzziero, 2008). You may simply know what to do without really thinking about it too much. Your supervisees, on the other hand, may lack the experience to intuitively see the ethical dimensions of situations, let alone navigate ethical dilemmas. Don't assume ethical issues are evident or obvious: look for opportunities to explicitly point out how ethical and legal considerations apply and explain why you do things the way you do (e.g., "No matter what, I start every initial counseling session with a discussion about the boundaries of confidentiality so that the student is fully informed about what will and will not stay between us.").

- **Think aloud**. One of the best ways to model ethical problem-solving is to walk your supervisee through what you are thinking as you work your way to a decision. Take those internal conversations and talk them out with your supervisee. Highlight the angles you are considering and the struggles you may be encountering as you try to identify the least bad of a set of undesirable options. This can normalize the emotional challenges of making tough ethical decisions and show supervisees that it is ok to struggle with them (Knapp & Sturm, 2002). The think aloud process could also include involving the supervisee in any consultations you have with colleagues, which models another aspect of good ethical problem-solving.

- **Find time to reflect**. The lack of time to process ethically challenging situations can be a barrier to learning for supervisees, as they may conclude that the dilemma (and all future ones like it) had a single right answer, or fail to appreciate the need to stop and consider even time-sensitive scenarios (Handelsman, Gottlieb, & Knapp, 2005). Certainly in some situations it is important for supervisors to take the lead and make a relatively quick decision, but not all ethically challenging situations are true crises. If you can find a way to slow down and discuss things, do so. If not, find time later in the day or during the next supervision session to process the experience, including ways in which similar situations might be prevented in the future.
- **Foster open dialogue about ethical issues**. A good contracting process emphasizes the importance of maintaining open communication, particularly about mistakes or behaviors that might constitute ethical violations. Making ethics a regular part of supervision discussions not only normalizes the experience of talking about ethical issues, it models strong ethical practice for supervisees and provides frequent opportunities for learning about and applying ethical concepts. By framing discussions of ethical struggles as learning experiences rather than deficits or failings, supervisors can provide positive opportunities for learning (Handelsman et al., 2005).
- **Provide developmentally appropriate support and challenge**. A first-year practicum student who has just completed (or may even still be taking) a course on ethics may be quite unfamiliar with the ins and outs of the ethics codes that guide school psychology practice. Such a supervisee may need explicit instruction in ethical principles and is likely not ready to tackle a dilemma independently. On the other hand, a second-semester intern with several years of experience may benefit tremendously from the opportunity to work through a challenge with only minimal guidance from a supervisor. Like any skill, you must assess your supervisee's level of ethical development and provide an appropriate balance of challenge and support to maximize growth. You can apply an "I do, we do, you do" approach to ethics by initially having the supervisee observe how you navigate a dilemma, eventually working through the problem-solving process together, and ultimately having the supervisee present his or her process and decision to you for feedback.

Ethical Supervision and Ethical Problem-Solving

Competence

Competence is a key ethical consideration for all aspects of school psychology practice (so much so that there is an entire Principle of the NASP ethics code devoted to it), but when it comes to supervision it takes on even greater importance. Competence refers to the fact that "school psychologists engage only in practices for which they are qualified" (NASP, 2010, p. 6). This means that you know what you need to know and can do what you need to do in all areas in which you practice. Sometimes this can be more challenging to determine than you might think. For example, I work with some credentialed school psychologists whose positions involve almost nothing but providing counseling services; are they "competent" to assess students? What about their competence to supervise trainees completing assessment cases? How much therapy training does a supervisor need to supervise school-based counseling? Often evaluating competence is a personal decision based on the specific parameters of the situation. Seeking consultation or confirmation from a trusted colleague is always an option when questions of competence arise.

As a supervisor, not only must you have sufficient competence in the domain(s) being supervised to provide effective supervision, you must also have competence in *supervision* itself. By pursuing information and training about supervision, you are taking positive steps to build supervision competence. Reading this book is a step in the right direction, but would not be enough to build true competence. Seeking ongoing meta-supervision is an ideal way to build and maintain competence.

Ethics Codes and Supervision

As was mentioned above, virtually all aspects of the National Association of School Psychologists [NASP] (2010) *Principles for Professional Ethics* (PPE) apply to the supervision of school psychology practice. Jacob, Decker, and Lugg's (2016) *Ethics and Law for School Psychologists* (7th Edition) provides a detailed review of how the code's broad ethical themes and more specific ethical principles apply to supervision. This resource should be on every school psychologist's bookshelf, as it addresses ethical and legal considerations across all domains of school psychology. But the NASP PPE does include some standards specific to the provision of supervision that should be familiar to all school psychology supervisors; these are highlighted in Box 8.2. Generally speaking, these standards speak to the importance of ensuring that recipients of services from preservice trainees understand that they are working with interns or practicum students; that supervising school psychologists are ultimately responsible for all the work and actions of their supervisees; that supervisors do not harass or discriminate against supervisees; and the general ethical obligation to contribute to the future of the field by supervising and mentoring future school psychologists.

BOX 8.2 SUPERVISION-RELATED STANDARDS FROM THE NASP *PRINCIPLES FOR PROFESSIONAL ETHICS*

Supervision and the NASP (2010) *Principles for Professional Ethics*

Standard I.1.3: School psychologists ensure that an individual providing consent for school psychological services is fully informed about the nature and scope of services offered ... Any service provision by interns, practicum students, or other trainees is explained and agreed to in advance, and the identity and responsibilities of the supervising school psychologist are explained prior to the provision of services.

Standard I.3.1: School psychologists do not engage in or condone actions or policies that discriminate against persons, including students and their families, other recipients of service, supervisees, and colleagues based on actual or perceived characteristics including race; ethnicity; color; religion; ancestry; national origin; immigration status; socioeconomic status; primary language; gender; sexual orientation; gender identity, or gender expression; mental, physical, or sensory disability; or any other distinguishing characteristics.

Standard II.2.4: When supervising graduate students' field experiences or internships, school psychologists are responsible for the work of their supervisees.

Standard III.3.3: Except when supervising graduate students, school psychologists do not alter reports completed by another professional without his or her permission to do so.

Standard III.4.3: School psychologists do not exploit clients, supervisees, or graduate students through professional relationships or condone these actions by their colleagues. They do not participate in or condone sexual harassment of children, parents, other clients, colleagues, employees, trainees, supervisees, or research participants. School psychologists do not engage in sexual relationships with individuals over whom they have evaluation authority, including college students in their classes or program, or any other trainees, or supervisees ...

Principle IV.4: Contributing to the Profession by Mentoring, Teaching, and Supervision: As part of their obligation to students, schools, society, and their profession, school psychologists mentor less-experienced practitioners and graduate students to assure high-quality services, and they serve as role models for sound ethical and professional practices and decision-making.

Standard IV.4.2: School psychologists who supervise practicum students and interns are responsible for all professional practices of the supervisees. They ensure that practicum students and interns are adequately supervised as outlined in the NASP *Graduate Preparation Standards for School Psychologists*. Interns and graduate students are identified as such, and their work is cosigned by the supervising school psychologist.

Standard IV.4.3: School psychologists who employ, supervise, or train professionals provide appropriate working conditions, fair and timely evaluation, constructive supervision, and continuing professional development opportunities.

The Eight-Step Ethical Problem-Solving Model

School psychology is a complex field that involves balancing the needs and rights of various groups and individuals. This can present a wide range of challenges that call for thoughtful problem-solving. When different ethical obligations collide—such as when your obligation to protect client privacy is in opposition to your need to ensure client safety, or your respect for client autonomy conflicts with your obligation to obtain parental consent for services—you have a dilemma on your hands and have to make difficult decisions. As a supervisor, you also have an opportunity to foster ethical development by modeling ethical problem-solving for your supervisees.

Ethical decisions are those that can be described as *principled, reasoned,* and *universalizable* (Haas & Malouf, 2005). This means that the ultimate course of action was (1) grounded in ethical principles, (2) based on thoughtful consideration of applicable principles, and (3) one that you would recommend to others in the same situation. Using a structured ethical problem-solving model is a great way to ensure that you arrive at a decision that meets these criteria. Jacob et al. (2016, p. 25) present an eight-step problem-solving model for addressing ethical dilemmas that was adapted for school psychology practice from steps originally outlined by Koocher and Keith-Spiegel (2008). Those eight steps are explained in Box 8.3. Simon and Swerdlik (2017) also offer a helpful and practical eight-step model that emphasizes using common sense in ethical decision-making.

BOX 8.3 ETHICAL PROBLEM-SOLVING MODEL

Applying an Eight-Step Problem-Solving Model for Ethical Dilemmas

1. **Describe the situation**. What is the problem? What's going on? Describe the issue in your own words.
2. **Define the potential ethical and legal issues**. What seem to be the relevant issues, off the top of your head? Sometimes what we *believe* to be unethical or illegal technically isn't (think about all the variation in state laws under the umbrella of complying with IDEA). By initially

outlining the things that your gut tells you are potential legal or ethical violations, you can organize the rest of your problem-solving.

3. **Consult ethics codes, legal mandates, and district policies**. Here's where you can confirm your suspicions. Go to the NASP and APA ethics codes to find the exact standards that apply. Check the language of state and federal laws (or better yet, consult with a knowledgeable attorney). And be sure to examine any school district or organization policies that may be relevant to the issue(s) at hand.

4. **Evaluate the rights and welfare of all affected parties**. Exactly who is involved in the situation (e.g., client(s), students, parents, teachers, colleagues, supervisees, administrators, community members), and how are they currently being affected? What might happen to them if things do not change? What rights do all involved individuals have? Keep in mind that various parties' rights may be in conflict with one another.

5. **Generate a list of alternatives**. Approach this like brainstorming: everything and anything is on the table. Don't worry if an idea seems too risky, too costly, or even just sounds crazy. As Koocher and Keith-Spiegel (2008) note, after making a complete list, you may see that an initially unattractive option emerges as less awful than all the others. And sometimes parts of different solutions can be packaged together into better ones (Gottlieb, 2006). Also, don't forget to include "do nothing right now" and "get more information" on the list; you should evaluate the risks and benefits of those options as well.

6. **Identify the potential positive and negative consequences of each option**. This is the time to get out your yellow legal pad for a good old pros-and-cons assessment. Take each idea from your list of alternatives and think through the potential short- and long-term effects that could occur for all the affected parties if you implemented that course of action. Consider psychological, social, and economic costs and factors that would affect individuals' dignity and your obligation to provide responsible caring.

7. **Assess how likely it is that these consequences will actually occur**. This risk–benefit analysis is an important, yet sometimes overlooked, step in the process. Particularly in an emotionally charged or crisis situation, we may panic and envision a laundry list of terrible outcomes. Take time to honestly assess the likelihood that the cons you identified will actually happen (e.g., are you *really* likely to be fired over this?) and also the potential that the positive outcomes you envisioned will occur.

8. **Make the decision, accept responsibility, and monitor conse-quences**. After this thorough analysis, it is time to formally decide what to do. This might mean waiting to see what happens, setting off to gather more information, or having a difficult phone call or tough conversation.

> Whatever you choose to do (or not do) you must accept responsibility for your actions, in accordance with NASP and APA ethics codes. <u>Document</u> what you decided to do and how you arrived at the decision, and be sure to follow up to monitor the outcomes of your decision.
>
> *Note*: based on Jacob et al. (2016)

Work Together

Navigating ethical dilemmas, like so many aspects of school psychology practice, can be really hard. The good news is that the collaborative nature of school psychology means that you don't have to work solo. Reaching out to colleagues for consultation or supervision is a normal, commonly used, and even ethically mandated strategy to engage when we are confronted with unfamiliar or challenging territory. Gottlieb (2006) presents a very helpful template for peer ethics consultation that highlights several important considerations to keep in mind when the phone rings and a colleague is asking you for advice. But as a supervisor you may have an additional option in your office when a tricky situation arises: your supervisees.

In addition to the valuable opportunities for learning that come with involving your supervisees in ethical problem-solving (remember—it's incredibly helpful to think aloud and externalize your thought processes), collaborating in this way has the potential to help you navigate the process in the best way possible. Depending on the supervisee's level of development, a trainee can actually be a fruitful source of information and creative solutions. Some supervisees may actually have more knowledge of some concepts than their supervisors, especially in areas that have undergone significant research and development since the supervisor was in graduate school. And supervisees, even if they have limited experience in the field, can bring a unique and potentially more objective perspective as relative outsiders, particularly to situations in which more experienced practitioners involved may be used to "business as usual" and unable to see things happening in a new way. This can be particularly invaluable for dilemmas involving diversity factors, in which perspective-taking and seeing the world through the eyes of others is essential.

Ethical Issues in the Supervision Relationship

Navigating Roles and Relationships

Multiple Relationships

Chapter 2 introduced the idea of potential multiple relationships in supervision. Ethical issues are most likely to arise due to the inherent power differential between supervisee and supervisor, along with the supervisor's responsibility to evaluate supervisee performance (Simon & Swerdlik, 2017). To prevent complications, supervisors are advised to carefully consider any factors that could potentially compromise objectivity and to discuss them openly in supervision. As was noted earlier in Box 8.1, highlighting the ethical dimensions of your work can provide a great learning opportunity for supervisees, and being straightforward about any possible conflicts from the beginning sets the stage for any additional conversations that might be needed as roles and relationships develop over time.

Socializing with Supervisees

Schools are inherently social environments that foster close relationships that may extend beyond the end of the academic day. As a supervisor, you're encouraged to build a close and supportive working relationship with your supervisee, but should doing so involve socializing outside of school hours? Like any other ethically involved question, the answer depends on a variety of factors: what kind of socializing are we talking about (e.g., participating in a faculty book club after school vs. going for happy hour drinks at a local bar)? How long have you been working with the supervisee? How mature and professional is the supervisee? Is there any risk of the supervisee interpreting an invitation to socialize as anything more than you intended it? How comfortable are you with carrying interactions over to post-school hours? Perhaps the single most important question a supervisor needs to consider in such circumstances is: does interacting in this way have the potential to affect my ability to objectively, fairly, and honestly evaluate this supervisee's performance? If there is even the slightest chance that the answer to that question might be "yes," it is probably best to maintain clear boundaries and focus solely on the professional side of your supervision relationship. See Chapter 2 for more on boundaries in supervision relationships.

Confidentiality Considerations

Confidentiality is complicated when it comes to supervision because, particularly for preservice supervisees who are not yet credentialed to practice independently, there may be times when you need to share information with others, such as university-based supervisors. Even clinical supervisors of practicing school psychologists may find themselves disclosing information gathered during supervision sessions if it becomes necessary to involve other administrators in addressing problematic behavior. As with so many other challenging aspects of supervision, clear communication of expectations from the start of the relationship can go a long way to prevent problems. As part of the supervision contracting process, discuss what will and will not stay confidential between you and your supervisee. Ask the supervisee about his or her expectations for privacy and share examples of things that might need to be disclosed to others and what would not. You can use the same skills you employ when explaining the limits of confidentiality to clients receiving mental health services.

Another confidentiality consideration unique to supervision impacts the clients your supervisees see. The NASP (2010) *PPE* stipulates that clients served by supervisees understand that services are being provided under supervision. This includes ensuring that clients understand that things they discuss within the context of the therapeutic relationship may be shared with the provider's supervisor. We are sometimes quick to say "what you say will be private and only between us," while also explaining the mandated reporting conditions that would require us to break confidentiality. But supervisees need to remember to note that their supervisors may also hear about those confidential conversations, and be prepared to answer any questions clients have about that possibility.

Providing Feedback and Evaluation

As was noted in Box 8.3, the NASP (2010) *PPE* explicitly state, "School psychologists who employ, supervise, or train professionals provide . . . fair and timely evaluation . . ." (p. 13). Evaluating supervisee performance is an essential role for supervisors, given that a primary purpose of supervision is to foster growth and learning, and one of the best ways to learn is to try something and get corrective feedback on your performance from someone with more experience. Despite the recognized importance of the evaluative role, many supervisors shy away from this responsibility. In fact, in one study more than a third of supervisees surveyed indicated that their supervisors had committed ethical violations related to evaluation of their performance (Ladany et al., 1999). Providing feedback and evaluating performance may be uncomfortable for some supervisors, particularly when the information that has to be delivered has the potential to cause negative feelings for the supervisee. After all, most of us who enter helping professions do so because we want to help people feel *better* about themselves. But as supervisors, we must follow through with our evaluative role in order to ensure that our supervisees build the skills they need to help current and future clients (or to protect potential clients from supervisees who are unable to attain a sufficient level of professional competence). Chapters 4 and 5 discuss feedback and evaluation in more detail and provide suggestions for navigating these sometimes tricky, but always essential, parts of your role as supervisor.

Case Examples

What discussion of ethics would be complete without some ethical dilemma vignettes? Review the scenarios presented in Box 8.4 and Box 8.5 and consider the questions that follow. Hypothetical situations like these can make for interesting ethical discussions in group or individual supervision sessions.

BOX 8.4 CASE EXAMPLE #1

Did He Cheat?

Your supervisee, Anna, is seeing a 16-year-old special education student, Henry, for counseling to address anxiety and build independent problem-solving skills. One day Henry discloses that while working on a take-home math test he consulted with several classmates to figure out some challenging problems. He happily reported that he got an A- on the test—the best grade he'd gotten in math all year. Anna was concerned that Henry's approach constituted cheating on the test, but Henry insisted that the teacher never said the students couldn't talk to each other.

Questions for Consideration

- What ethical, moral, and/or legal considerations are relevant in this situation?
- What would you want Anna to learn about ethics and ethical problem-solving from this experience? How would you help her do so?
- How would you help Anna apply an ethical problem-solving model to decide what steps (if any) to take next?

BOX 8.5 CASE EXAMPLE #2

Report Problems?

You are providing clinical supervision to Jack, a first-year credentialed school psychologist who was hired by your district at the start of the school year to work in another building. Jack is friendly and personable and has quickly built close relationships with many teachers, as well as the Principal and the Director of Special Services. The administrators seem to be particularly impressed with how well Jack has done plowing through the long list of initial and triennial evaluations left behind by the previous school psychologist. One of Jack's goals was to improve his assessment skills. Mid-year, you suggest he bring a report to supervision so you could review the case together. Glancing at the report, you immediately notice several serious errors (e.g., the reported FSIQ could not possibly be accurate based on the index and subtest scores presented). Feeling a bit stunned, you offer to review the report more closely before your next supervision session so you can provide Jack with specific feedback. You find a number of other problems with the report, from simple typos to significantly flawed interpretations of the data.

Questions to Consider

- What are the potential ramifications to consider if this report is representative of Jack's work, and not an unusually flawed example?
- How should you address this with Jack?
- Do you need to alert anyone else about this situation?
- How would your role and approach in this situation be different if Jack were an intern, rather than a credentialed school psychologist?

Supervisor's Summary

- As a supervisor, you are an important ethical role model for your supervisees.
- By highlighting the ethical dimensions of your work, thinking aloud as you navigate ethical dilemmas, reflecting and discussing ethical challenges with your supervisees, and providing a developmentally appropriate level of support for navigating ethically complex situations, you can help foster ethical development and ethical problem-solving skills.
- You have an ethical obligation to be competent not only in all areas of practice you supervise, but also in supervision itself.
- Supervisors must be knowledgeable of relevant ethics codes and ethical problem-solving models.
- Seek support, consultation, and meta-supervision when dealing with difficult situations. By involving your supervisee in problem-solving, you can both benefit!
- Ethical supervision requires careful navigation of roles and relationships, including thoughtful decisions about whether and how to interact with supervisees outside of work hours. Diligent contracting and open communication can help to prevent problems.
- When it comes to supervision, confidentiality considerations include understanding what will and will not remain private between you and your supervisees, and ensuring that the supervisee's clients understand that what they share with the supervisee may also be shared with the supervisor.
- Providing frequent, helpful feedback and fair evaluation are some of a supervisor's most important, yet regularly overlooked or avoided, ethical obligations.

FINAL REFLECTIONS

- Reflecting on competence, in what areas do you feel your skills are strongest? Where could you use more professional development? What short- and long-term goals can you set for enhancing your skills?
- What strategies do you currently use to navigate ethical dilemmas? How well does your current approach work for you? What, if anything, could you do better with respect to ethical problem-solving?
- How do you handle multiple relationships in your work? Do these approaches apply equally well to your supervision relationships? What might you need to do differently to manage your supervisory role in the most ethical way possible?
- How do you feel about the process of evaluating supervisees? Do you need to change your approach to evaluation to uphold your ethical obligation to evaluate supervisees in a fair, honest, and meaningful way?

References

Gottlieb, M. C. (2006). A template for peer ethics consultation. *Ethics & Behavior, 16*(2), 151–162. doi:10.1207/s15327019eb1602_5.

Haas, L. J., & Malouf, J. L. (2005). *Keeping up the good work: A practitioner's guide to mental health ethics* (4th ed.). Sarasota, FL: Professional Resource Press.

Handelsman, M. M., Gottlieb, M. C., & Knapp, S. (2005). Training ethical psychologists: An acculturation model. *Professional Psychology: Research and Practice, 36*(1), 59–65.

Harvey, V., & Struzziero, J. (2008). *Professional development and supervision of school psychologists: From intern to expert* (2nd ed.). Bethesda, MD: National Association of School Psychologists.

Jacob, S., Decker, D. M., & Lugg, E. T. (2016). *Ethics and law for school psychologists* (7th ed.). New Jersey: John Wiley Publishers.

Knapp, S., & Sturm, C. (2002). Ethics education after licensing: Ideas for increasing diversity in content and process. Ethics & Behavior, 12(2), 157–166.

Koocher, G. P., & Keith-Spiegel, P. (2008). *Ethics in psychology and the mental health professions: Standards and cases.* New York: Oxford.

Ladany, N., Lehrman-Waterman, D., Molinaro, M., & Wolgast, B. (1999). Psychotherapy supervisor ethical practices: Adherence to guidelines, the supervisory working alliance, and supervisee satisfaction. *The Counseling Psychologist, 27*(3), 443–475. doi:10.1177/0011000099273008.

National Association of School Psychologists. (2010). *Principles for professional ethics.* Bethesda, MD: Author.

Simon, D. J., & Swerdlik, M. E. (2017). *Supervision in school psychology: The developmental, ecological, problem-solving model.* New York: Routledge.

9

PREVENTING BURNOUT THROUGH SELF-CARE

In order to be a good supervisor to others, you must care for yourself. The job of a school psychologist can be extremely stressful, and it is essential to have resources to cope with the demands. This chapter will discuss burnout and the importance self-care. As a supervisor who is vicariously liable for the practice of preservice supervisees or responsible for the functioning of credentialed school psychologists, you must be attuned to the self-care practices of supervisees as an ethical imperative. Furthermore, you are helping to lay the foundation for another school psychologist's future self-care practices; modeling healthy self-care habits is as important a part of your responsibility as building assessment, consultation, or counseling skills.

School Psychologists and Burnout

Burnout has long been conceptualized as a feeling of depletion resulting from intense or chronic stress (Suran & Sheridan, 1985). Burned-out workers are exhausted, cynical, and feel ineffective (Maslach, 2017). Table 9.1 provides an overview of some signs and symptoms of burnout. Stress and burnout are not unique to the helping professions, but it does seem that those working in such careers may be at high risk. For example, 42% of physicians recently reported being burned out (Peckham, 2018) and more than 90% of teachers in one study reported high levels of stress (Herman, Hickmon-Rosa, & Reinke, 2018). It's particularly upsetting to note that teacher stress has been linked to stress in *students*: kids with teachers reporting burnout have demonstrated higher levels of cortisol, a biological indicator of stress, at the start of their school day (Oberle & Schonert-Reichl, 2016).

Doctors are burned out, teachers and students are stressed ... why should school psychologists be any different? Despite the fact that a meta-analysis of

TABLE 9.1 Signs of Burnout

Physical Symptoms	Emotional/Cognitive Symptoms	Social/Behavioral Symptoms
• Chronic fatigue, exhaustion	• Difficulty concentrating	• Isolation from coworkers, friends, family
• Trouble sleeping	• Lack of focus	• Detachment
• Chest pain, palpitations	• Memory problems	• Lack of productivity
• Headaches	• Anxiety	• Poor work performance
• Dizziness	• Depression	• Avoidance (e.g., calling in sick frequently)
• Gastrointestinal pain	• Irritability, anger	
• Frequent illness	• Loss of enjoyment (of work or personal life)	
• Changes in appetite		
• Overuse of alcohol, caffeine, drugs	• Pessimism, hopelessness, apathy	

Source: Carter (2013)

research from the 1980s and 1990s determined that almost 85% of school psychologists were satisfied or even very satisfied with their jobs (VanVoorhis & Levinson, 2006), in a more recent study of burnout more than half of school psychologists reported feeling seriously ineffective and 37% were emotionally exhausted (Boccio, Weisz, & Lefowitz, 2016). On the positive side, only 5% of respondents indicated high levels of depersonalization, or feeling detached from or cynical towards their clients. Understandably, these school psychologists also indicated less job satisfaction and a desire to leave their job, or even the field, altogether. This trend is a serious concern, given the already existing shortage of school psychologists nationwide (Castillo, Curtis, & Tan, 2014).

School psychologists may be vulnerable to burnout for a variety of reasons. For example, administrative pressure to act in unethical ways (e.g., to withhold recommendations that might be expensive or support an overly restrictive special education placement) has been linked to higher rates of burnout (Boccio et al., 2016). Leung and Jackson (2014) identified four sources of burnout for school psychologists: (1) inadequate administrative support, (2) resistance from consumers (teachers, parents, administrators), (3) experiencing a limited impact on students due to things like bureaucratic or societal structural barriers, and (4) the sheer intensity of the workload (both the amount of work and its emotional intensity). Whatever the source, the problem of burnout is real: as a school psychologist once posted on social media, "Have [you] ever felt so underappreciated and so overworked it makes [you] physically sick?"

School Psychologists and Resilience

As school psychologists we are experts at reframing difficulties, so let's examine the other side of the burnout coin: resilience. "Resilience" is a term that has been defined in a variety of ways, but as Prince-Embury (2012) put it, resilience can be thought of as, "the ability to weather adversity or to bounce back from negative experience" (p. 10). We often think about resilience in terms of how children and adolescents respond to challenging experiences and circumstances, but we can also turn that view on ourselves as professionals. Often working in diverse roles with competing priorities and high-stakes decisions to make, school psychologists definitely need to be resilient to survive.

Working from a resiliency model allows school psychologists to apply principles from positive psychology to promote effectiveness and life satisfaction (Leung & Jackson, 2014). One of the most encouraging aspects of this model is that, while resiliency researchers acknowledge that to some extent resilience may be an inherent personal trait, it is possible to *learn* to become more resilient (Higgins, 1994). This is critically important for supervisors to understand, because it means not only can you continually work to build your own resiliency reserves, but you also have the potential to foster resilience in supervisees through teaching and modeling. Nurturing resilience in your supervisees can help build better adjusted, more effective school psychologists who may stay in the field longer and help more children and families throughout their careers.

Leung and Jackson (2014) present a framework for building resiliency based on three protective factors: self-awareness, balance, and lifelong learning. These authors articulate a variety of "resiliency builders" that school psychologists across the career span can use to promote professional satisfaction. Some of these suggestions are integrated into Table 9.2, which highlights ways for everyone from graduate students to veteran practitioners to stay energized and engaged in their work as school psychologists. Think about ways you can incorporate some of these ideas into your own efforts to combat burnout and how you can encourage supervisees to do the same.

Self-Care for Supervisors and Supervisees

A Definition of Self-Care

Dorociak, Rupert, Bryant, and Zahniser (2017) define self-care as, "a multi-dimensional, multifaceted process of purposeful engagement in strategies that promote healthy functioning and enhance well-being" (p. 326). This means it involves a variety of components and behaviors that are executed in a thought-out, planful manner. As a respected colleague of mine once said, "it's more than just getting a massage" (Jacobs, Kaplan, Silva, & Murphy, 2018). As Box 9.1 highlights, this definition also emphasizes that self-care is a *process* that requires reflection and periodic adjustments based on personal and professional development and changes in circumstances. I know that for me, self-care looked pretty different when I was a new school psychologist in my late 20s than it does now that I'm a working mother and professor in my early 40s. We need to regularly reappraise what we need in terms of self-care and adapt accordingly.

BOX 9.1 SELF-CARE: BIG IDEAS

Self-care...

- Is multidimensional
- Is multifaceted
- Is purposeful
- Is a process
- Promotes healthy functioning
- Enhances well-being

Note: from Dorociak et al. (2017)

The framework of mindfulness-based positive principles and practices (Wise, Hersh, & Gibson, 2012) emphasizes four foundational ideas that can help guide our self-care efforts:

1. Focus on *flourishing* rather than surviving.
2. *Intentionally* choose self-care.
3. Recognize that your self-care efforts *reciprocally* benefit supervisees and clients.
4. *Integrate* self-care into existing practices, rather than adding it on as something extra.

Be a Role Model: Care for Yourself

We often turn to the "oxygen mask" metaphor when considering self-care: that idea that you have to help yourself first in order to be available to help others in need. This really is true when it comes to supervision. Think about the worst supervisor you ever had, and then check out the list of burnout symptoms in Table 9.1. How many of those descriptors fit? Were they irritable? Cynical? Frequently absent? Lacking awareness of current research and developments in the field? Not all bad supervisors are burned out, but probably most burned-out supervisors are bad at supervision. That's because supervising future or fellow school psychologists takes time, patience, energy, and an enthusiasm for the field that includes a commitment to professional development and lifelong learning. Supervisors who don't engage in sufficient self-care to cope with the stress and demands of the job are unlikely to be available to provide quality supervision.

TABLE 9.2 Fostering Resilience across a School Psychologist's Career

	Inner Direction (Know Yourself)	Sharpen the Saw (Need for a Balanced Life)	Love of Learning (Lifelong Learner)
Preservice (graduate school, internship)	• Begin developing personal vision of school psychology • Identify preferences and areas of interest • Identify domains of strength across NASP (2010) Practice Model • Identify preferred work settings, populations	• Lay the foundation for self-care by establishing good habits from the very beginning and maintain them throughout your career • Make time each week for interests, friends, and family • Get regular physical activity (try different things each week) • Eat a balanced diet (try learning new cooking techniques as a hobby!) • Practice good sleep hygiene	• Join professional organization(s); attend local, regional, and national conferences • Cultivate a growth mindset; embrace challenges or setbacks as opportunities for learning • Take advantage of professional development opportunities on campus
Early career (1–8 yrs)	• Cultivate a long-term view (change doesn't happen overnight) • Find open doors to change: build relationships with teachers willing to try new things • Internalize students' successes; learn from failures • Look for ways to work "smarter not harder"	• Find time to get out of the office (e.g., visit classrooms) • Try to balance direct-service roles (e.g., testing, counseling) with indirect service or other domains of practice • Pursue school-level leadership opportunities or special projects that foster change	• Maintain membership in professional organizations; attend conferences for learning and networking • Pursue/maintain national certification • Stay connected with your graduate school network of faculty and classmates • Mentor or supervise interns or practicum students
Midcareer (10–18 yrs)	• Identify roles that fulfill you and make time for them	• Seek strategies to balance work and caregiving responsibilities	• Pursue leadership positions in professional organizations

	• Set realistic goals that build on strengths • Focus on successes • Consider the long-term impact you have had on clients' lives	• Eat lunch every day • Do as much paperwork as possible at school • Set limits on commitments; devote your time to roles that fulfill you	• Mentor or supervise interns or practicum students • Pursue additional or specialized training to enhance skills • Guest lecture or teach for a graduate program
Veteran (19+)	• Seek out challenging opportunities in areas of professional interest • Acknowledge and accept inherent limitations/barriers beyond your control • Recognize evidence of both short-term and long-term successes	• Continue to engage in practices that promote health and fitness • Schedule quality time with loved ones • Build new personal and professional connections, or reconnect with past colleagues • Engage in peer supervision to network and enhance skills • Pursue opportunities in areas of professional interest	• Continue or pursue leadership positions in professional organizations • Provide professional development opportunities for other school psychologists • Supervise other school psychologists and/or trainees • Pursue an advanced degree or specialized credential • Teach as an adjunct professor

Note: Based on framework from Leung and Jackson (2014)

Another extremely important reason that supervisors must attend to self-care is that they often serve as key role models for supervisees. The habits and strategies you employ may become the very same behaviors your supervisees adopt, be they effective or maladaptive. This is why it's essential to not only "talk the talk" but also "walk the walk" when it comes to self-care. Are you encouraging your supervisee to head home to relax after a long day, but staying at the office until 8pm to finish your own stack of work? Stressing the importance of taking breaks as you eat lunch while working on a report? It's important to step back and examine your own behavior as part of a coordinated approach to self-care that can benefit both you and your supervisees.

Methods of Self-Care

Remember: what constitutes effective self-care is different for everyone and likely changes over the course of one's training and career. Therefore, having a broad sense of what might work can help you develop effective self-care plans year after year. The literature on self-care emphasizes some common themes that can help organize the wide range of strategies that might work for you or for different supervisees (see Dorociak et al., 2017; Norcross & Guy, 2007; Walsh, 2011; Wise et al., 2012).

Professional Support

Sometimes the best way to cope with the stresses of being a school psychologist is to talk to other school psychologists. Who else could possibly understand the insanity of annual-review season or the stress of being pressured by an administrator to agree to a decision that you don't think is right? Professional support as self-care includes strategies such as seeking your own supervision, engaging with professional organizations (NASP, APA, and state/regional school psychology associations), and attending conferences or pursuing other forms of professional development. Anything that connects you with other school psychologists could constitute professional support.

Personal Support

As much as we need to talk with other school psychologists to cope with the demands of the job, there are also those times when the *last* thing you want to do is talk about school psychology. Or you want to talk about work with someone who can provide an outsider's perspective. Having friends, family, and other loved ones to turn to is an essential component of self-care. Research has established that relationships are key to physical and mental health, and good relationships are associated with important qualities like resilience (Walsh, 2011). Of course, for some of us quiet time alone is an essential form of self-care; that can certainly have its place. But if you find yourself, or observe a supervisee, becoming noticeably isolated from interpersonal connections, it can be a warning sign that something needs to change.

Work–Life Balance

We talk a lot about maintaining balance, but it's often much easier said than done. It's important to recognize that balance is an ongoing process. Sometimes it helps to focus on maintaining balance on a broad level, other times it's on a day-by-day or even a minute-by-minute basis. So this could be everything from planning a big vacation for a school break, to taking five minutes off from the report you've been working on for hours to play an online game to standing up to walk the halls in between back-to-back IEP meetings. It also involves setting boundaries. This may mean that you commit yourself to not checking email after a certain point in the day or doing everything possible to leave work at work. Finally, balance is as much about time allocation as it is balancing the types of activities you engage in, professionally and personally. If you are testing students all day, every day and don't find that rewarding, balance means looking for opportunities to shift your role a bit. Finding balance is a very personal thing that depends on many factors, such as whether you're responsible for caring for other people, the working conditions at your job, and how efficiently you're able to work at a given stage of your career. It's also something that takes practice and won't always go smoothly. When you find yourself out of balance, part of self-care is acknowledging it and accepting it, and working to get the see-saw to tilt back in the other direction.

Cognitive Strategies

If you've had even minimal experience with cognitive behavioral therapy (CBT), you likely understand that our thoughts affect our feelings and behaviors. It's important to remain aware of our thoughts and feelings and monitor triggers that are likely to make us vulnerable to stress (Dorociak et al., 2017). When change is needed, the principles of CBT may be helpful. Disputing and changing unhelpful thoughts is something we often try to help students do; this approach can be a form of self-care for school psychologists themselves. When you find yourself up against a tough case thinking, "I'm useless," think about all the students, teachers, and families you *have* helped in your work. Or if you feel overwhelmed by the pressures and frustrations of working in a bureaucratic system, empower yourself by remembering why you *chose* the job you did and why you choose to stay. Many of the techniques we use to encourage struggling students can do double duty as strategies for caring for ourselves when confronting challenging situations.

Physical Self-Care

We sometimes think about things like taking time to exercise, eating right, and getting enough sleep as the basics of self-care. And for good reason: these strategies are good for pretty much all human beings! But they're some of the first things to go when work gets busy. Personally, I've found two strategies helpful for incorporating more physical activity into my self-care regimen: scheduling it and multitasking it. I actually block out time in my calendar a few times a week to go to the gym or for a run, or I sign up (and pay in advance for) workout classes. Something about seeing that "appointment" in my schedule makes me more committed to following through on being active and less likely to agree to meetings that would conflict with those plans. It doesn't always work, but it's more effective than just telling myself I'm going to do it. And when I do go to the gym, sometimes I try to get other things done while I'm there. I'm probably one of the few people on the elliptical machines who's reading psychology journal articles or reviewing reports or papers! Or alternatively, I'll use the time on the workout machine to give myself a mental break and stream a TV series I want to catch up on, or read the news. How I manage it depends on the day, time of year, and my mood, but it almost always helps my mental and physical state.

Another aspect of physical self-care that sometimes comes up in the literature is the importance of experiencing nature. As Walsh (2011) notes, spending lots of time indoors is associated with disruptions in mood and sleep, as well as impairments in attention and cognition. Depending on where in the world you are, getting out into the woods, the mountains, or the beach may be easier said than done, but if you find yourself in a place where you can step outside for some physical activity, it's like another self-care two-for-one. Even something as simple as a walk around the outside of your building, or maybe a few laps around the high school track at lunchtime can break up the day, get you out of your office, and help reset your mind and body for the afternoon rush. When I worked in an elementary school I tried to pop out to the playground for recess a few times a week to check in on students, observe behaviors and social interactions, and enjoy the hilarious things kindergarteners had to say. Again, this felt like multitasking; I was getting some daylight and fresh air while also keeping an eye on my students.

Box 9.2 provides examples of strategies that tap into some of these self-care methods.

BOX 9.2 MULTIPURPOSE SELF-CARE IDEAS

Bang for Your Buck: Multipurpose Self-Care Ideas

- **Join a team**. Whether it's softball, soccer, dance, or roller derby, making a commitment to a group or team activity helps build connections with others and provides physical activity. Plus you'll have scheduled games or meets, which will make you more likely to follow through and show up.

- **Coach a team**. I know a number of school psychologists who coach after school. Not only is this a source of additional income, but it provides opportunities for physical activity, connections with other adults in education, and the chance to see students strive and thrive in a non-academic setting that is potentially quite rewarding.

- **Advise a club**. Similar to coaching, serving as an advisor to a student organization provides opportunities to connect with students outside the classroom and give back to the school community.

- **Get a (group) hobby**. Joining a group with shared interests promotes the kinds of interpersonal connections that constitute good self-care. A book club, garage band, theater group, or community service organization might be just the thing to promote relaxation and meaningful connections with others.

- **Visit recess**. If you work in any elementary schools try to take a few minutes to get out to the playground. This will get you out of your office, break up the day, get you some fresh air and natural light, and provide the opportunity to do some informal behavior observations of students on your caseload or coach emerging social skills.

- **Eat lunch**. How ridiculous does this sound? But I know for some school psychologists it's tempting to work on reports or return emails while shoveling down a meal. Even if it's just once or twice a week, stepping away from your desk to eat can provide a much-needed break. Whether or not to eat with colleagues is an individual decision; if visiting the teachers' lounge means you'll be bombarded with requests, it may not be the best self-care move. But if you can spend the time connecting with others without making it about work, go for it! Another efficient alternative is to hold a "lunch bunch" group and eat with students while simultaneously working on social skills (assuming you find that time with students enjoyable and not stressful).

- **Practice mindfulness**. There are few topics hotter than mindfulness these days, and you may already be incorporating such concepts into your work with young people. But do you apply these ideas to your own life? Learning about mindfulness can contribute to your professional development by keeping you current on developments in the field, and you can reap the benefits by teaching students to practice mindfulness and participating right alongside them. Win, win, win!

- **Go to a conference.** There's nothing that gets me more excited about being a school psychologist than attending the annual NASP convention. Not only is it a wonderful opportunity to learn new skills and content by attending sessions, but also to contribute to the professional development of others by presenting. And catching up with friends from graduate school, making new professional connections, and seeing new cities doesn't hurt either. If a national conference isn't realistic for you, maybe there's a state or regional meeting closer to home to check out. Either way, you can reap multiple self-care benefits in terms of professional development and building your interpersonal professional support network.

- **Undergo therapy.** As school psychologists we appreciate and promote the value of mental health, yet we can be surprisingly reluctant to seek support ourselves. Participating in therapy not only has the potential to build coping resources and help address problems that may contribute to stress and diminished functioning, but also gives us a better understanding of what it's like for our students and their families to take the step of seeking treatment.

Assessing Self-Care

I have learned that checking in on how [supervisees] are feeling and their level of stress is important and something that should be routinely discussed.

(A.M., First-time supervisor)

What do school psychologists love more than data-based decision making? Not much. With that in mind, you may be wondering if there's a way to measure self-care needs and behaviors. The Professional Self-Care Scale (PCSC; Dorociak et al., 2017) was recently developed as a tool for research on self-care, but it could easily be used to promote self-reflection and organize conversations around self-care. At 21 items, it is relatively brief and it has emerging evidence of reliability and validity. As an alternative, Handout 9.1 presents a questionnaire you could use to structure reflections on your own self-care, and prompt discussions about self-care with supervisees.

In addition to comprehensively assessing self-care for longer-term planning purposes, it's important to monitor self-care on a frequent basis. A quick self-care check-in can be part of every supervision session. This normalizes discussions of self-care and emphasizes its importance. You can even make it a collaborative effort and model good practices by asking, "How are *we* doing on self-care this week?"

The Self-Care Plan

Preparing and planning ahead for quality self-care can be far more effective than trying to react when you begin to notice that you or your supervisee is beginning to burn out. Just like a supervision contract, a written self-care plan (SCP) documents and organizes what's going to happen and can help keep you accountable, even if only to yourself. Personally, I find I'm almost always more likely to follow through with something that I've written down. Like a remediation plan, you can approach an SCP like a behavior plan, because the goal of the SCP is to encourage and reinforce healthy self-care behaviors. And like a BIP, it has to include things that are actually reinforcing in order to work. So if you absolutely hate going to the gym, including that as a strategy in your self-care plan isn't likely to be effective.

Because our self-care needs change over time and according to circumstances, SCPs should be revisited and revised on a regular basis, such as at the start and end of the school year, or during particularly stressful periods, such as annual-review season. For supervisees, self-care planning could be done in conjunction with summative evaluations and within the broader context of professional development planning.

A template for an SCP and a sample plan are provided as Handout 9.2. The first step towards improved self-care is to develop your plan! After doing so, you will be in the perfect position to encourage supervisees to do the same.

Supervisor's Summary

- Self-care is an ethical imperative for school psychology supervisors, who are role models for supervisees and responsible for monitoring their effectiveness.
- Burnout is a feeling of depletion resulting from intense or chronic stress that leaves individuals feeling exhausted, cynical and ineffective. Without effective self-care, teachers and school psychologists are susceptible to burnout.
- Working from a resiliency model allows school psychologists to apply principles from positive psychology to promote effectiveness and job satisfaction.
- Self-care is a multidimensional, multifaceted, purposeful process that promotes healthy functioning and enhances well-being (Dorociak et al., 2017)
- Methods of self-care can be organized around professional support, personal support, work–life balance, cognitive strategies, and physical self-care.

- Assessment of self-care practices can be used to inform the development of an SCP, which organizes and formalizes plans for implementing a range of self-care strategies.

FINAL REFLECTIONS

- How would you rate your commitment to self-care at this moment in your career?
- What have been the most effective self-care strategies for you?
- How involved do you feel you should be in your supervisees' self-care planning?
- Consider the symptoms of burnout presented in this chapter. How many of them have you experienced? Have you noticed them in supervisees or coworkers?

References

Boccio, D. E., Weisz, G., & Lefowitz, R. (2016). Administrative pressure to practice unethically and burnout within the profession of school psychology. *Psychology in the Schools, 53*(6), 659–672. doi:10.1002/pits.21931.

Carter, S. B. (2013). The telltale signs of burnout . . . Do you have them? *Psychology Today,* November 26. Retrieved from www.psychologytoday.com/us/blog/high-octane-women/201311/the-tell-tale-signs-burnout-do-you-have-them.

Castillo, J. M., Curtis, M. J., & Tan, S. Y. (2014). Personnel needs in school psychology: A 10-year follow up study on predicted personnel shortages. *Psychology in the Schools, 51* (8), 832–849. doi:10.1002/pits.21786.

Dorociak, K. F., Rupert, P. A., Bryant, F. B., & Zahniser, E. (2017). Development of the Professional Self-Care Scale. *Journal of Counseling Psychology, 64*(3), 325–334. doi:10.1037/cou0000206.

Herman, K. C., Hickmon-Rosa, J., & Reinke, W. M. (2018). Empirically derived profiles of teacher stress, burnout, self-efficacy, and coping and associated student outcomes. *Journal of Positive Behavior Interventions, 20*(2), 90–100. doi:10.1177/1098300717732066.

Higgins, G. O. (1994). *Resilient adults: Overcoming a cruel past.* San Francisco, CA: Jossey-Bass.

Jacobs, D. B., Kaplan, J., Silva, A., & Murphy, C. (2018, February). Be good to yourself: Fostering self-care and psychological hardiness. Paper presented at the annual meeting of the National Association of School Psychologists, Chicago, IL.

Leung, B. P., & Jackson, J. (2014). Best practices in maintaining professional effectiveness, enthusiasm, and confidence. In P. L. Harrison & A. Thomas (Eds.), *Best practices in school psychology: Foundations* (pp. 641–650). Bethesda, MD: National Association of School Psychologists.

Maslach, C. (2017). Finding solutions to the problem of burnout. *Consulting Psychology Journal: Practice and Research, 69*(2), 143–152. doi:10.1037/cpb0000090.

Norcross, J. C., & Guy, J. D. (2007). *Leaving it at the office: A guide to psychotherapist self-care.* New York: Guilford Press.

National Association of School Psychologists. (2010). *Model for comprehensive and integrated school psychological services*. Bethesda, MD: Author.

Oberle, E., & Schonert-Reichl, K. A. (2016). Stress contagion in the classroom? The link between classroom teacher burnout and morning cortisol in elementary school students. *Social Science & Medicine, 159*, 30–37. doi:10.1016/j.socscimed.2016.04.031.

Peckham, C. (2018, January 17). Medscape national physician burnout & depression report 2018. Retrieved from www.medscape.com/slideshow/2018-lifestyle-burnout-depression-6009235#2

Prince-Embury, S. (2012). Translating resilience theory for assessment and application with children, adolescents, and adults: Conceptual issues. In S. Prince-Embury & D. H. Saklofske (Eds.), *Resilience in children, adolescents, and adults: Translating research into practice* (pp. 9–16). New York: Springer.

Suran, B. G., & Sheridan, E. P. (1985). Management of burnout: Training psychologists in professional life span perspectives. *Professional Psychology: Research and Practice, 16*(6), 741–752. doi:10.1037/0735-7028.16.6.741.

VanVoorhis, R. W., & Levinson, E. M. (2006). Job satisfaction among school psychologists: A meta-analysis. *School Psychology Quarterly, 21*(1), 77–90. doi:10.1521/scpq.2006.21.1.77.

Walsh, R. (2011). Lifestyle and mental health. *American Psychologist, 66*(7), 579–592. doi:10.1037/a0021769.

Wise, E. H., Hersh, M. A., & Gibson, C. M. (2012). Ethics, self-care and well-being for psychologists: Reenvisioning the stress-distress continuum. *Professional Psychology: Research and Practice, 43*(5), 487–494. doi:10.1037/a0029446.

HANDOUT 9.1 SELF-CARE ASSESSMENT

Name:		Date:	

How would you describe your self-care efforts right now (circle a rating from 1–10)?

Poor	I'm hanging on, but I need help			Sufficient		I'm doing pretty well...			Excellent
1	2	3	4	5	6	7	8	9	10

Consider the following options and indicate whether/how often you use the strategy.

	I do this often	I do this sometimes	I do this rarely/ never
I engage in supportive *professional* relationships with other school psychologists.			
I engage in supportive *professional* relationships with non-school psychologists (e.g., teachers, administrators, other mental health professionals).			
I engage in supportive *personal* relationships (e.g., family, friends, partner).			
I engage with professional organizations in the field.			
I pursue ongoing professional development opportunities to enhance my existing skills and/or build new ones.			
I look for ways to maximize opportunities to do the parts of my job that I like best.			
I periodically think about what situations or aspects of my job are most likely to trigger stress for me and consider ways to avoid or limit them.			
I take time to reflect on the good parts of my job (e.g., positive impact on students, families, teachers).			

(*Continued*)

(Cont).

I take breaks and leave my office or workspace for at least a few minutes a few times each day.			
I leave work at the office.			
I ask for help from colleagues or supervisors when I need it.			
I get outside and spend time in nature.			
I engage in mindfulness exercises or meditation, even if just briefly.			
I engage in physical activity (e.g., walk, go to the gym, yoga).			
I maintain healthy sleep habits and get sufficient rest.			
I try to eat balanced meals and nutritious foods.			
I engage in a hobby or interest that is enjoyable to me.			
I participate in volunteer work/service that contributes positively to others.			

What are your current self-care goals?

Note: Developed from review of Dorociak et al. (2017); Norcross and Guy (2007); Walsh (2011); Wise et al. (2012)

SAMPLE SELF-CARE PLAN
For September 2018 through June 2019
SPECIFIC SELF-CARE TO-DO TASKS

What	*By When*	*Completed?* ✓
I will download a mindfulness/meditation app for my phone	September 1st	
I will meet my former supervisor for coffee	December 15th	
I will attend this year's state school psychology conference	May 15th	

ONGOING SELF-CARE GOALS

What	When	Where	How Much/ How Often?	Evaluation
I will practice mindfulness	When I arrive at school	In my office	Daily for 5 minutes	☐ **I did this consistently** ☐ **I did this intermittently** ☐ **I did this not often or at all**
I will attend Pilates class	Tuesdays at 4:30pm	Pilates Plus	Weekly	☐ **I did this consistently** ☐ **I did this intermittently** ☐ **I did this not often or at all**

(Continued)

(Cont).

I will visit a kindergarten classroom	During afternoon free play time	Mrs. Kindergarten Teacher's room	Twice a month for 20 minutes	☐ **I did this consistently** ☐ **I did this intermittently** ☐ **I did this not often or at all**
I will get a massage	At the end of the semester	The spa in Anytown, USA	Twice per school year	☐ **I did this consistently** ☐ **I did this intermittently** ☐ **I did this not often or at all**
I will attend group supervision with other district psychologists	First Friday of each month	Central office building	Monthly for 90 minutes	☐ **I did this consistently** ☐ **I did this intermittently** ☐ **I did this not often or at all**

NOTES (e.g., things that worked, things that didn't, things to add or change)

September	
October	
November	
December	
January	

(*Continued*)

(Cont).

February	
March	
April	
May	
June	

HANDOUT 9.2 SELF-CARE PLAN

For _____ through _____

SPECIFIC SELF-CARE TO-DO TASKS

What	By When	Completed?

ONGOING SELF-CARE GOALS

What	When	Where	How Much/How Often?	Evaluation
				☐ I did this consistently ☐ I did this intermittently ☐ I did this not often or at all
				☐ I did this consistently ☐ I did this intermittently ☐ I did this not often or at all
				☐ I did this consistently ☐ I did this intermittently ☐ I did this not often or at all
				☐ I did this consistently ☐ I did this intermittently ☐ I did this not often or at all
				☐ I did this consistently ☐ I did this intermittently ☐ I did this not often or at all

NOTES (e.g., things that worked, things that didn't, things to add or change)

September	
October	
November	
December	
January	
February	
March	
April	
May	
June	

10

TECHNOLOGY AND SUPERVISION

With Dan Florell

Technology has become an integral part of school psychology practice. For supervisors, this can be very helpful for important tasks such as recording and reviewing sessions or editing reports. But, as is so often the case, there are pros and cons to the ways we use technology for supervision. This chapter will provide an overview of some important considerations for supervisors when it comes to using technology and will highlight helpful resources.

Protecting Sensitive Information

All school psychologists are ethically obligated to protect clients' private information, but supervisors have the added responsibility of ensuring that supervisees do so as well. And given the need for supervisees and supervisors to exchange drafts of reports, share case notes, or send electronic recordings of sessions, there are additional considerations involved. Technology can make it easier to do these things, but also presents some important factors to keep in mind.

Communication

As a supervisor you probably exchange a lot of emails with supervisees. However, this mode of communication is notoriously bad for keeping information private and confidential. For one thing, it's just too easy to type in the wrong email address or have people forward messages to others. Also, employers can go through employee emails for content (Kanz, 2001; Wilczenski & Coomey, 2006). To play it safe, try to reserve email for clerical and administrative communication related to supervision such as scheduling sessions or making sure documents were received (Barnett, 2011; Cummings, 2002). Email *can* be secured and used for discussing students' personal information but it is not simple to do. For those who would still like to use email in supervision, try Hushmail (www.hushmail.com), which is HIPAA-compliant, but has a fee for use.

Text messaging is little better than email and should really be avoided when discussing clients, as it has the same issues regarding privacy and confidentiality. It also runs the risk of devolving into a less formal, or even unprofessional, mode of communication. That said, texting can be used through an app that uses encryption and an anonymizer to ensure security. Such options include Telegram, TigerText, TextSecure, and Wickr.

Cloud Computing

Much of the most important information in our lives is "in the cloud" these days, including sensitive information about our clients. Ideally, a medical system that is HIPAA-compliant would be the best place to store reports, videos, assessments, and clinical notes. With regard to notes, a popular system for psychologists is Therapy Notes (www.therapynotes.com), though this requires a monthly fee for use. Many schools today are using G-Suites by Google, which includes an amazing array of utilities. G-Suites can be HIPAA-compliant, but caution should be used by encrypting files. Other popular cloud storage options include Dropbox (www.dropbox.com) and Box (www.box.com/home).

Remember, "loose lips sink ships." Even though most cloud storage companies have options for HIPAA secure services, these companies only guarantee that the *system* is secured. The security becomes compromised the moment people allow access to any files on the cloud beyond themselves or those outside the school district or organization.

File Sharing

Electronically transferring reports or other documents that include personal information is fraught with the risk of violating student privacy. One low-tech way to prevent problems is to only exchange draft documents that are stripped of any and all identifying information. Names, birthdates, and any other identifying or sensitive information can be added in at the last moment before printing or submitting the finalized version. Even better, encrypting documents makes them unreadable by anyone without the "key" or password to the file. There are services, such as Boxcryptor (www.boxcryptor.com), that will encrypt documents in a safe and secure manner. Note that this does *not* include email. Another option is Hightail (www.hightail.com), which allows file sharing by emailing a time-limited link to the document for the recipient to download. After the link has expired, the file is deleted.

Using Technology to Support Supervision

If you consider yourself tech-savvy it may be tempting to look for ways to integrate it into all aspects of work and life. However, when it comes to supervision, don't get enamored with using technology for technology's sake; rather, consider how technology can be used to *enhance* the supervision process (Florell, 2016). Online learning and networking are two examples of areas in which the digital age can really help support supervision.

Social Networking

Social networks and listservs provide ample expertise on a variety of issues. With a few keystrokes you can connect with school psychologists across the country or around the world to get guidance on tricky issues or encouragement on a tough day. The NASP website even includes a wealth of information on using social media to promote school psychology (see www.nasponline.org/membership-and-community/social-media). However, there are some things to keep in mind before you or your supervisee create a post. First, consider the qualifications of the members in the group and be mindful of how private (or not) the setting is (Florell, 2016). Are you posting to the Trainers of School Psychologists listserv (https://tsp.wildapricot.org/page-18179)? Probably an excellent forum to ask questions about graduate education or supervision. An open Facebook group for school psychologists (e.g., School Psychology Forum: www.facebook.com/groups/141798755860302)? A great place to get intervention ideas from members with a wide range of experiences. Wherever you may be posting or connecting, always be sure to de-identify any personal data before posting questions or anecdotes, and be extremely thoughtful if you post any photos (Myers, Endres, Ruddy, & Zelikovsky, 2012). Ask yourself if there is *any* chance that a subject of the post might be identifiable, even if you're saying something nice!

Accessing Research

School psychologists, and particularly school psychology supervisors, must be up to date on current research related to the field. Google Scholar (https://scholar.google.com/) can be a helpful resource for tracking down articles, and supervisees enrolled in university training programs likely have access to professional journal databases loaded with a vast array of psychology and education publications. NASP members can access current and past issues of *School Psychology Review* as well as *School Psychology Forum*.

With respect to evidence-based interventions, there are several helpful (and free!) sites that supervisors and supervisees should be sure to bookmark for their own access, as well as to share with teachers and parents. See Box 10.1 for a description of some of these options.

BOX 10.1 HELPFUL INTERVENTION WEBSITES

- **Intervention Central** (www.interventioncentral.org). An excellent place to get resources for RTI, with sections on various empirically validated academic and behavioral interventions. The academic interventions are organized by IDEA category, making it easy to find options that link with specific deficits. For behavior interventions, there are several resources for common issues such as de-escalating, increasing motivation, and assisting with self-management.
- **What Works Clearinghouse** (https://ies.ed.gov/ncee/wwc). Loaded with resources on everything from reading and math to science to English learners, the goal of the WWC is to help educators made evidence-based decisions.
- **National Center on Intensive Intervention** (https://intensiveintervention.org). Provides resources on how to implement intensive interventions in literacy, math, and behavior for students with a high level of need. The site ascribes to a data-based individualization (DBI) approach, which integrates assessment data, validated interventions and intensive strategies.
- **Florida Center for Reading Research** (www.fcrr.org). A multidisciplinary research center at Florida State University, FCRR conducts and disseminates research related to literacy assessment and instruction for grades pre-K to 12.
- **The IRIS Center** (https://iris.peabody.vanderbilt.edu). This site supports education outcomes for all children, particularly those with disabilities. It highlights empirically validated practices and interventions for academic and behavioral problems along with an RTI/MTSS focus. Training modules on topics such as FBA can be helpful for teachers, parents, and supervisees.
- **Understood** (www.understood.org/en). Maintained by a collaborative of non-profits for parents who have children with learning and attention issues, this site provides tips on the special education process, perspectives from other parents, and expert opinions on various issues.
- **Reading Rockets** (www.readingrockets.org). Designed for parents and teachers, this site focuses on assisting young readers and provides a wealth of resources for parents, including suggestions of books to read and techniques that can be used at home.
- **Khan Academy** (www.khanacademy.org). This site can help parents understand math concepts and the way they are currently taught in school. It also includes history resources.

Professional Development

Online learning is easy to do and supervisors can immediately send supervisees to pertinent trainings on issues that arise. Some sites to try:

- **NASP Online Learning Center** (https://nasp.inreachce.com). Provides a wide variety of training options on school psychology topics, including webinars like "Applied Tips for Behaving Ethically with Today's Technology."
- **Schoolpsych.com** (https://schoolpsych.com). Allows access to various online webinars with a focus on using technology.
- **AATBS** (www.aatbs.com). Presents a broader sampling of online trainings that include more clinical topics.
- **Test Publishers**. Companies like Pearson (www.pearsonclinical.com), Psychological Assessment Resources (www.parinc.com), and MHS (www.mhs.com), among others, often offer *free* training on specific test instruments.

Telesupervision

The ability to conduct virtual meetings has the potential to increase access to supervision and mentoring for school psychologists through telesupervision, or supervision conducted via technology such as videoconference software. This is great news, considering the general lack of access to supervision that has persisted for decades (Silva, Newman, Guiney, Valley-Gray, & Barrett, 2016). However, there are pros and cons to this modality (see Table 10.1) and virtual supervision may be better for working with advanced supervisees or providing mentoring rather than for the supervision of preservice school psychologists or ECSPs (early career school psychologists). In fact, certification or licensure requirements may stipulate that only a specific portion of such supervision may be provided via video or audioconference, so be sure you are clear on what's permissible for each organization and/or state for which the supervisee plans to seek credentialing.

It's important to note that effective telesupervision requires more than just videoconferencing software. This is recognized in APA's *Guidelines for the Practice of Telepsychology*[1] and the practice guidelines available from the American Telemedicine Association,[2] two comprehensive documents that provide expert consensus regarding clinical videoconferencing. To summarize, what follows are some important considerations for providing telesupervision:

- **Mimic in-person supervision**. The closer technology can resemble live supervision, the more likely it will be accepted as part of the supervision process (Gammon, Sorlie, Bergvik, & Hoifodt, 1998). Now that videoconferencing has become more reliable and less expensive, it can be a helpful means

TABLE 10.1 The Pros and Cons of Telesupervision

Pros	Cons
• Videoconferencing comes close to mimicking in-person supervision • Increased accessibility for supervisees in rural and/or remote areas • Lowers cost of supervision • Greater flexibility for scheduling supervision • Enables increased peer consultation • Group supervision of supervisees' practices in different locations enhances exposure to diverse experiences and populations • Supervision can be recorded and documented easily • Ability to access primary research and intervention websites in session	• Easy to violate client confidentiality • Variability in how states define location of services and how licensure/certification/scope of practice applies • Telesupervision may not fit professional organizations' or government agencies' definitions of supervision; may not count towards licensure/certification requirements • Technology can glitch through unreliable connections or firewall interference

Note: adapted from Florell (2016)

of approximating in-person supervision, provided participants have sufficient connectivity to support the technology (Conn, Roberts, & Powell, 2009; Nelson, Nichter & Henriksen, 2010).

• **Use hybrid supervision to transition from face-to-face (F2F) to telesupervision** (Conn et al., 2009; Wood, Miller, & Hargrove, 2005). Whenever possible, start by establishing an in-person relationship between the supervisee and supervisor. Once you have a solid working relationship, incorporate more telesupervision as needed.

• **Check your tech**. Conduct a speed test (www.speedtest.net) to ensure your connection is sufficient to support videoconference software. This can vary based on time of day, so test regularly. You will need at least 1 Mbps upload and download speed for quality video conferencing for one-on-one sessions, and the ability to share a screen. Generally, the higher quality of video and the more participants on a video session, the more bandwidth you will need. Try to connect using a direct wired connection rather than Wi-Fi, as these are more stable and ensure a better connection. You will also need a webcam capable of producing high quality video and a computer with at least 1 GB of RAM and a dual core processor.

• **Remember to protect sensitive information**. Ensure data security and use of encryption for any technology that is going to be used (Rousmaniere, Russell, Kovnot, Norton, & Cloutier, 2014).

- **Choose your platform**. There are a variety of options available for "meeting" online. For example, VSee is a free option that provides HIPAA-compliant video conference software that allows for adequate privacy in live video interactions. For supervisors working with multiple supervisees in various sites (e.g., interns in different states), VSee is an option for conducting group supervision. It allows for sharing screens, so participants can see one another's case presentations or other information. Avoid the more popular video conference programs such as Skype, Facetime, or YouTube as they either do not ensure adequate privacy or are limited in their functionality, such as sharing screens or allowing multiple locations. Other videoconferencing options are presented in Table 10.2.
- **Prepare in advance**. As part of the transition from F2F to telesupervision, participate in in-person training with your supervisee to learn about the technology that is going to be used, if needed. Always test connections and technology early on when you're not pressed for time. Troubleshoot issues by trying a hypothetical case discussion in order to test equipment and get comfortable with the technology. Contact IT staff about issues regarding firewalls, bandwidth, and usage restrictions.
- **Consider travel restrictions**. If supervisee and/or supervisor travel to various locations, the portability of technology needs to be considered. Can your laptop support videoconferencing technology, or do you need to be at your desk tethered to your Ethernet cord to have access to a quality webcam? Also keep in mind that the technology needs to work smoothly across various platforms such as desktop computers, laptops, and smartphones (de Weger, Macinnes, Enser, Francis, & Jones, 2013).
- **Use good videoconferencing etiquette**. Box 10.2 reviews some basic guidelines that both supervisors and supervisees should follow to help telesupervision proceed smoothly.

TABLE 10.2 Videoconferencing Options

Name	Link
VSee	https://vsee.com
Zoom	https://zoom.us
Doxy	https://doxy.me
Wecounsel	www.wecounsel.com
Thera-Link	www.thera-link.com

BOX 10.2 VIDEOCONFERENCING ETIQUETTE 101

- Pick a location that is private and will not have other people coming in during the session.
- Position the camera so that facial expressions are visible.
- Turn off or silence other mobile devices such as smart phones.
- Use headphones with a microphone instead of relying on the computer's microphone, as audio will be more consistent and clear.
- Avoid placing anything too close to the microphone, particularly smartphones.
- Avoid making unnecessary movements while on screen.
- Avoid having side conversations.

Telesupervision and Contracting

When telesupervision is going to be part of your supervision plan your contract should include a few additional components. Contracting is all about clarifying expectations and details to prevent problems or confusion, so specifying certain details is likely to be helpful (also see Stretch, Nagel, & Anthony, 2012 for a list of contract considerations). First, designate a back-up plan if videoconferencing is unavailable by indicating phone numbers (including landlines) that the supervisor and supervisee can use to reach one another. Second, be sure to outline security procedures for clients and the supervisee and arrange for a local supervisor to be available in case of an emergency (Abbass et al., 2011; Panos, Panos, Cox, Roby, & Matheson, 2002). Finally, specify exactly how technology will be used for telesupervision (Rousmaniere, 2014). This includes explicitly stating the technology to be used to back up clinical notes and reports, and how personally identifiable information will be stored and safeguarded (Stretch et al., 2012).

Telesupervision and Informed Consent

As part of our ethical obligations as school psychologists, it is important that clients be aware that telesupervision is being used, so you will need to add language to existing informed consent documents if you are going to use this modality. Be sure to explicitly state what technology will be utilized as part of supervision. This should include that confidential information will be transmitted electronically and stored on a cloud server of a third-party company (Abbass et al., 2011; Baker & Bufka, 2011; Smith et al., 2011), how that information is going to be used, and what steps will be taken to ensure that their data remains confidential (Byrne & Hartley, 2010; Wood et al., 2005). Informed consent should address whether client sessions will be recorded and if they are to be used in the telesupervision sessions (Rousmaniere et al., 2014). If so, the form should cover how the video will be secured, de-identified, and encrypted. Box 10.3 presents a list of sample sections that can be used for such an informed consent document.

BOX 10.3 TELESUPERVISION INFORMED CONSENT COMPONENTS

- Types of Information We Collect and How We Collect It
- Definition of Personally Identifiable Information
- Effective Date and Changes to Privacy Notice
- Outline of Parent Rights re: Child Records

  - Types and location of information
  - Who information will be shared with
  - Requests to limit what is shared
  - Requested communication method
  - Other uses of information
  - Withdrawing consent
  - Filing a complaint

- Uses of Records by District
- When We Share Information without Prior Consent

Supervisor's Summary

- Technology can increase access to supervision and help make many aspects of it more convenient, but supervisors and supervisees must attend to concerns like protecting clients' privacy and ensuring the security of electronic records.
- Social networking and convenient access to online learning opportunities represent ways technology can enhance supervision.
- Telesupervision can make it possible to provide support to more school psychologists (particularly those beyond the ECSP stage), but it requires sufficient technology infrastructure.
- Hybrid supervision helps facilitate the transition from face-to-face supervision to telesupervision.
- Telesupervision requires attention to some additional contracting and informed consent considerations and specific etiquette concerns to facilitate an effective meeting.

FINAL REFLECTIONS

As you reflect on what you've learned about technology and supervision, consider these important questions that supervisors should be able to answer:

- Where are your records being stored? By which company?
- Who owns the information you have stored "in the cloud?" Who has access to it?
- For how long is your information going to be stored?
- What level of security do your cloud storage services (e.g., Google, Dropbox) have?
- What safeguards are in place to protect your stored information?

Notes

1 Available at www.apa.org/practice/guidelines/telepsychology.aspx.
2 Available at http://hub.americantelemed.org/resources/telemedicine-practice-guidelines.

References

Abbass, A., Arthey, S., Elliott, J., Fedak, T., Nowoweiski, D., Markovski, J., & Now-oweiski, S. (2011). Web-conference supervision for advanced psychotherapy training: A practical guide. *Psychotherapy*, *48*(2), 109–118. doi:10.1037/a0022427.

Baker, D. C., & Bufka, L. F. (2011). Preparing for the telehealth world: Navigating legal, regulatory, reimbursement, and ethical issues in the electronic age. *Professional Psychology: Research and Practice*, *42*(6), 405–411. doi:10.1037/a0025037.

Barnett, J. E. (2011). Utilizing technological innovations to enhance psychotherapy supervision, training, and outcomes. *Psychotherapy*, *48*(2), 103–108. doi:10.1037/a0023381.

Byrne, A. M., & Hartley, M. T. (2010). Digital technology in the 21st century: Considerations for clinical supervision in rehabilitation education. *Rehabilitation Education*, *24*, 57–68. doi:10.1891/088970110805029912.

Conn, S. R., Roberts, R. L., & Powell, B. M. (2009). Attitudes and satisfaction with a hybrid model of counseling supervision. *Educational Technology and Society*, *12*, 298–306. Retrieved from www.jstor.org/stable/jeductechsoci.12.2.298.

Cummings, P. (2002). Cybervision: Virtual peer group counselling supervision—Hindrance or help? *Counselling and Psychotherapy Research*, *2*(4), 223–229. doi:10.1080/14733140212331384705.

de Weger, E., Macinnes, D., Enser, J., Francis, S. J., & Jones, F. W. (2013). Implementing video conferencing in mental health practice. *Journal of Psychiatric and Mental Health Nursing*, *20*, 448–454. doi:10.1111/j.1365-2850.2012.01947.x.

Florell, D. (2016). Web-based training and supervision. In J. K. Luiselli & A. J. Fisher (Eds.), *Computer-assisted and web-based innovations in psychology, special education, and health* (pp. 313–337). London: Elsevier.

Gammon, D., Sørlie, T., Bergvik, S., & Sørensen Høifødt, T. (1998). Psychotherapy supervision conducted via videoconferencing: A qualitative study of users' experiences. *Nordic Journal of Psychiatry, 52*(5), 411–421. doi:10.1080/08039489850139445.

Kanz, J. E. (2001). Clinical-supervision.com: Issues in the provision of online supervision. *Professional Psychology: Research & Practice, 32*(4), 415–420. doi:10.1037/0735-7028.32.4.415.

Myers, S. B., Endres, M. A., Ruddy, M. E., & Zelikovsky, N. (2012). Graduate training in the era of online social networking. *Training and Education in Professional Psychology, 6*(1), 28–36. doi:10.1037/a0026388.

Nelson, J. A., Nichter, M., & Henriksen, R. (2010). On-line supervision and face-to-face supervision in the counseling internship: An exploratory study of similarities and differences. Retrieved from http://counselingoutfitters.com/vistas/vistas10/Article_46.pdf.

Panos, P. T., Panos, A., Cox, S. E., Roby, J. L., & Matheson, K. W. (2002). Ethical issues concerning the use of videoconferencing to supervise international social work field practicum students. *International Social Work, 38*(3), 421–437. doi:10.1080/10437797.2002.10779108.

Rousmaniere, T. (2014). Using technology to enhance clinical supervision and training. In C. E. Watkins Jr. & D. L. Milne (Eds.), *The Wiley international handbook of clinical supervision* (pp. 204-237). West Sussex, UK: John Wiley & Sons.

Rousmaniere, T., Abbass, A., Frederickson, J., Henning, I., & Taubner, S. (2014). Video-conference for psychotherapy training and supervision: Two case examples. *American Journal of Psychotherapy, 68*(2), 231–250. doi:10.1176/appi.psychotherapy.2014.68.2.231.

Silva, A. E., Newman, D. S., Guiney, M. C., Valley-Gray, S., & Barrett, C. A. (2016). Supervision and mentoring for early career school psychologists: Availability, access, structure, and implications. *Psychology in the Schools, 53*(5), 502–516. doi:10.1002/pits.21921.

Smith, R. E., Fagan, C., Wilson, N. L., Chen, J., Corona, M., Nguyen, H., . . . Shoda, Y. (2011). Internet-based approaches to collaborative therapeutic assessment: New opportunities for professional psychologists. *Professional Psychology: Research and Practice, 42*(6), 494–504. doi:10.1037/a0025392.

Stretch, L. S., Nagel, D. M., & Anthony, K. (2012). Ethical framework for the use of technology in supervision. *Therapeutic Innovations in Light of Technology, 3*(2), 39–45. Retrieved from http://onlinetherapyinstitute.com/wp-content/uploads/2013/08/EthicalFramework_FEATURE_Vol3_Issue213_FINAL3-4.pdf.

Wilczenski, F., & Coomey, S. (2006). Cyber-communication: Finding its place in school counseling practice, education, and professional development. *Professional School Counseling, 9*, 327–331. Retrieved from www.jstor.org/stable/42732693.

Wood, J. V., Miller, T. W., & Hargrove, D. S. (2005). Clinical supervision in rural settings: A telehealth model. *Professional Psychology: Research and Practice, 36*(2), 173–179. doi:10.1037/0735-7028.36.2.173.

SECTION IV

Developmentally Responsive Supervision

11

SUPERVISING INTERNS AND PRACTICUM STUDENTS

For supervisees who are still completing graduate training, supervisors in the field share responsibility with university-based supervisors. This is something of a symbiotic relationship: each needs the other to be successful and both parties benefit from the experience. Field sites need well-trained practicum students and interns who have developmentally appropriate skills for their level of experience, and training programs need field sites that provide the necessary breadth and depth of training, along with quality supervision, to move students' learning from the classroom to the "real world" (Sullivan, Svenkerud, & Conoley, 2014). Although almost all the topics addressed in this book apply to the supervision of interns and practicum students (see, in particular, sections on supervision contracts [Chapter 2] and supervision planning [Chapter 3]), this chapter will touch on some specific considerations for supervisors working with these populations of supervisees. Readers are also referred to Harvey and Struzziero's (2008) comprehensive text on supervision in school psychology, which addresses special considerations for the supervision of practicum students and interns (see pp. 202–206). And Newman's (2013) *Demystifying the School Psychology Internship* is a wonderful resource for all things internship-related. Finally, NASP (2014a) also provides guidelines for high-quality intern supervision that all internship supervisors are encouraged to review.

Getting off to a Strong Start: Facilitating Entry into the Field Site

Perhaps one of your most important roles as a supervisor for practicum students and interns is to help your supervisee make a comfortable and successful transition to your school or district. Particularly for practicum students, who may have limited experiences in schools beyond having attended them for K-12 education, the process can be overwhelming. Even fundamental considerations like finding the bathroom can be challenging when one is new to a school. So before planning training experiences or setting goals, you can help supervisees by reviewing nuts and bolts like where to park, how to get any required credentials like an ID badge, what time to arrive and how late to stay, where to store belongings, and how to navigate the building. Introducing the supervisee to key stakeholders such as administrators, front-office staff, custodians, teachers, other special services staff, and any other trainees at the site is also extremely helpful for facilitating entry. Kelly and Davis (2017) provide a useful checklist for orientation to a field site that includes these and other suggestions, such as introducing your supervisee to the school staff via a welcome email, having the supervisee attend a faculty meeting, and providing information about school demographics.

Collaborating with the University

To facilitate a collaborative working relationship, a university-based supervisor is typically designated as the point person for maintaining regular contact with the field site (NASP, 2014b). This individual could be a full-time core faculty member from the school psychology training program (as I am) or a part-time person whose sole responsibility is to oversee students completing field experiences. Some may be more involved than others, depending on the nature of the position and the training program, but as a field supervisor you should feel comfortable reaching out to the university any time you need support or have to advocate for your needs or those of your supervisee.

I've found that collaborating with field supervisors sometimes feels like co-parenting: we both want the same outcome for the supervisee—to develop the necessary knowledge, skills, and behaviors to be successful—but we may have different perspectives on how to get to that finish line, and we definitely play different roles in the process. Table 11.1 highlights some of the differences between university-based and field-based supervisors. Understanding each party's roles and responsibilities at the outset of the training experience can help to prevent confusion and frustration along the way.

Communication

As a field supervisor, ideally you should have somewhat regular contact with your co-supervisor at your supervisee's training program. This doesn't mean you need to talk every day, or even every month, but it's nice to

TABLE 11.1 Supervisor Roles and Responsibilities

University-Based Supervisor	Field-Based Supervisor
• Indirect oversight of supervisee's progress and performance • Knowledge of training program requirements and policies • Knowledge of state and national school psychology certification requirements • Communicate general goals and specific expectations for required training experiences • Maintain communication with field supervisor to broadly monitor progress and performance	• Direct oversight of supervisee's activities • Knowledge of school/district/ training site policies and norms • Monitoring and confirmation of attendance and activities (e.g., approving hours logs) • Identify appropriate activities/ assignments/cases to build skills • Provide ongoing formative feedback and summative evaluation based on observations of performance

touch base every so often—even if things are going well! Just like a parent, I love hearing positive feedback from my students' supervisors. But certainly when things *aren't* going smoothly, it's extremely important to reach out as soon as possible, because the university supervisor can't do anything to help with problems they don't know about. And without any reason to believe otherwise, university supervisors are likely to assume no news is good news (Guiney, 2018).

Site Visits

In my role as university-based supervisor for internships, I typically make two or three site visits a year to see my interns and their field supervisors (because practica are less intensive, there is not such a high level of on-site monitoring). For sites that are a significant distance from campus, sometimes we conduct these meetings by phone or web-based conference. Site visits include an initial meeting at the start of the experience to set expectations and discuss the training plan, a mid-year meeting to review the first semester evaluation and plan for activities that need attention during the latter half of the field experience, and a final visit at the end of year to review progress made towards goals and plan for ongoing professional development. These visits are usually very pleasant and eye-opening for me, but some are more productive than others. Because everyone's time is valuable, you want to make the most of the time spent on these meetings. Box 11.1 shares some tips that can help site visits go smoothly.

BOX 11.1 TIPS FOR SUCCESSFUL SITE VISITS

- **Preview concerns.** If there are delicate issues that need to be addressed during a site visit meeting, it's helpful to let the university-based supervisor know about them in advance. This helps you both to be prepared to engage in a productive group conversation with the supervisee.
- **Secure space.** Particularly if anything sensitive needs to be discussed, like concerns about a student's competence or any specific cases, it's essential to have a private location for your meeting. If you share an office, try to reserve an alternative space for the meeting.
- **Make introductions.** If possible, try to introduce the field supervisor to any administrators who are available. In addition to sending a message that the internship experience is an important collaboration with the university, it's a chance to remind them that you're volunteering your time for an important professional development opportunity!
- **Offer a tour.** Personally, I love getting a tour of the school during an initial visit to a new practicum or internship site. It's a great way to better understand the student's training experience and the learning opportunities available. If you have the time, offer to show the university supervisor around the building. If you don't have the time, have the supervisee conduct the tour!
- **Speak up for what you need.** As a university-based supervisor, my job is to help field experiences go smoothly. If I'm not aware of a problem, I'm not able to help. Don't hesitate to speak up if there are things the university supervisor can do to support you.
- **Ask questions.** Particularly at the start of the field experience, be sure to ask the university supervisor if there is anything in particular you should know to help things go smoothly. If you've never supervised a student from the training program before this is particularly important, but even if you've been working with the program for years, ask if any requirements or expectations have changed.

Working Together to Address Problems

As much as I love the positive stories from the field, there's no denying that the majority of interactions I have with supervisors between these visits center around problems. Much like we would tell supervisees that they should speak up as soon as they think there might be something going on with a case, field supervisors should never hesitate to reach out to the university, even if there's just a vague sense that a problem might be brewing. Box 11.2 lists some examples of times when you should definitely make that call or send that email to the training program. I've been contacted about everything from concerns about assessment skills, to interns being too forward in meetings, to attendance problems, to worries about interns' mental health. It's the university supervisor's job to help you navigate these tricky situations, and with your direct observations of on-site behavior and the faculty member's knowledge of academic performance and history on campus, together you have a lot of information to share with one another.

BOX 11.2 WHEN TO CONTACT THE UNIVERSITY SUPERVISOR

- **Attendance problems**. If your supervisee is arriving late, leaving early, or not coming in as scheduled, it's important to take action. Early intervention provides an opportunity to discuss professional behavior and to explore any difficulties (e.g., health problems, transportation issues) that might be affecting attendance. Even if you choose to address the issue yourself initially, if the supervisee doesn't exhibit behavior change after hearing your feedback, it's a good idea to get the university supervisor involved.
- **Unethical behavior**. For preservice interns, the university is usually responsible for certifying that graduates are ready to practice independently. If a supervisee lacks the judgment to behave ethically, the university supervisor needs to know!
- **Concerns about competence**. Whenever you feel uneasy about a student's skills, particularly if you've provided feedback and it hasn't resulted in noticeable improvement, seeking guidance from the training program is a good idea. In some cases, a conversation about the curriculum and expectations for competence is enough to put things in perspective and set your mind at ease.
- **Changes in your availability**. School years are long and sometimes unpredictable; it's not unheard of for supervisors to be reassigned or even hired elsewhere during a student's training experience. If you know you are not going to be able to continue to supervise your intern or practicum student, definitely work with the university-based supervisor to come up with an alternative plan as soon as you become aware of the issue.
- **Significant events on-site**. If there is a school crisis or other situation that might be unusually challenging for your supervisee and/or yourself, the university-based supervisor can provide an extra source of

support. It's also good for program faculty to be aware of such events that might be upsetting, or even provide valuable learning opportunities for other members of the training cohort through group supervision on campus.

- **Any time**! Whenever you feel yourself wondering if you should contact the university, it probably means you should. Remember that the university-based supervisor is your partner in the supervision of students on field placements: you don't have to go it alone!

Finishing Strong: A Word about Terminating Internship/ Practicum Supervision

The DEP model of supervision for school psychologists (Simon & Swerdlik, 2017) pays special attention to how supervisees grow and change over the course of a supervision relationship and emphasizes taking this into consideration at the end of the experience. One particular consideration that the model highlights with respect to terminating supervision is the importance of talking specifically about how the nature of your relationship with the supervisee will change following the end of the experience. Particularly when working with interns, who may seem more like junior colleagues than supervisees by the time all is said and done, termination should include a discussion of whether and how you will maintain contact in the future.

Documentation and Data Collection

If you've supervised an intern or practicum student, particularly one from a nationally-accredited program, you may have marveled at the amount of paperwork and documentation that's involved. Affiliation agreements, contracts, training plans, logs, evaluation forms, more evaluation forms ... I'm sure my field supervisors feel like it never stops. But take comfort in the fact that it's all for good reason: documentation ensures that high-quality training experiences are taking place, ideally consistent with NASP's (2010c) *Standards for Graduate Preparation of School Psychologists*. What may seem like red tape is really a means of developing effective school psychologists. At the start of any field experience it's a good idea to talk with your supervisee about their plans and goals regarding certification and licensure to ensure you will be able to meet any specific requirements that might need to be documented down the road. For example, doctoral students who plan to pursue licensure for independent practice must typically be supervised by someone who is themselves licensed. Such details are definitely best considered at the start of any supervised field experience.

Training Broadly

Depending on your state and the level of training your supervisee is completing, there are specific requirements that need to be met for state certification for school-based practice or licensure to practice independently. These regulations govern the number of hours of practicum and internship that must be completed, the amount of supervision that must be provided, and often the types of training experiences students need to have to meet standards. For example, NASP-approved programs must document that their graduates are well-trained in all 10 domains of the *Model for Comprehensive and Integrated School Psychological Services* (NASP, 2010a). Such programs need to train students consistent with national standards for the field, as opposed to just local norms that reflect the role of the school psychologist.

Collaborating with Colleagues to Meet Requirements

Meeting the need to train broadly can be challenging at times, particularly when supervisors or their districts see school psychologists as having primarily an assessment role, as opposed to being providers of prevention and mental health services. In such situations, it's essential to work collaboratively with your university-based supervisor to discuss ways that training requirements can be met while still working within the realities of your position. For example, interns might collaborate with a behavior specialist to work on a functional behavioral assessment if that's not part of your role. Or in New Jersey, where school psychologists often don't conduct educational testing, my students have been known to team up with special education teachers to gain experience administering standardized academic measures.

Letters of Recommendation

When supervising practicum students or interns, you are one of a fairly short list of professional contacts who has direct knowledge of their work. Aside from faculty, you are likely to be a top source of requests for letters of recommendation when it comes time to apply for future field experiences or jobs. Writing such letters can be more challenging than it sounds, whether you've had a great or a terrible supervisee. On the one hand, because letters of recommendation have become so universally positive, it can be difficult to help a truly strong supervisee stand out from the pack. On the other, when you've had a supervisee who struggled during a field experience, it's a delicate job to address shortcomings without being overly negative. Two sample letters are presented as appendices to give some guidance for navigating reference letter requests. Appendix J is an example of how you can help a strong supervisee stand out, while Appendix K addresses how to provide a reference for an intern or practicum student who has struggled.

Basic Considerations

Newman (2013) and Corey, Haynes, Moulton, and Muratori (2010) provide some helpful tips for writing letters of recommendation, such as:

- Know the deadline for when the letter is needed and be sure to meet it (I ask students to email me their requests and then "flag" them in my inbox for follow-up until the letter is completed).
- Be clear, concise and direct.
- Address both strengths and weaknesses, but don't over- or understate your points.
- Remember that the first and last paragraphs will probably get the most attention.
- Proofread. You don't want to send a letter with the wrong name or spelling errors!
- Keep a copy.

From my own personal experience as someone who writes a number of recommendations each year I would add the following suggestions:

- **Ask for a copy of the supervisee's resume or CV** when they request a letter of recommendation. Even though I usually know quite a bit about a supervisee's previous experiences when I sit down to write a letter, I like being able to use the exact names of previous field experience sites when highlighting interests or linking past work to current projects. Sometimes I even learn new and impressive things about a supervisee when I read such materials, such as the time I discovered that a student had worked with children in Romania as a volunteer. This provided me with a new perspective on a student I already considered to be independent and committed to gaining a diverse range of experiences.
- **Highlight at least one specific example** that illustrates a strength the supervisee exhibits. Whether it's a particular case they handled well, an area of interest they pursued with independence, or a unique personal quality or skill, I try to point out something about the student that might stick in the brain of someone who is reading dozens of letters.

- **Remind students to tell you if they use you as a reference** for any of the sites or institutions that might be receiving your letter. I always appreciate a heads-up if someone has been on an interview and given my name as a reference so I can be ready to speak with someone about the things I included in my letter of recommendation.

Helping Strong Supervisees Stand Out

When you've supervised a truly remarkable practicum student or intern you are probably very invested in seeing them succeed as they move on to their next professional experience. Aside from the fact that you may simply like the supervisee very much, you have invested time, energy, and other resources into helping build this individual into a budding professional. After all that you want to see them get that internship, job, or post-doc position they desire. But with letters of recommendation being so universally positive as to not be very useful (Stedman, Hatch, & Schoenfeld, 2009), it can be a challenge to communicate just how truly great *your* supervisee is. Appendix J presents an example of a letter of recommendation for a stellar student, based on an actual supervisee I was lucky enough to work with.

Based on both my experience writing letters of recommendation and reading them as part of the graduate admissions process, I would argue the following considerations might help you drive home your point that your supervisee is really amazing:

- **Be specific**. Instead of saying, "Jane has strong assessment skills," highlight how you know her skills are strong (e.g., "Jane is one of only two interns out of the dozens I have supervised whose first protocol of the year was completely error-free.").
- **Share an anecdote**. A unique story can catch a reader's eye and break up the monotony of reading about all the placements applicants have had over the years. Be sure to keep it brief, but try to tell a memorable story about something that highlights your supervisee's talents or positive attributes.
- **Highlight potential for growth**. Talk about what you see as the supervisee's next steps for honing skills, highlighting ways that this individual would be an asset to the next site that is smart enough to snap them up. Again, specifics are better than generalities!

When Supervisees Have Struggled

There's no doubt it can be uncomfortable to write a letter of recommendation for a student who has experienced difficulties or exhibited deficiencies as a supervisee. But keep in mind that our codes of ethics demand that we are honest in our interactions, respect other professionals, and do no harm, in addition to serving as gatekeepers who ensure only qualified individuals enter the field prepared to help clients (APA, 2017; NASP, 2010b). For these reasons you are obligated to address weaknesses when serving as a reference for a supervisee. However, you are *not* obligated to write every letter of recommendation that is requested of you. If you feel that you truly could not write a balanced letter that acknowledges a supervisee's struggles while also highlighting strengths and improvements, then it is best to explain this to the requester and respectfully decline to provide a letter of recommendation.

When writing a letter for a student who had difficulties or even needed formal remediation, keep in mind the following considerations (Newman, 2013):

- **Be transparent**. Have a direct conversation with the supervisee about what you will need to include in the letter. They should understand what the letter will say before you proceed with writing it.
- **Do your paperwork**. Be clear about whether you need to sign any release forms for the institution receiving the letter and if you are supposed to submit it directly to the site or to the supervisee.
- **Don't beat around the bush**. Describe areas of difficulty directly and as specifically and objectively as possible.
- **Have a growth mindset**. Highlight efforts the supervisee made to remediate difficulties and discuss specific changes in behavior you observed as a result.

Appendix K presents an example of a letter written for a student who had difficulties.

Supervisor's Summary

- Field- and university-based supervisors work together, in slightly different roles, to support practicum students and interns completing preservice training experiences.
- Regular communication with the university-based supervisor (via email, phone, or site visits) is important for supporting interns and practicum students, especially when problems arise.
- Site visits are an opportunity to help the university-based supervisor better understand the nature of your training site, review plans for learning experiences, and discuss evaluation results. Being prepared and proactive will make these visits productive.
- When concerns arise, it is important to contact the university-based supervisor to address issues as proactively as possible.
- There can be a lot of paperwork and documentation involved in supervising students; be sure you know what you're responsible for and ask questions when unsure.

- Training requirements may extend beyond your typical role and job responsibilities; collaborate with colleagues if supervisees need experiences you can't provide.
- Letters of recommendation have become so universally positive that it can be hard to make a strong student stand out. Try to highlight specific, unique experiences or skills that set your stellar supervisee apart from the pack.
- If a supervisee who struggled requests a letter of recommendation, be upfront about the fact that you will need to address deficiencies in the letter. Note weaknesses in specific, objective terms, and highlight the results of remediation efforts.

FINAL REFLECTIONS

- How much support or involvement do you want from a student's training program? Do you want to truly co-supervise, or would you prefer to be left alone (or somewhere in between)?
- What kinds of concerns would lead you to contact the university-based supervisor?
- Given your current role as a school psychologist, are there any limitations that might prevent you from providing an experience that addresses all domains of school psychology practice? If so, who can you partner with at your site to fill in those gaps?
- Have you ever been asked to write a letter of recommendation for someone you felt you could not wholeheartedly recommend? How did you handle it? Would you do anything differently if you could go back?

References

American Psychological Association. (2017). *Ethical principles of psychologists and code of conduct.* Washington, DC: Author. Retrieved from www.apa.org/ethics/code/ethics-code-2017.pdf.

Corey, G., Haynes, R., Moulton, P., & Muratori, M. (2010). *Clinical supervision in the helping professions: A practical guide* (2nd ed.). Alexandria, VA: American Counseling Association.

Guiney, M. C. (2018). Addressing problems of professional competence: Collaborating with university training programs to support struggling supervisees. *Communiqué, 46*(6), 4, 6–7.

Harvey, V. S., & Struzziero, J. A. (2008). *Professional development and supervision of school psychologists: From intern to expert* (2nd ed.). Bethesda, MD: National Association of School Psychologists.

Kelly, K. K., & Davis, S. D. (2017). *Supervising the school psychology practicum: A guide for field and university supervisors.* New York: Springer.

National Association of School Psychologists. (2010a). *Model for comprehensive and integrated school psychological services.* Bethesda, MD: Author.

National Association of School Psychologists. (2010b). *Principles for professional ethics.* Bethesda, MD: Author.

National Association of School Psychologists. (2010c). *Standards for graduate preparation of school psychologists.* Bethesda, MD: Author.

National Association of School Psychologists. (2014a). *Best practice guidelines for school psychology intern field supervision and mentoring.* Bethesda, MD: Author.

National Association of School Psychologists. (2014b). *Best practice guidelines for school psychology internships.* Bethesda, MD: Author.

Newman, D. S. (2013). *Demystifying the school psychology internship: A dynamic guide for interns and supervisors.* New York: Routledge.

Simon, D. J., & Swerdlik, M. E. (2017). *Supervision in school psychology: The developmental, ecological, problem-solving model.* New York: Routledge.

Stedman, J. M., Hatch, J. P., & Schoenfeld, L. S. (2009). Letters of recommendation for the predoctoral internship in medical schools and other settings: Do they enhance decision making in the selection process? *Journal of Clinical Psychology in Medical Settings, 16*(4), 339–345. doi:10.1007/s10880-009-9170-y.

Sullivan, J. R., Svenkerud, N., & Conoley, J. C. (2014). Best practices in the supervision of interns. In A. Thomas & P. Harrison (Eds.), *Best practices in school psychology: Foundations* (pp. 527–540). Bethesda, MD: National Association of School Psychologists.

12

SUPPORTING EARLY CAREER SCHOOL PSYCHOLOGISTS

Although supervision is typically mandated for preservice school psychologists, upon completing training and obtaining the necessary credentials, practitioners may not be formally required to access supervision, particularly if they are not pursuing licensure for independent practice. However, supervision is recommended as best practice for school psychologists at *all* levels of experience (NASP, 2018) and during the early career years it is particularly important. The concepts and strategies highlighted throughout this book generally apply to supporting this population, but a clear understanding of the characteristics of these school psychologists is needed to apply them most effectively. This chapter will address considerations specific to early career school psychologists (ECSPs) in order to help supervisors and mentors provide the kind of strategic support that these individuals may need. Readers are also referred to Simon and Swerdlik's (2017) text, which includes a chapter that specifically addresses how the DEP model can be applied to the supervision of credentialed psychologists.

Supervision vs. Mentoring vs. Postgraduate Professional Support

Before getting too deep into the unique features of the early career period and why support is so important for school psychologists at this level, let's start by clarifying some of the terms that this chapter will use to address the various ways more experienced professionals can support ECSPs.

Supervision

Remember that one of the classic definitions of supervision in school psychology is, "an interpersonal interaction between two or more individuals for the purpose of sharing knowledge, assessing professional competencies, and providing objective feedback with the terminal goals of developing new competencies, facilitating effective delivery of psychological services, and maintaining professional competencies" (McIntosh & Phelps, 2000, pp. 33–34). It typically includes a distinct focus on evaluation and may involve vicarious liability for supervisors along with gatekeeping responsibilities, such as determining (at the graduate training level) whether someone should be recommended for independent practice, or deciding (for credentialed school psychologists) about advancements such as promotion or tenure. After internship, ECSPs are less likely to receive this type of *clinical supervision*, or supervision of their school psychology practice, than *administrative supervision*, which tends to focus on the "nuts and bolts" of getting the job done, like hiring decisions or whether reports are being completed on time (Silva, Newman, Guiney, Valley-Gray, & Barrett, 2016). Of course, this is if they are receiving any supervision at all, which is, unfortunately, the exception and not the norm.

Mentoring

This chapter will use the term "mentoring" somewhat generally to refer to all the kinds of support that might be provided to new school psychologists. As Simon and Swerdlik (2017) define it, mentoring "involves structured support from a senior staff psychologist to a junior colleague who is early in his or her career or new to a particular assignment or setting" (p. 202). It is a non-evaluative supportive relationship in which the mentee, a credentialed professional, retains liability for the welfare and progress of clients while the mentor provides guidance that helps improve practice. Table 12.1 compares and contrasts supervision and mentoring in school psychology to highlight their similarities and differences.

Postgraduate Professional Support

PGPS is an umbrella term that could refer to *either* supervision or mentoring; it's any kind of support or oversight that a credentialed school psychologist might receive to guide their practice. NASP's (2016) *Guidance for Postgraduate Mentorship and Professional Support*[1] describes PGPS in more detail and shares specific considerations that can help guide supervision and mentoring for ECSPs (more on that later).

Benefits of Mentoring

Although there is not a large body of research on the effects of mentoring for ECSPs, it has received attention with respect to new teachers, who share some similarities with new school psychologists. A comprehensive review of

TABLE 12.1 Types of Professional Support

Type of Support	Definition/Features
Administrative supervision (see Harvey & Struzziero, 2008; NASP, 2018)	Oversight of the "nuts and bolts" or logistics of service delivery with a focus on consumer satisfaction. Includes responsibilities such as hiring, firing, and assigning staff; conducting performance evaluations; assigning caseloads; and monitoring legal responsibilities (e.g., compliance with special education mandates). May be provided by a school psychologist or a professional not trained in school psychology.
Clinical supervision (see Bernard & Goodyear, 2014; NASP, 2018)	Supervision focused specifically on building professional skills with the goal of enhancing professional competence. Involves evaluating progress towards training goals and monitoring the quality of service delivery to ensure that supervisees are sufficiently well trained to practice independently at the end of the supervision relationship.
Mentoring (see NASP, 2016)	Similar in goals and purpose to clinical supervision but without an evaluative or "gatekeeping" component. Mentees are credentialed to practice independently and retain responsibility for their own work.
Postgraduate professional support (see NASP, 2016)	Broader term that incorporates both mentoring and supervision for in-service school psychologists who are credentialed to practice.

research on teacher mentoring programs (Ingersoll & Strong, 2011) found that such supports had positive impacts on teacher retention, classroom instructional practices, and student achievement. The retention component is particularly salient in light of the current shortage of school psychologists that many regions of the country are confronting (Castillo, Curtis, & Tan, 2014); any interventions with the potential to keep ECSPs in the field deserve attention.

Both formal and informal mentors have been found to play important roles for new teachers (Desimone et al., 2014). Formal mentors—those assigned by the school or district to work with (and typically observe and evaluate) novice teachers—can often provide professional support in areas such as curriculum and instruction. On the other hand, informal mentors, or individuals teachers sought out on their own, were found to spend time discussing things like teacher expectations, parent involvement, and the emotional aspects of teaching. These findings suggest that ECSPs, like new teachers, may benefit from opportunities to connect with more experienced professionals who are formally assigned to support the development of their school psychology skills (i.e., a clinical supervisor) while also building connections with other colleagues who can understand the challenges and stresses of the job and help ECSPs "learn the ropes" in a new school or district.

The Early Career: A Distinct Period

In 2009, NASP created the Early Career Committee to address and advocate for the needs of school psychologists in their first five years of credentialed practice. Other professional organizations define "early career" differently; for example, APA's Office on Early Career Psychologists (established in May of 2016) seeks to address the needs of psychologists in the first 10 years following graduate school (APA, n.d.). It is evident that leading professional organizations representing school psychologists have become actively engaged in supporting ECSPs over the past decade. This attention is warranted, as the early career years are marked by some particular characteristics that make them different from graduate school and later periods of practice.

Endings and Beginnings

Some might think that obtaining that school psychology degree represents the *end* of training, but in fact it is really just the *beginning* of what should be a career of lifelong learning (Fouad et al., 2009; Simon & Swerdlik, 2017). Because every school and district is unique, every school psychologist's role can be different, and there are so many various contexts in which to serve widely ranging populations of students, ECSPs inevitably have gaps in training to fill after completing internship. In fact, my own former students have repeatedly told me that after finishing our program and starting their "real world" jobs, they quickly realized how much more there was to learn. Supervision or mentoring, along with continuing professional development, can serve important protective factors for ECSPs during a critical phase (Silva, Newman, & Guiney, 2014).

The Novice Professional Phase

As was noted in Chapter 1, Rønnestad and Skovholt (2003) proposed a theory of therapist and counselor development that includes six distinct professional phases based on interviews with 100 therapists at different points in their careers, from graduate students to veteran professionals. Their findings indicated that therapists in the initial years following graduate training tend to experience some or all of the following, which change and evolve as the early career years progress:

- Intense and eager exploration of self and the profession
- Realization that it is ok to express personality and sense of humor in the work

- A desire to confirm the accuracy of training, and disillusionment upon realizing that not everything taught in graduate school applies in the "real world"
- Dismay at perceived lack of preparation for the challenges of practice; frustration upon recognizing gaps in training
- Difficulty applying a singular theoretical orientation uniformly to all cases
- Dependence on client feedback as a measure of effectiveness
- Challenges setting boundaries and determining how much to take on; trying to "do it all"
- Sense of inadequacy when clients don't make sufficient progress; questioning effectiveness and even career choice
- Exploration "outward" to find work settings and roles that best fit.

As much as these findings highlight the enthusiasm and energy that ECSPs may have as they tackle entry into the profession, it is clear that this novice professional phase is also marked by significant confusion, disillusionment, and stress. Fortunately, Rønnestad and Skovholt's (2003) work revealed that many novice therapists and counselors sought out mentors for support and guidance during these turbulent years. However, the extent to which such professional support is available to school psychologists is of some concern.

Access to Supervision for Early Career School Psychologists

A recent survey of supervision and mentoring for ECSPs (Silva et al., 2016) highlighted some notable trends. Of the 700 ECSPs who participated, only 38% reported having access to clinical supervision and only about half received administrative supervision. Just 55% had access to mentoring. These results highlight how limited access to PGPS can be during the critical early career years. Overall, 68% of respondents indicated that they wanted access to more support. One of the most noteworthy findings from this study was that nearly a third of ECSP participants admitted that they felt pressured to practice outside their boundaries of competence due to a lack of access to supervision or mentoring. Thus, there is an ethical imperative to provide greater access to support for ECSPs as they transition into independent practice.

Transitions during the Early Career

As Green and Hawley (2009) noted, "a mentor is someone who understands a mentee professionally as well as personally" (p. 208). This is worth remembering because the early career period is marked by a number of significant professional and personal transitions: from graduate student to credentialed professional, supervised trainee to independent practitioner, and in some cases, from emerging adult to full-blown grownup (see Silva et al., 2014 for a thorough consideration of early career transitions). Taken together, these factors can make for a somewhat turbulent time in a school psychologist's career.

Professional Transitions

The early career period may be a time of multiple position changes, depending on things like the economy and regional differences in job markets. Some professional transitions occur by choice, such as when an ECSP opts to leave one job to pursue a more desirable opportunity. Others, not so much: under the "last in first out" tradition of school staffing decisions, ECSPs may be among the first to go when budgets get tight (Silva et al., 2014). Sometimes an ECSP may want to stay in a position but not have the option, as occasionally happens to my students who take temporary leave replacement positions that end when the permanent school psychologist returns to work. Given these potential changes, ECSPs may find themselves anxious about everything from fundamental concerns such as financial security to professional challenges like navigating entry into multiple schools or systems, or developing new skill sets needed for working with new populations. Access to professional support from a mentor or supervisor can be extremely helpful in such challenging times.

Personal Transitions

Although not all ECSPs are in their 20s and 30s, those who entered graduate school immediately or soon after completing their undergraduate degrees often are. This represents a unique life stage that can be marked by milestones such as establishing long-term relationships and starting families, prompting transitions from single person to partner or childless person to parent. However, ECSPs who entered the field later in life may bear the burden of caring for aging parents, which can be a tremendously stressful transition, or even confronting their own health issues that come with aging. As Green and Hawley (2009) note, early career psychologists also face financial pressures due to high levels of educational debt, and may be navigating burdensome licensure requirements if seeking additional credentials. In other words, ECSPs may be dealing with more transitions than simply the adjustment to professional life.

Supporting ECSPs

By now it should be clear that, for a variety of reasons, ECSPs need support. Recognizing the benefits of PGPS, NASP recently instituted a requirement that first-time Nationally Certified School Psychologists (NCSPs) receive at least one year of support (supervision or mentoring) before the end of the three-year renewal cycle for the credential. The requirement was accompanied by *Guidance for Postgraduate Mentorship and Professional Support* (NASP, 2016), a document that provides a variety of suggestions for structuring effective mentoring relationships, including considerations regarding the use of technology for long-distance mentoring. The full document is essential reading for all ECSPs and those who support them, but some key considerations derived from the *Guidance* are highlighted in Box 12.1.

BOX 12.1 SUPPORTING ECSPs THROUGH POSTGRADUATE PROFESSIONAL SUPPORT

Supporting ECSPs

(see NASP's 2016 *Guidance for Postgraduate Mentorship and Professional Support*)

- **Be committed to mentoring**. Mentors should be sure they have sufficient time (e.g., one hour per week) to provide support to mentees.
- **Use structure to prevent problems**. Like a supervision contract, a mentorship agreement that outlines basic expectations can be extremely helpful for promoting an organized and positive experience. Address things like when, how often, and by what means (in person, phone, via the web) you will meet. When are unexpected phone calls acceptable? What numbers should and should not be used?
- **Be flexible, but accountable**. Working school psychologists are extremely busy, and things certainly come up that may necessitate that the mentor or mentee reschedule meetings. But if sessions are regularly being moved or missed, take time to consider how you might restructure things to be sure you are meeting your commitment as a mentor. Try laying out a set schedule at the start of the year and entering sessions into your calendars to avoid conflicts.
- **Consider a group**. Mentorship at the postgraduate level can be effective when conducted in a group setting, where ECSPs can learn from one another *and* a more experienced mentor simultaneously. Co-mentoring a group can also provide backup if last-minute scheduling conflicts come up, so try teaming up with a colleague to guide a group of new school psychologists.
- **Set specific goals**. Take time at the start of the relationship to identify specific areas for growth and goals for the experience. ECSPs can use NASP's *Self-assessment for School Psychologists Survey* (available through the NASP website) to identify areas in need of professional development. Consider how progress towards goals will be monitored.

- **Keep notes**. If you're participating in a district- or state-mandated mentoring program, you may be required to keep some notes, but it's great practice even if not mandatory. Even if you're not formally evaluating a mentee, looking back at notes from earlier mentoring meetings can help highlight growth and progress.
- **Provide feedback**. Both ongoing (formative) and mid-year and year-end (summative) feedback is essential for mentees to grow. Highlight successes and help identify goals for continued improvement.
- **Model ethical practice**. Use "think aloud" techniques to highlight the ethical problem-solving process and model self-reflection. Support ECSPs through the process of developing as an ethical practitioner.
- **Seek feedback**. To continue to improve as a mentor, ask mentees what is working and what is not. "What could I do more of to be helpful to future mentees?" can be a helpful question to ask.
- **Promote self-care**. Establishing healthy self-care habits in the early career years is critical for preventing burnout and retaining ECSPs. Highlight your self-care strategies to help the mentee recognize how important it is to maintain work–life balance and physical and mental health.

Areas to Address

As much as ECSPs are embarking on a lifelong journey of learning the content and skills needed to be effective psychologists, there is more to know than just the domains of school psychology practice. Given their unique needs as recent graduates and new professionals, ECSPs can benefit from guidance about a number of topics that more advanced psychologists may have experience navigating. For example, Green and Hawley (2009) highlight several specific areas in which mentors can support early career psychologists, including:

- **Career**: navigating transitions, negotiating salary, pursuing specialized training or advanced credentials
- **Networking**: introducing mentee to colleagues, sharing resources
- **Finance**: understanding loan repayment, guidance on financial planning
- **Balancing personal and professional identity**: modeling balance, highlighting teachable moments, sharing strategies for managing both family and career
- **Leadership**: how to be involved in the profession, setting boundaries on involvement, developing leadership skills.

Building Supervision Skills

The developmental component of the DEP model emphasizes the importance of cultivating supervision skills in students and ECSPs (Simon & Swerdlik, 2017). Despite the fact that supervision skills are viewed as a foundational professional competency (APA, 2015; NASP, 2018), only 15–20% of school psychologists receive specific training on supervision (Cochrane, Salyers, & Ding, 2010; Flanagan & Grehan, 2011). This stems from the fact that school psychologists are able to practice at the pre-doctoral level; APA-accredited doctoral programs are required to provide coursework on supervision, but at the non-doctoral level, school psychology programs do not have to include any instruction on supervision at all. Because about 70% of school psychologists are trained at the master's or specialist level (Curtis, Castillo, & Gelley, 2012), a majority of school psychology supervisors aren't learning how to supervise through graduate training—they're learning on their own once in the field. This means that as a mentor to an ECSP, you can be a powerful source of modeling and learning with the potential to impact the future supervisees of your mentee. You can help by sharing and discussing key resources, like the APA (2015) *Guidelines for Clinical Supervision in Health Service Psychology*, and providing meta-supervision for ECSPs embarking on initial experiences providing supervision.

Case Example

After completing her internship at a high school in an ethnically and socio-economically diverse suburban district, Molly secured a job at Shadyside Elementary School, a K-5 building in a wealthy, primarily white community. The building housed a self-contained classroom for students with serious emotional and behavioral concerns—a population with which Molly had little previous experience. The district was also in the process of transitioning to a multi-tiered system of supports (MTSS) model for identifying and addressing reading problems, which thrilled Molly, as her graduate training had heavily emphasized such practices.

Thanks to a state-mandated mentoring requirement, Molly was assigned to meet monthly with Marcus, the school psychologist who had served Shadyside for 10 years before being moved to a different building. He reached out to Molly to arrange a meeting on the day before school started. After covering basics like where and how often they would meet, he started by asking Molly about her goals and needs. Although Molly had a long list of goals, together they prioritized three: (1) build strong working relationships with teachers, administrators, and parents at Shadyside; (2) develop the necessary knowledge and skills to work with children with emotional and behavioral disorders; and (3) support the implementation of MTSS. They identified some specific short- and long-term objectives that would help Molly achieve these goals (e.g., attend the first PTA meeting of the year, complete readings and online trainings about emotional disorders, deliver a successful in-service training on curriculum-based assessment) and discussed how they would evaluate progress towards goals over the year. They agreed upon a set monthly meeting time (8:30am on the first Friday of each month) and entered all the dates for the year into their respective calendars to avoid scheduling conflicts. Then Marcus walked Molly around Shadyside, introducing her to teachers and staff members. He also took time to fill her in on cases that would be carrying over from the year before, highlighting the ones that were particularly complex or contentious. Finally, they worked together to draft a joint letter to parents introducing Molly as the new Shadyside school psychologist. Molly felt pretty overwhelmed, but was relieved to have such an active and supportive mentor.

Over the first six weeks of the year, Marcus checked in with Molly regularly to see how things were going. He repeatedly encouraged her to reach out to him with questions, especially about specific cases, and she did so frequently. In conjunction with their scheduled mentoring meeting for October, they arranged for Marcus to come to Shadyside and sit in on Molly's weekly group counseling session with the students in the self-contained class. They co-led the group, giving Molly a chance to observe Marcus's style and techniques, while Marcus was later able to highlight things Molly did well with the group and give her constructive feedback for future sessions.

As the year progressed, Marcus was amazed at the growth in skills and confidence Molly demonstrated, and he was sure to tell her as much during their meetings. He also noticed that she went from calling and emailing him on an almost daily basis in the fall to now checking in only occasionally between mentoring sessions. When she tried to downplay her success, he referred back to his supervision notes from earlier in the year to highlight how far she had come. However, by February, Marcus observed that Molly seemed pretty tired, stressed, and even sick. That month's meeting was devoted to an extended discussion of self-care during which Marcus and Molly worked on developing their own respective self-care plans. This included implementing "moving mentoring" sessions for the spring, during which they walked around the Shadyside sports field as they talked.

By June, when Marcus and Molly evaluated progress towards goals set in September, Molly was a well-known member of the Shadyside community and a valuable member of the MTSS team. Despite some challenges with the self-contained class, Molly's principal was pleased with how the year had gone for the students and several parents expressed great satisfaction with the program. Marcus and Molly celebrated these successes, identified goals for the following year, and agreed to continue to keep in regular contact as Molly navigated the district's tenure review process.

Supervisor's Summary

- Supervision is recommended for school psychologists at all stages of the career span and is especially important for ECSPs.
- Experienced school psychologists can support ECSPs through supervision or mentoring: two forms of PGPS that differ in ways such as level of structure and formality.
- Mentoring has documented benefits for educators, including the retention of early career professionals.
- Both formal and informal mentors can play an important role in the professional development of ECSPs.
- The early career period is a unique one filled with challenges and potential transitions, making mentoring or supervision extremely important for ECSPs.
- Many ECSPs don't have access to PGPS, but they indicate that they'd like more support.
- Mentors can support ECSPs as they continue to build their knowledge and skills across the domains of school psychology practice, as well in areas such as career development, networking, understanding finances, finding personal–professional balance, and developing leadership skills.
- During the early career years, mentors can play a key role in helping new school psychologists to learn the skills needed to supervise others.

FINAL REFLECTIONS

- What do you remember about your early years as a school psychologist?
- What challenges did you encounter as you transitioned out of internship? What kind of support did you have to help with the process? What was helpful?
- In what areas did you need the most additional development when you started working as a school psychologist? How did you gain the additional knowledge and skills you needed?
- If you didn't have access to formal supervision training in graduate school, how have you learned about supervision? Did your supervisors do anything specific to help you build supervision skills?

Note

1 Available at www.nasponline.org/Documents/Standards%20and%20Certification/Certification/Guidance_Postgraduate

References

American Psychological Association. (2015). Guidelines for clinical supervision in health service psychology. *American Psychologist, 70*(1), 33–46. doi:10.1037/a0038112.

American Psychological Association. (n.d.). Contact the office on early career psychologists. Retrieved from www.apa.org/careers/early-career/contact.aspx.

Bernard, J. M., & Goodyear, R. K. (2014). *Fundamentals of clinical supervision* (5th ed). Upper Saddle River, NJ: Pearson.

Castillo, J. M., Curtis, M. J., & Tan, S. Y. (2014). Personnel needs in school psychology: A 10-year follow-up study on predicted personnel shortages. *Psychology in the Schools, 51* (8), 832–849. doi:10.1002/pits.21786.

Cochrane, W. S., Salyers, K., & Ding, Y. (2010). An examination of the preparation, supervisor's theoretical model, and university support for supervisors of school psychology interns. *Trainer's Forum: Journal of the Trainers of School Psychologists, 29* (1), 6–22.

Curtis, M. J., Castillo, J. M., & Gelley, C. (2012). School psychology 2010: Demographics, employments, and the context for professional practices—Part 1. *Communiqué, 40*(7), 1, 28–30.

Desimone, L. M., Hochberg, E. D., Porter, A. C., Polikoff, M. S., Schwartz, R., & Johnson, L. J. (2014). Formal and informal mentoring: Complementary, compensatory, or consistent? *Journal of Teacher Education, 65*(2), 88–110. doi:10.1177/0022487113511643.

Flanagan, R., & Grehan, P. (2011). Assessing school psychology supervisor characteristics: Questionnaire development and findings. *Journal of Applied School Psychology, 27*, 21–41. doi:10.1080/15377903.2011.540504.

Fouad, N. A., Grus, C. L., Hatcher, R. L., Kaslow, N. J., Hutchings, P. S., Madson, M. B., ... Crossman, R. E. (2009). Competency benchmarks: A model for understanding and measuring competence in professional psychology across training levels. *Training and Education in Professional Psychology, 3*, S5–S26. doi:10.1037/a0015832.

Green, A. G., & Hawley, G. C. (2009). Early career psychologists: Understanding, engaging, and mentoring tomorrow's leaders. *Professional Psychology: Research and Practice, 40*(2), 206–212. doi:10.1037/a0012504.

Harvey, V. S., & Struzziero, J. A. (Eds.). (2008). *Professional development and supervision of school psychologists: From intern to expert* (2nd ed.). Bethesda, MD: National Association of School Psychologists.

Ingersoll, R. M., & Strong, M. (2011). The impact of induction and mentoring programs for beginning teachers: A critical review of the research. *Review of Educational Research, 81*(2), 201–233. doi:10.3102/0034654311403323.

McIntosh, D. E., & Phelps, L. (2000). Supervision in school psychology: Where will the future take us? *Psychology in the Schools, 37*(1), 33–38. doi:10.1002/(SICI)1520-6807(200001)37:1<33::AID-PITS4>3.0.CO;2-F.

National Association of School Psychologists. (2016). *Guidance for postgraduate mentorship and professional support.* Bethesda, MD: Author.

National Association of School Psychologists. (2018). *Supervision in school psychology [Position statement].* Bethesda, MD: Author.

Rønnestad, M. H., & Skovholt, T. M. (2003). The journey of the counselor and therapist: Research findings and perspectives on professional development. *Journal of Career Development, 30*, 5–44. doi:10.1023/A:1025173508081.

Silva, A., Newman, D. S., & Guiney, M. C. (2014). Best practices in early career transitions. In A. Thomas & P. Harrison (Eds.), *Best practices in school psychology: Foundations* (pp. 553–556). Bethesda, MD: National Association of School Psychologists.

Silva, A. E., Newman, D. S., Guiney, M. C., Valley-Gray, S., & Barrett, C. A. (2016). Supervision and mentoring for early career school psychologists: Availability, access, structure, and implications. *Psychology in the Schools*, *53*(5), 502–516. doi:10.1002/pits.21921.

Simon, D. J., & Swerdlik, M. E. (2017). *Supervision in school psychology: The developmental, ecological, problem-solving model.* New York: Routledge.

13

ENHANCING PROFESSIONAL GROWTH FOR ADVANCED SUPERVISEES

While the needs of practicum students and interns are often the focus of the supervision literature, professionals at all stages of the career lifespan can benefit from supervision. As NASP's (2018) *Position Statement on Supervision in School Psychology* states, "NASP strongly promotes the supervision of school psychologists by school psychologists at all levels of practice (i.e., trainee, early career, and expert) as a means of ensuring effective practices to support the educational attainment of all children" (p. 1). This chapter will consider the unique supervision needs of mid-career and veteran school psychologists and present several options for providing professional support to this population. Readers are also referred to Simon and Swerdlik's (2017) DEP model of school psychology supervision, which, as an explicitly developmental model, applies across the career span.

Why Do Advanced School Psychologists Need Supervision?

In the previous chapter we established that the end of graduate school is only the beginning of the real learning process for school psychologists. This process continues throughout the career lifespan. School psychologists need to be lifelong learners, and supervision is an essential part of ongoing professional development. Box 13.1 highlights some reasons that school psychologists need access to supervision from graduation through retirement.

BOX 13.1 WHY ADVANCED SCHOOL PSYCHOLOGISTS NEED SUPERVISION

- **There's so much to know.** School psychologists are typically generalists who are required to be competent in broad array of domains across both psychology and education. That's a lot for anyone at any career stage!
- **What we learned in graduate school rapidly becomes outdated.** It's currently anticipated that within less than nine years after completing graduate training, half of the knowledge school psychologists learned through graduate coursework will be obsolete (Neimeyer, Taylor, Rozensky, & Cox, 2014).
- **Our field is always changing.** A mid-career school psychologist who completed graduate school a decade or more ago may never have heard the term "MTSS" during training and likely didn't learn about the needs of transgender students. School psychologists can benefit from access to supervision to help navigate our ever-changing field.
- **Our society is always changing.** As our nation becomes increasingly diverse (see Frey, 2018), so do our schools. School psychologists need professional development and supervision to strengthen and maintain their ability to provide responsive services to students of all cultural backgrounds and identities (see Chapter 7).
- **Anyone can become a novice at any time.** Even with many years of experience, if a school psychologist is assigned to a new position with different demands, supervision can be critical to learning the knowledge and skills that are necessary for competent practice.
- **It can help battle burnout.** Not only does career-long supervision promote advanced skill development and maintenance of current knowledge, as a method of self-care it can serve an important restorative function and protect against burnout. Furthermore, because school psychologists may be the only professionals of their kind in a given school or district, the job can be rather isolating. The ability to connect with a supervisor who understands the role and experience can be encouraging and restorative (Simon & Swerdlik, 2017).

Developmental Characteristics of Advanced School Psychologists

The unique developmental features of mid-career and veteran school psychologists will affect the kind of supervision they need and what's most likely to be effective.

Unlike the early career stage, which is limited to the first three to ten years of practice, the mid- to late-career period could span decades of development. Different models describe this process in various terms, but generally speaking, with time and experience professionals achieve at least a basic level of competence. Some, but not all, move on to become proficient school psychologists and maybe even achieve true expertise over the course of the career span. But remember that development isn't always necessarily even: in a field like school psychology, where practitioners tend to be generalists who must have skills and knowledge across a wide range of domains, it is important to recognize that individuals may be competent or proficient in some areas, and expert in others. Thus, the supervision needs of advanced professionals are likely to vary depending on the area being supervised, including the provision of supervision itself.

Competence

What It Looks Like

After surviving the early career years, members of the helping professions typically enter into Rønnestad and Skovholt's (2003) Experienced Professional Phase. This is a time of increasing authenticity and confidence, as well as flexibility, as practitioners move beyond trying to strictly apply the "rules" of a given theory or model. Practice becomes more organized, automatic, purposeful, and goal-oriented (Harvey & Struzziero, 2008). In terms of self-care, at this stage professionals are often better than their novice peers at setting and negotiating boundaries and may have the confidence and experience to transition to a work setting that better fits their goals and needs, if necessary. Although there is still a risk of the work–life balance tipping too far in the work direction, Rønnestad and Skovholt's study found that the work of many therapists at this point was enhanced by experiences from their personal lives.

Supervision Considerations

With at least three years of experience, school psychologists are eligible to supervise interns or practicum students (NASP, 2014). Thus, the initial years following the early career period may find the advanced school psychologist providing supervision as well as receiving it. At this stage meta-supervision, the supervision *of* supervision, can be extremely valuable. Additionally, supervision for competent school psychologists can address considerations such as navigating transitions, enhancing existing skills, and developing specialized expertise in an area of interest or need for the school or district, as well as focusing on self-care needs such as improving or maintaining work–life balance. Supervisees should be actively involved in structuring supervision at this stage to facilitate the acquisition of new techniques and methods that are needed for effective practice (Harvey, Struzziero, & Desai, 2014).

Proficiency

What It Looks Like

The work of school psychologists who achieve proficiency is more efficient and streamlined than it was when they were merely competent. With years of experience, these professionals are able to recognize patterns, quickly identify the most salient features of a complex situation, understand the implications of different factors, and generally make decisions more easily (Harvey & Struzziero, 2008). More so than ECSPs or even their competent peers, proficient professionals are able to "see the forest for the trees" and make decisions without laboring over a long list of alternative options. This ability to see the big picture lends itself well to addressing systems-level issues, which can be beneficial for school-based practitioners working in progressive environments, or quite frustrating for those in settings that are not open to innovation.

Supervision Considerations

Despite having well-developed skills, proficient school psychologists can benefit from supervision as much as any others. Rather than analyzing the minutiae of individual cases or decisions, examining opportunities for systems-level change and supporting the proficient school psychologist's efforts towards such endeavors may be helpful (Harvey & Struzziero, 2008). Particularly if change is difficult to achieve (as it so often is in schools) supervision can be an outlet for processing frustration, recognizing even small successes, and seeking alternative routes to achieve progress. And as always, supervision can serve a valuable restorative function. Experienced professionals may be subject to feelings of disillusionment that there's nothing new to learn or that they're seeing the same wheel reinvented (Rønnestad & Skovholt, 2003); supervision targeted to the enhancement of existing skills or development of specialized expertise has the potential to keep school psychologists at this level challenged and engaged.

Expertise

What It Looks Like

Harvey and Struzziero (2008) present a picture of expert school psychologists as coherent professionals who are comfortable in complex environments. Not everyone in the helping professions achieves true expertise, but those who do are able to analyze situations and solve problems even more rapidly and efficiently than proficient individuals. Work is more intuitive after learning from years of study, feedback, and experience. Experts may use their extensive skills and knowledge to foster high-level change through public policy efforts.

Supervision Considerations

Expert-level school psychologists are likely functioning at either Rønnestad and Skovholt (2003) Experienced Professional Phase or the final phase of their model: the Senior Professional Phase. Many senior professionals have been practicing for several decades and may be approaching retirement. This life stage presents its own unique considerations for supervision and self-care, including the fact that professionals at this point in their careers may have experienced the loss of significant prior supervisors and mentors, and even professional peers. Some of the disillusionment of the experienced professional phase may persist and even manifest as cynicism; as one veteran therapist in Rønnestad and Skovholt's study put it, "it can be frustrating to the senior therapist to see people make a big fuss about something he/she has known about for years" (p. 26). Thus, senior professionals and experts may need to actively seek out supervision from peers with comparable experience to stay engaged and rejuvenated. Of course, these school psychologists have the potential to share their valuable expertise with future generations by providing, as well as receiving, supervision.

Using Self-Assessment to Plan Advanced Supervision

As Simon and Swerdlik (2017) note, "number of years practicing is not the only factor that determines a supervisee's professional supervision needs" (p. 209). Advanced supervisees must be actively engaged in assessing their evolving areas for growth for several reasons. First, as has been noted previously, school psychologists are expected to be competent across a wide range of domains, and each of us, no matter how experienced, is stronger in some areas and weaker in others. There is also variability across roles that makes some practices more essential to day-to-day practice than others (e.g., a school psychologist working in a preschool may not do as many suicide risk assessments as one based at a high school). So any school psychologist who transitions to a new assignment or role may suddenly have new professional development needs. Finally, our skills evolve with increased experience, but our field is ever-changing as well, and it is essential to remain aware of how our professional development plans may need revising. Regular self-assessment that takes into account the context in which a school psychologist practices is necessary to identify knowledge and skills that need to be enhanced or acquired (Armistead, 2014). Advanced supervisees can work in conjunction with supervisors to identify and access meaningful learning experiences and supplement self-assessment with the insights of others who have observed their work.

The NASP (2010) Practice Model provides an organizing framework for assessing professional development needs. Handily enough, NASP (n.d.) developed a Self-assessment for School Psychologists[1] that can be completed online to identify areas of practice that are in "low," "medium," or "high" need of professional development. This is a *self* assessment: you complete the ratings so it prompts reflection on competence. With results in mind, NASP members can complete a professional growth plan (PGP)[2] and receive one NASP-approved continuing professional development credit per year for completing it. The PGP identifies specific goals in the areas of knowledge, skills, and professional work characteristics and delineates the action steps, required resources, and anticipated timeline for attainment of objectives. The process of developing and executing such a PGP could organize and guide supervision of school psychologists at all levels, including advanced supervisees.

Professional Support Options for Advanced School Psychologists

A range of modalities are available for supervision and professional support as school psychologists advance beyond the early career stage. They vary in level of structure or formality, such as how regularly sessions occur and whether they are scheduled or happen more spontaneously. At this level of development finding professional support in groups can be particularly beneficial, both because it is efficient and because it provides the benefit of learning from multiple experienced professionals at once. But sometimes formalized supervision may not be available, due to factors such as district size, financial resources, or lack of support for the importance of devoting time to supervision. In these instances school psychologists may need to be more self-directed in their professional development. A range of options are presented below to help advanced school psychologists develop effective professional growth plans.

Clinical Supervision

The most formal type of support for school psychologists at all levels is clinical supervision, which is the primary focus of most of this book. Although for advanced supervisees clinical supervision is unlikely to involve the kinds of vicarious liability and evaluation considerations that it does for preservice practicum students and interns, it is still a relatively structured, long-term, well-planned relationship within which the supervisor is expected to provide feedback to enhance the supervisee's practice. Unfortunately, this type of support tends to be the exception rather than the norm for school psychologists: results from the most recent survey of NASP members indicated that less than half of respondents had access to any form of systematic professional support (Walcott & Hyson, 2018).

For the majority of school psychologists who do not have access to individual clinical supervision, group supervision can be an efficient alternative. Personally, I have had the opportunity to participate in such a group, and I found it extremely beneficial. In particular, it was helpful to hear about my colleagues' challenges (and realize that I wasn't the only one struggling with certain issues), and to benefit from their diverse backgrounds and experiences as we discussed cases. Rather than getting the singular perspective of a clinical supervisor, group members were able to hear varied ideas about case conceptualization or intervention from individuals with varied expertise. Of course, group supervision is about more than just throwing a bunch of school psychologists into a room together; certain considerations should be kept in mind to facilitate an effective group. See Box 13.2 for ideas to keep in mind when arranging group supervision.

BOX 13.2 SUGGESTIONS FOR EFFECTIVE GROUP SUPERVISION

- **Limit group size**. Supervision groups should ideally consist of between four and eight members of relatively similar levels of development (Harvey & Struzziero, 2008).
- **Schedule in advance**. Whether the group meets weekly, bi-weekly, or monthly, set a schedule for the school year and block out the time to avoid last-minute cancellations. Crises certainly come up, but group members should try to prioritize supervision time over other conflicts as much as possible.
- **Have an agenda**. Like any effective meeting, a supervision session benefits from structure. As good as it can feel to vent frustrations, a supervision meeting that devolves into a group complaining session isn't likely to result in effective learning or problem-solving. Starting out with a plan for how time will be allocated and goals for what participants hope to get out of the session can help make the precious supervision time productive.
- **Plan ahead**. It's helpful to know in advance who will be presenting at a given supervision session. How you identify presenters may depend on the goal of supervision. For groups focused on professional learning, group members can sign up well in advance to present on topics of particular expertise. If supervision is meant to serve a problem-solving function, it may make more sense to plan closer to the last minute, when participants can identify pressing issues that need attention. An email circulated a week before the meeting date can serve as a reminder notice and a call for presenters.
- **Address confidentiality concerns**. At the outset, have an open discussion about the limits of confidentiality, particularly if any group members or the supervisor are not employed by your district. Be guided by the "need to know" principle when sharing sensitive information, and ask group members to limit what they say to things that are necessary for effective supervision. Discussing cases in hypothetical

---

terms can be helpful for avoiding the release of private information (Gottlieb, 2006).

• **Use good listening skills.** Busy and supportive school psychologists may find it hard to resist the urge to jump in with advice and solutions soon after a colleague begins sharing a difficult problem. Try to listen carefully and ask clarifying questions to help the supervisee *explore* what's going on before rushing to, "I had a case just like that and this is what worked!" Similar to consultation, sometimes the real learning in supervision comes from the exploration of the problem, rather than the solution.

Structured Group Supervision

Structured peer group supervision (SPGS; Newman, Nebbergall, & Salmon, 2013) is another option for groups of school psychologists in need of professional support. As the name implies, it involves a formal set of steps that guide participants through a methodical supervision process. It begins with a request for help from the supervisee, followed by a period of clarifying questions from group members. Once the request for help is clear, participants provide feedback about how to address the problem. This is followed by a break, during which time the supervisee reflects on the feedback and prepares for the next step, which is a response statement that addresses whether each group member's feedback was helpful. The process ends with a summary of next steps. The group may opt to engage in a discussion of the overall process if time permits. Newman et al. (2013) demonstrated the applicability of the SPGS model for supervision of consultation; they even provide a training video[3] that illustrates how the process works. School psychologists looking to strengthen their consultation skills may find this approach extremely helpful.

My students have successfully implemented a structured group supervision (SGS) process for meta-supervision and peer supervision. From observing the interactions of cohorts over several years and reviewing course evaluation feedback, it is clear to me that following a step-by-step process prevents group members from rushing to solutions or advice-giving and promotes thoughtful and productive support. It also provides valuable opportunities for peer supervisors to hone their communication skills by asking clarifying questions and paraphrasing the presenter's concerns. Students have overwhelmingly indicated that they find the SGS helpful, both for processing challenges they experienced as supervisors and considering difficult situations from their work as school psychologists. Handout 13.1 provides an overview of the SGS process that could be adapted for peer supervision of school psychologists.

Meta-Supervision

> This [experience] also highlighted . . . the value and importance of meta-supervision groups, or peer supervision groups. Supervision encourages continued growth as a supervisor, promotes continuing education/professional development, and assists in the continued development of best practice in school psychology.
>
> *(Anonymous first-time supervisor)*

After exiting the early career stage, school psychologists may find themselves in the role of supervisor for the first time. No matter how advanced or expert you are, taking on such a new role comes with challenges. As Harvey and Struzziero (2008) put it, "all supervisors are novices when they begin to act as a supervisor" (p. 32). Advanced school psychologists who supervise trainees or other school psychologists can benefit from meta-supervision, or supervision of supervision. This type of support can be extremely helpful, particularly for professionals at the expert stage who are working with beginners or novice professionals. As Rønnestad and Skovholt's (2003) model of therapist development highlights, for experienced professionals sometimes the work becomes so second-nature that a supervisor might forget all the specific steps and unique nuances that a novice must go through in approaching a particular problem. Or experts may overestimate a student's knowledge or level of development and assign overly challenging cases or expect too much. Furthermore, school psychologists at this level may not be true experts across all domains of practice; for example, someone whose role involves primarily assessment may not be equally competent at running groups or implementing systems-change efforts. In such cases, supervising in those less familiar areas can be a challenge.

Meta-supervision provides the opportunity to enhance supervision skills, process challenges, and develop new knowledge by engaging with another professional (or professionals). It may be hierarchical in nature, particularly if the meta-supervisor is someone in a position of greater authority, like a director of a service unit, but it can also be collegial. Personally, I have found it tremendously helpful to participate in a meta-supervision group with colleagues at my institution. Together we have engaged in professional development by examining, studying, and practicing new assessments published in recent years and we are able to consult with one another when questions arise about cases. Furthermore, because group members have individualized deep expertise in areas as varied as reading development, autism, neuropsychology, and school-based mental health, we are able to support supervisees across a wide range of domains. I have also seen my own students benefit tremendously from participation in meta-supervision groups. Individually or in a group format, meta-supervision can be a wonderful learning opportunity for advanced school psychologists.

Peer Consultation and Mentoring

As helpful as structured supervision can be for school psychologists across the career span, supportive peer relationships can be an important component of a professional's network as well. Because they are mutually beneficial, meaning both participants are equally able to give and receive support, peer relationships are different from hierarchical relationships in which the supervisee is a recipient of the supervisor or mentor's expertise. Such peer relationships have been found to provide friendship and emotional support in ways that mentoring relationships do not (Kram & Isabella, 1985). Different kinds of peer relationships develop in professional settings—some are relatively impersonal and primarily involve information exchange, others are more collegial and include a bit more personal disclosure, and a small number resemble true friendships and involve support regarding both professional and personal issues (Kram & Isabella, 1985). Having a variety of these kinds of peers to turn to provides a network of support for navigating a range of challenging situations.

Providing Peer Consultation

When navigating a tricky case or tackling an unfamiliar situation, a school psychologist may choose to consult with a peer. I know that in my school-based practice as well as my faculty position, I've relied heavily on trusted colleagues for advice. This may be particularly important when dealing with ethical dilemmas. Gottlieb (2006) offers a template for peer ethics consultation that outlines several important questions to ask when a friend or colleague asks for help. These questions can be applied to requests for peer consultation of all kinds. They are outlined in Box 13.3 for reference.

BOX 13.3 QUESTIONS TO CONSIDER WHEN PROVIDING PEER CONSULTATION

- Am I sufficiently qualified and competent to provide consultation on this topic?
- Can I be objective with this colleague in this situation?
- Do I have enough time for this?
- Do I have the resources I need to be helpful?
- Do I have any conflicts of interest regarding this situation?

- Are there any legal considerations I need to think about given the nature of my relationship with this colleague (e.g., the conversation is likely not privileged communication)?
- Am I comfortable accepting responsibility for my role in this consultation?
- Is there any reason I should decline this request for consultation?

Note: based on Gottlieb (2006)

Peer Mentoring

In addition to spontaneously turning to a colleague when a problem arises, school psychologists can participate in more formalized peer mentoring relationships to maintain competence. For example, Zins and Murphy (1996) investigated peer support groups, or "a small group of professionals with a common area of interest who meet periodically to learn together, to share their expertise, and to support one another in their ongoing professional [development]" (p. 176). These groups provide social support in addition to opportunities to learn new knowledge and techniques and can serve the same kind of restorative function as supervision. Participants reported that group members improved their skills and school psychology knowledge base, increased their enthusiasm, and in some cases even increased their involvement in professional organizations.

The concept of *relational mentoring* (Johnson, Barnett, Elman, Forrest, & Kaslow, 2013) highlights the power of peer mentoring relationships. Such interactions are reciprocal and mutually beneficial, and dyad members are able to flexibly trade the roles of teacher and learner. This type of supportive relationship involves sufficient trust to allow members to make themselves vulnerable enough to share their weaknesses. They are such powerful interactions that they not only serve to improve professional skills but can also positively affect non-work domains as well.

Johnson et al. (2013) present relational mentoring within the context of a *competence constellation*, or the collection of individuals who are engaged in supporting a psychologist's competent practice. They note, "a dyad is stronger and consequently more competent than an individual" (p. 346). Because we may not always be entirely accurate in self-evaluating competence, surrounding ourselves with peers who can provide a more objective view can serve as a detection mechanism for flagging signs of trouble if we are starting to slip.

Case Example

The Westvale School District was undergoing a number of changes. A new Director of Special Education, Dr. Campbell, was recently hired and several school psychologists were going to be reassigned for the upcoming school year. One was Linda, who was moving to Westvale High School (WHS) after working at the elementary level for 15 years. Linda was an experienced and capable practitioner, but she recognized that this change was going to be an adjustment. For one thing, WHS had a high rate of students experiencing anxiety and depression, and Linda knew the psychologists in the building spent a lot of time completing suicide risk assessments; Linda had done only a handful of such interviews since her internship. And while Linda was certainly familiar with the basics of adolescent development, after working with K-3 students for well over a decade she was going to have to adjust to counseling more mature clients. Furthermore, one of the reasons Linda had been reassigned was because she had been a key player in bringing an effective RtI/MTSS system to the elementary level; district administrators wanted her to help the high school implement a successful pre-referral intervention system.

Dr. Campbell recognized that access to quality supervision would be an essential component of navigating the transitions her team was experiencing. One of her first actions as director was to meet with the district's ten school psychologists to plan for the following year. They developed a schedule for monthly group supervision meetings and appointed one team member to be in charge of emailing the group a week before each month's meeting to collect agenda items. The group also scheduled monthly meetings for the K-5 and 6–12 psychologists to discuss cases, so each psychologist was engaging in group supervision every two weeks. The first meeting of the year would include training in the SGS process so that subsequent meetings would have structure and provide opportunities to strengthen communication and problem-solving skills. Although a few folks in the room grumbled about this new time commitment, everyone involved locked the dates into their calendars and agreed to attend supervision unless a true crisis occurred.

After the group meeting Dr. Campbell met individually with Linda to discuss her transition to WHS and develop an individual supervision plan that included a mix of self-directed professional development and ongoing peer support. During the summer Linda would complete online training to refresh her suicide risk assessment skills. Once the year was underway, she would observe Dave, her colleague at the high school, completing his first assessment and then trade roles and be observed when conducting her own interview with an at-risk student. She also planned to take some time to read research articles on the implementation of MTSS at the secondary level. Dr. Campbell was supportive of these plans and vowed to find money in the budget to reimburse Linda for the professional development costs. She also offered to meet with Linda on a monthly basis for individual supervision, which Linda greatly appreciated.

During the summer Linda scheduled a lunch with a friend from graduate school who worked at a high school and had fun catching up while also gathering some insights into current issues confronting adolescents and the adults who work with them. They agreed to keep in touch by email over the year and to try to attend the state school psychology conference together in December. Once the year began, Linda worked closely with Dave to get oriented to the building. Dave was supervising an intern for the first time that year, and after working with more than a dozen graduate students over the years Linda was more than happy to provide meta-supervision to Dave in appreciation of all the time he spent helping her adjust to her new role. They both learned a great deal from one another: Dave appreciated Linda's expertise on MTSS as they worked to bring the system to WHS, and Linda benefited from knowledge such as Dave's experience working with LGBTQ students at the high school level. Despite the increased time commitment, both Linda and Dave found that after their bi-monthly group supervision meetings they left feeling relieved and supported; they felt more connected to their colleagues in the district and were able to learn strategies that generalized to their own work when they weren't presenting cases. With the support of her peers and supervisor, Linda made a successful transition to WHS.

Supervisor's Summary

- Advanced school psychologists need access to supervision to maintain competence, build new skills, and prevent burnout.
- School psychologists at the competence stage and beyond should be highly involved in structuring supervision to meet their professional growth and self-care needs.
- Supervision for proficient school psychologists may focus on systems-level issues and enhancing specialized skills.
- Expert school psychologists can benefit from peer supervision with highly experienced colleagues and can stay engaged in the field by providing supervision to others.
- Self-assessment of knowledge and skills is an essential component of planning supervision for advanced supervisees; online tools such as the NASP Self-Assessment for School Psychologists and Professional Growth Plan are available for organizing such efforts.
- A range of professional support options are available to advanced school psychologists, including (from most- to least-structured): individual clinical supervision, group clinical supervision, structured group supervision, meta-supervision, peer mentoring, and peer consultation. An effective professional growth plan for an advanced school psychologist is likely to include a mix of these alternatives.

FINAL REFLECTIONS

- How would you rate your level of overall development as a school psychologist? How does your level of expertise vary across the domains of school psychology practice? Where are you strongest? Where you could develop further?
- What would it be like to supervise someone who is more experienced than you are in a given domain?
- What supervision modalities do you currently use for professional development? Why? What could you add to enhance your own access to supervision?
- Which of the professional support options discussed in this chapter would you feel most comfortable providing as a supervisor? Which would be the least familiar to you?

Notes

1 Available at http://apps.nasponline.org/standards-and-certification/survey/survey_launch.aspx.
2 Available at www.nasponline.org/Documents/Professional%20Development/NASP_Professional_Growth_Plan.pdf.
3 Available at www.youtube.com/watch?v=OxhzkgEIz5k.

References

Armistead, L. D. (2014). Best practices in continuing professional development for school psychologists. In A. Thomas & P. Harrison (Eds.), *Best practices in school psychology: Foundations* (pp. 611–626). Bethesda, MD: National Association of School Psychologists.

Frey, W. H. (2018). The US will become 'minority white' in 2045, Census projects, March 14. Retrieved from www.brookings.edu/blog/the-avenue/2018/03/14/the-us-will-become-minority-white-in-2045-census-projects.

Gottlieb, M. C. (2006). A template for peer ethics consultation. *Ethics & Behavior, 16*(2), 151–162. doi:10.1207/s15327019eb1602_5.

Harvey, V. S., & Struzziero, J. A. (Eds.). (2008). *Professional development and supervision of school psychologists: From intern to expert* (2nd ed.). Bethesda, MD: National Association of School Psychologists.

Harvey, V. S., Struzziero, J. A., & Desai, S. (2014). Best practices in supervision and mentoring of school psychologists. In A. Thomas & P. Harrison (Eds.), *Best practices in school psychology: Foundations* (pp. 567–580). Bethesda, MD: National Association of School Psychologists.

Johnson, W. B., Barnett, J. E., Elman, N. S., Forrest, L., & Kaslow, N. J. (2013). The competence constellation model: A communitarian approach to support professional competence. *Professional Psychology: Research and Practice, 44*(5), 343–354. doi:10.1037/a0033131.

Kram, K. E., & Isabella, L. A. (1985). Mentoring alternatives: The role of peer relationships in career development. *Academy of Management Journal, 28*(1), 110–132. doi:10.5465/256064.

National Association of School Psychologists. (2010). *Model for comprehensive and integrated school psychological services.* Bethesda, MD: Author.

National Association of School Psychologists. (2014). *Best practice guidelines for school psychology intern field supervision and mentoring.* Bethesda, MD: Author.

National Association of School Psychologists. (2018). *Supervision in school psychology* [Position statement]. Bethesda, MD: Author.

National Association of School Psychologists (n.d.). Self-assessment for school psychologists. Retrieved from http://apps.nasponline.org/standards-and-certification/survey/survey_launch.aspx.

Neimeyer, G. J., Taylor, J. M., Rozensky, R. H., & Cox, D. R. (2014). Diminishing durability of knowledge in professional psychology: A second look at specializations. *Professional Psychology: Research and Practice, 45*(2), 92–98. doi:10.1037/a0036176.

Newman, D. S. (2013). *Demystifying the school psychology internship: A dynamic guide for interns and supervisors.* New York: Routledge.

Newman, D. S., Nebbergall, A. J., & Salmon, D. (2013). Structured peer group supervision for novice consultants: Procedures, pitfalls, and potential. *Journal of Educational and Psychological Consultation, 23*(3), 200–216. doi:10.1080/10474412.2013.814305.

Rønnestad, M. H., & Skovholt, T. M. (2003). The journey of the counselor and therapist: Research findings and perspectives on professional development. *Journal of Career Development, 30,* 5–44. doi:10.1023/A:1025173508081.

Simon, D. J., & Swerdlik, M. E. (2017). *Supervision in school psychology: The developmental, ecological, problem-solving model.* New York: Routledge.

Walcott, C. M., & Hyson, D. (2018). *Results from the NASP 2015 membership survey, part one: Demographics and employment conditions.* [Research report]. Bethesda, MD: National Association of School Psychologists.

Zins, J. E., & Murphy, J. J. (1996). Consultation with professional peers: A national survey of the practices of school psychologists. *Journal of Educational and Psychological Consultation, 17*(1–2), 175–184. doi:10.1207/s1532768xjepc0701_5.

HANDOUT 13.1 STRUCTURED GROUP SUPERVISION STEPS

Step 1: Request for Help
The supervisee states, "I need your help with …" and briefly states the problem before explaining the situation in more detail. If relevant data is available, a written summary is provided to group members. Audio or video recordings can also be shared, if appropriate.

Step 2: Question Period
Group members ask clarifying questions and paraphrase their understanding to try to better understand the problem. This process is purposeful and organized: each member asks one question at a time until no one has any remaining questions. The supervisee answers the questions as objectively and nondefensively as possible without explaining or providing any rationale for why things were done or past decisions were made.

Step 3: Feedback
Again proceeding one at a time, group members provide suggestions for how the supervisee might proceed, beginning each feedback statement with "If this were my case/student I would …." The **supervisee remains silent** and takes notes about each suggestion.

- Break -
A break of at least two to ten minutes is given for the supervisee to reflect on the feedback and prepare his or her response statement. During the break group members do not speak to the supervisee.

Step 4: Response Statement
The supervisee responds to each group member's suggestions, explaining what was helpful, what was not helpful, and why. This is done in a respectful manner. Now **group members remain silent** until the supervisee completes all responses.

Step 5: Discussion
Time permitting, the discussion leader facilitates a discussion of the process, including what worked, what could have gone better, and any other reactions group members had regarding the experience.

Note: from Newman (2013)

Appendix A
RECOMMENDED READING

American Psychological Association. (2014). *Guidelines for clinical supervision in health service psychology.* Retrieved from http://apa.org/about/policy/guidelines-supervision.

Bernard, J. M., & Goodyear, R. K. (2014). *Fundamentals of clinical supervision* (5th ed.). Upper Saddle River, NJ: Pearson.

Harvey, V. S., & Struzziero, J. A. (Eds.). (2008). *Professional development and supervision of school psychologists: From intern to expert* (2nd ed.). Bethesda, MD: National Association of School Psychologists.

Joyce-Beaulieu, D., & Rossen, E. (2016). *The school psychology practicum and internship handbook.* New York: Springer.

Kelly, K. K., & Davis, S. D. (2017). *Supervising the school psychology practicum: A guide for field and university supervisors.* New York: Springer.

Newman, D. S. (2013). *Demystifying the school psychology internship: A dynamic guide for interns and supervisors.* New York: Routledge.

Simon, D. J., & Swerdlik, M. E. (2017). *Supervision in school psychology: The developmental, ecological, problem-solving model.* New York: Routledge.

Appendix B

SAMPLE PROFESSIONAL DISCLOSURE STATEMENT

Professional Disclosure Statement

Meaghan Curran Guiney, PhD., NCSP	
Address: Fairleigh Dickinson University 1000 River Rd., T–WH1-01 Teaneck, NJ 07666	Phone: (201) 692-2310 Email: mguiney@fdu.edu

Education

- Ph.D., School Psychology (Fordham University, 2010)
- P.D., School Psychology (Fordham University, 2007)
- M.Ed., Therapeutic Interventions (Fordham University, 2007)
- B.A., Psychology (Bowdoin College, 2000)

Licensure and Certifications

- Licensed Psychologist (NY)
- Nationally Certified School Psychologist
- State certification: New York and New Jersey

Relevant Professional Experience

- Assistant Professor, School of Psychology, Fairleigh Dickinson University (2018 to present)
- Clinical Assistant Professor, School of Psychology, Fairleigh Dickinson University (2012–2018)

- School Psychologist, Katonah Lewisboro School District (2007–2009)
- School Psychology Intern, Ossining Union Free School District (2006–2007)
- Psychology Extern, Child and Adolescent Psychiatric Evaluation Service (CAPES), New York State Psychiatric Institute (NYSPI)/Columbia Presbyterian Hospital (2005–2006)
- Graduate Assistant, The College Board, Office of Services for Students with Disabilities (2004–2006)

Domains of Supervision

Given my training as a school psychologist I am comfortable supervising **assessments of learning problems for children and adolescents**, particularly those involving possible learning disabilities or attention issues. I participate in a meta-supervision group and regularly consult with colleagues regarding these cases. I have particular expertise with respect to requests for standardized testing accommodations, as I previously worked at the College Board assisting with reviews of documentation for such cases. I will supervise cases involving mild to moderate social-emotional concerns, such as anxiety or depression. For cases involving more serious clinical concerns I have engaged in co-supervision, involving colleagues with expertise in the diagnosis of more severe psychopathology. I am a licensed psychologist, but particularly for cases involving classroom-based difficulties, I tend to focus more on educational implications and potential eligibility for special education services via the Individuals with Disabilities Education Act (IDEA) than DSM-5 diagnosis.

I have a degree in therapeutic interventions and background providing school-based counseling to students in both general education and a self-contained program for children with behavioral and emotional difficulties. I am comfortable supervising **child and adolescent counseling cases involving behavioral difficulties or mild to moderate social-emotional concerns**, but would not feel competent supervising intensive therapy with adults. I have experience supervising **therapy cases for the FDU COMPASS program**, which provides support to college students on the autism spectrum. Such work has addressed concerns including building independent living and academic skills and navigating social difficulties.

I have considerable training in the area of **school-based consultation**, as I completed an extensive year-long practicum in a consultation-focused district, provided consultation services as a practicing school psychologist, taught graduate courses on consultation, and publish research on consultation.

My primary area of research, scholarship, and teaching is in the **supervision of school psychologists**. I provide meta-supervision to supervisors-in-training and participate in my own meta-supervision with fellow faculty members.

Supervision Training and Experience

I completed a course on psychology supervision as part of my doctoral training. This involved a practicum through which I provided supervision to a less-experienced graduate student. For six years I have been providing supervision to doctoral students completing practicum experiences in assessment and therapy (the latter involving cases from the FDU COMPASS program described above). I serve as the university-based supervisor for all interns in FDU's School Psychology programs and co-supervise these experiences with school psychologists in the field. I have taught a doctoral course on supervision and provided meta-supervision to my students as they supervise interns or MA students completing a psychoeducational evaluation since 2013. I have published research and presented at national conferences on supervision.

Philosophy of Supervision

My approach to supervision is informed by a developmental perspective. I strive to adapt my supervision to meet the needs of the supervisee, providing sufficient support to promote security while also encouraging supervisees to solve problems independently, and even make mistakes, to foster learning. I expect supervisees to make mistakes, but also to learn from them and not make the same mistakes multiple times. Although I practice almost exclusively in a university setting, my supervision is guided by the Developmental Ecological Problem-solving (DEP) model (developed by Mark Swerdlik and Denis Simon), the only model of supervision specific to the practice of school psychology. I value the importance of culturally responsive practice in all that we do as school psychologists and expect to discuss diversity factors in supervision.

Supervision and Confidentiality

I respect the privacy of my supervisees and safeguard what is discussed during supervision. However, I do engage in meta-supervision and seek consultation with colleagues regarding challenging cases and to improve my own supervision skills. When supervising doctoral practicum students, I complete formal evaluations of knowledge, skill development, and professional work characteristics that are shared with course faculty. At times I may informally consult with the practicum course instructor regarding supervisee performance, if it is appropriate to support learning. I respect the obligation to break confidentiality in any instance in which I suspect or become aware of circumstances that might put a supervisee or client(s) at risk of harm, or when ordered to do so as part of a legal proceeding.

Appendix C

SAMPLE CONTRACT FOR SUPERVISION

This is an agreement between _____ and Dr. Meaghan Guiney.

    Both parties agree to the following:

1. This supervisory arrangement is established for the purpose of skill development during advanced graduate training.
2. The term of supervision will be from the start of the fall 2018 semester through the end of the spring 2019 semester, unless otherwise negotiated at a later date.
3. The supervisee is expected to meet with the client once per week for 50 minutes while FDU is in session (i.e., during the fall and spring semesters).
4. Supervision sessions will occur weekly for approximately 30 minutes. The scheduled day and time will be _____.
5. In the event that the supervisor or supervisee is unable to attend supervision, all efforts will be made to inform the other party as soon as possible and the session will be rescheduled for as soon as is feasible for both parties.
6. Technology-assisted supervision (i.e., video or phone conference) may be substituted for live supervision if necessary but is not intended to be the primary mode of supervision.
7. Supervisee and supervisor will adhere to the standards set forth in the NASP *Principles for Professional Ethics*, including (but not limited to): respect for the client's and supervisee's rights to privacy, confidentiality, and informed consent.
8. Supervision methods may include (but are not limited to): case conferences, review of audio or video recordings, review of progress notes, role plays, or (with client's consent) in-vivo supervision.

9. Ongoing formative feedback will be provided during weekly supervision sessions. Formal summative evaluation will be based on the Advanced Practicum Evaluation Form provided by the practicum course instructor to inform grading.

The supervisor agrees to:

1. Be available on an as-needed basis between scheduled supervision sessions in the event that an emergency occurs with the client or supervisee.
2. Maintain a transparent process for evaluation of the supervisee's performance and skill development.
3. Maintain supervisory discussions as confidential, with the exception of circumstances in which the client, supervisee, or another party may be at risk for injury or harm or for instances in which meta-supervision (i.e., supervision of supervision) or peer consultation is deemed in the best interest of the client or supervisee.

The supervisee agrees to:

1. Inform the supervisor immediately of any instances in which the client may be at risk of harm from self or others, or any other situations deemed to be emergencies.
2. Maintain open communication with the supervisor throughout the supervisory relationship, particularly around issues of possible ethical transgressions or ethically questionable behavior.
3. Complete any "homework" assignments or other activities deemed relevant for purposes of skill development in the supervisee and/or provision of high-quality services for the client.
4. Inform the supervisor of any concerns or issues related to supervision and/or the supervisor's management of supervision.

_____   _____
         Print name: Meaghan C. Guiney, PhD, NCSP

The Basics of Supervision with Dr. Guiney

Keep These Guidelines in Mind and Things Should Go Smoothly!

- **Maintain open communication**. Whether it's regarding an ethical dilemma, cultural considerations, or questions about basic procedures, honest communication is essential to effective supervision. You can usually reach me relatively quickly by email; I will aim to respond to all messages within 24 hours but it is typically much less than that. Just be sure not to include any identifying information about clients when communicating via email. On days when I have office hours feel free to call my campus line with any questions or concerns. <u>Please use my cell phone number only for emergencies.</u>

- Anything you ever feel hesitant to raise in supervision is probably the first thing you should bring up. Specifically . . .

  - **Keep me informed about your case(s)**. As your supervisor I am ultimately responsible for the welfare of any clients you see, so it is essential that I am fully apprised of all that goes on with your cases. Please be sure to keep me up to date on all that is going on. For testing cases, when we're not formally meeting on a regular basis, it's helpful to make at least weekly contact by email to keep me posted on the progress of your attempts to contact the family, your testing, and your report writing.
  - **Contact me in an emergency**. Any time you suspect potential danger or harm to your client, contact me immediately. My cell phone number is (123) 555–1234. Even if you are not sure your suspicions are correct, get in touch right away so we can discuss the situation.
  - **Share your mistakes**. If you think you made a mistake—be it an error in department procedures, a major ethical transgression, or anything in between—please tell me right away.
  - **Communicate about supervision**. For our supervision experience to be productive, it is important that we are able to talk about the process itself. If you have any concerns about your experience in supervision, including things I said or did that offended you or made you uncomfortable, or suggestions for things I could do more of or less of to improve the effectiveness of supervision, please do not hesitate to share them.

- **Know the department handbook**. Be sure to have a physical and/or electronic copy of the handbook readily accessible. Always consult it when uncertain about procedures, but don't hesitate to ask for guidance. Just be prepared for my initial response to be, "Did you check the handbook about that?"
- **Know your ethics codes**. Be sure you are familiar with NASP and APA ethical guidelines regarding, among other things, informed consent, confidentiality, multiple relationships, and respect for human dignity. Do not hesitate to ask questions when you are uncertain about an ethical issue and always speak up if you think an ethical transgression or violation may have occurred.

I look forward to a productive supervision experience!
Meaghan Guiney

Appendix D
SELF-ASSESSMENT TOOL

Before identifying specific goals and objectives for your learning experience, take time to reflect on your current level of development and competency across the NASP Domains of Practice. **Be sure to keep a copy of this form**. These ratings will be revisited at mid-year and at the end of the experience, so it is important to keep a copy with your previous ratings for review each time you re-assess. For each domain, rate yourself according to the following criteria:

New (N) = skills just being learned (i.e., beginner)

Developing (D) = functionally knowledgeable, but not yet proficient (i.e., advanced beginner)

Competent (C) = skills are commensurate with those of entry-level practitioner (i.e., competent)

Domain	Beginning of Year	Mid-Year	End of Year
Domain 1: Data-Based Decision-Making and Accountability	N D C	N D C	N D C
Domain 2: Consultation and Collaboration	N D C	N D C	N D C
Domain 3: Interventions and Instructional Support to Develop Academic Skills	N D C	N D C	N D C
Domain 4: Interventions and Mental Health Services to Develop Social and Life Skills	N D C	N D C	N D C

(Continued)

(Cont.)

Domain	Beginning of Year	Mid-Year	End of Year
Domain 5: School-Wide Practices to Promote Learning	N D C	N D C	N D C
Domain 6: Preventive and Responsive Services	N D C	N D C	N D C
Domain 7: Family-School Collaboration Services	N D C	N D C	N D C
Domain 8: Diversity in Development and Learning	N D C	N D C	N D C
Domain 9: Research and Program Evaluation	N D C	N D C	N D C
Domain 10: Legal, Ethical, and Professional Practice	N D C	N D C	N D C

Which 3–4 of these domains would your prioritize as your greatest areas in need of development during the coming year?

1.
2.
3.
4.

Professional Work Characteristics

1. Respect for Human Diversity	Beginning of Year	Mid-Year	End of Year
I take time to reflect on the impact of my upbringing and background on my view of the world and of others.	N D C	N D C	N D C
I seek out opportunities to gain experience working with clients who are culturally different from me.	N D C	N D C	N D C
I am comfortable discussing issues related to diversity in supervision.	N D C	N D C	N D C

To continue to improve in this area I need to ...

Beginning of Year	Mid-Year	End of Year

2. Effective Communication Skills	Beginning of Year	Mid-Year	End of Year
I engage in active listening with clients, consultees, supervisors, and others with whom I am communicating.	N D C	N D C	N D C
I communicate clearly with others.	N D C	N D C	N D C
I am able to assert my opinion in a respectful way.	N D C	N D C	N D C

To continue to improve in this area I need to ...

Beginning of Year	Mid-Year	End of Year

3. Effective Interpersonal Relations	Beginning of Year	Mid-Year	End of Year
I relate effectively with teachers.	N D C	N D C	N D C
I relate effectively with parents.	N D C	N D C	N D C

(Continued)

(Cont.)

3. Effective Interpersonal Relations	Beginning of Year	Mid-Year	End of Year
I relate effectively with supervisors.	N D C	N D C	N D C
I know when to listen, when to ask questions, and when to share my ideas and opinions.	N D C	N D C	N D C

To continue to improve in this area I need to ...

Beginning of Year	Mid-Year	End of Year

4. Ethical Responsibility	Beginning of Year	Mid-Year	End of Year
I possess a thorough knowledge of the NASP and APA ethics codes.	N D C	N D C	N D C
I consult relevant ethics codes when faced with ethical dilemmas.	N D C	N D C	N D C
I know when to seek consultation with others regarding ethical dilemmas or practice that is beyond my boundaries of competence.	N D C	N D C	N D C
I use a step-by-step ethical problem-solving model when faced with ethical dilemmas.	N D C	N D C	N D C
I act in a manner consistent with ethical standards.	N D C	N D C	N D C

To continue to improve in this area I need to ...

Beginning of Year	*Mid-Year*	*End of Year*

5. Flexibility	Beginning of Year	Mid-Year	End of Year
I can adapt when my planned schedule for the day needs to change.	N D C	N D C	N D C
I become flustered when things do not go the way I expected they would.	N D C	N D C	N D C
I listen to the ideas and opinions of others and can see situations from multiple perspectives.	N D C	N D C	N D C
I possess sufficient knowledge and skills to try a new technique or approach when what I'm doing doesn't seem to be working.	N D C	N D C	N D C

To continue to improve in this area I need to ...

Beginning of Year	*Mid-Year*	*End of Year*

6. Initiative and Dependability	Beginning of Year	Mid-Year	End of Year
I actively seek out new learning opportunities.	N D C	N D C	N D C
I am pretty much always busy doing something throughout the day.	N D C	N D C	N D C
If I find myself without an assigned task to complete, I ask my supervisor or other members of the team what I can do to help.	N D C	N D C	N D C
I consistently follow through on tasks I am assigned or on things I've told others I will do.	N D C	N D C	N D C
I have an effective organization system in place to manage my time and materials.	N D C	N D C	N D C

To continue to improve in this area I need to ...

Beginning of Year	Mid-Year	End of Year

Participation in Supervision	Beginning of Year	Mid-Year	End of Year
I am present for all supervision sessions and arrive on time for supervision.	Y N	Y N	Y N
If I am unable to attend supervision I notify my supervisor as soon as possible.	Y N	Y N	Y N
I come prepared for supervision with case summaries/data/other information requested by my supervision and questions.	Y N	Y N	Y N
I actively strive to incorporate supervisor feedback into my work and practice.	Y N	Y N	Y N

To continue to improve in this area I need to ...

Beginning of Year	*Mid-Year*	*End of Year*

Which of the following statements best describes you? Check one option during each self-assessment period.

	Beginning of Year	*Mid-Year*	*End of Year*
I need to build more confidence in my abilities.			
At times I may project more confidence in my abilities than is appropriate given my current level of skill development.			
I have a developmentally appropriate level of confidence in my abilities.			

Other thoughts or comments?

Beginning of Year	*Mid-Year*	*End of Year*

Appendix E
SAMPLE INTERNSHIP TRAINING PLAN

Domain	Goal(s) Related to Domain	Specific Objectives Related to Domain	Evaluation: I will know I met my goal when . . .
Domain 1: Data-Based Decision-Making and Accountability	• Improve skills in administration and interpretation of cognitive assessment measures • Increase knowledge of RTI processes (e.g., benchmarking, progress monitoring)	• Complete at least five comprehensive evaluations • Assist the RTI team with fall and spring benchmarking assessments and gather progress-monitoring data for at least two students	• My supervisor tells me that my evaluation reports have improved and/or I notice that I'm not making the same mistakes multiple times • I am able to independently administer and interpret benchmarking and progress-monitoring tools
Domain 2: Consultation and Collaboration	• Become more effective and comfortable engaging in consultation	• Complete at least two consultation cases this year: one focused on an academic	• Through self-reflection I recognize that I feel more comfortable and effective as a consultant

(Continued)

(Cont.)

Domain	Goal(s) Related to Domain	Specific Objectives Related to Domain	Evaluation: I will know I met my goal when . . .
	• Become more capable of following the four-step problem-solving model (problem ID, problem analysis, intervention, evaluation) to address consultee concerns	concern, one on a behavioral issue	• Feedback from at least one consultee indicates that I was helpful • Data gathered to monitor client functioning indicates improvement in the area of identified difficulty
Domain 3: Interventions and Instructional Support to Develop Academic Skills	• Become more proficient at implementing interventions to support academic skills	• Create at least one academic intervention plan • Collect progress-monitoring data for at least one academic intervention • Engage in a consultation case around an academic issue	• My supervisor's feedback indicates improvement in this area • Progress-monitoring data demonstrates measurable progress towards student client's goal(s)
Domain 4: Interventions and Mental Health Services to Develop Social and Life Skills	• Learn more counseling techniques • Feel more comfortable counseling students	• Lead a social skills group • Provide individual counseling to at least three students	• I have a binder of resources for use in future counseling sessions • My supervisor tells me I appear comfortable in counseling sessions
Domain 5: School-Wide Practices to Promote Learning	• Gain knowledge of how social-emotional learning principles can be used to promote positive school climate	• Participate as a member of the school climate team • Help implement a grade-wide social-emotional learning curriculum	• Pre- and post-data indicates that students endorse a more positive school climate after the grade-level intervention

(*Continued*)

(Cont.)

Domain	Goal(s) Related to Domain	Specific Objectives Related to Domain	Evaluation: I will know I met my goal when . . .
Domain 6: Preventive and Responsive Services	• Learn about crisis response • Learn how to conduct a suicide risk assessment	• Serve on the school crisis team • Observe my supervisor and/or other team members conducting risk assessments • Conduct at least two risk assessments independently	• My supervisor observes me conducting a risk assessment and says I did so effectively • I have resources on crisis teams for use in future practice
Domain 7: Family-School Collaboration Services	• I will feel comfortable presenting evaluation results to parents • I will collaborate with parents to coordinate implementation of effective behavior intervention plans at school and home • I will improve my parent interviewing skills	• Present assessment findings to parents for each evaluation conducted • Complete at least one behavior consultation case that involves collaboration with parents	• Progress-monitoring data indicates that a home-school intervention resulted in improved behavior for the student client • My supervisor observes my work with parents and indicates that I am comfortable and effective
Domain 8: Diversity in Development and Learning	• I will understand more about the experiences of English language learner students	• Complete assessment case with ELL student; collaborate with ESL teacher • Co-lead counseling group for LGBTQ	• I have successfully completed an assessment of an ELL student • I have resources and knowledge for working with LGBTQ students

(Continued)

Domain	Goal(s) Related to Domain	Specific Objectives Related to Domain	Evaluation: I will know I met my goal when . . .
	• I will gain knowledge of strategies for working with LGBTQ students	students at the high school	
Domain 9: Research and Program Evaluation	• Become fluent at finding and interpreting high-quality research to inform educational practice	• Research the F & P reading assessment system, synthesize findings, and present to CST	• The CST members and my supervisor indicate that my presentation was effective
Domain 10: Legal, Ethical, and Professional Practice	• Be skilled at designing legally defensible IEPs	• Actively participate in compliant IEP meetings • Write as least one complete IEP • Seek out professional development opportunities in this area	• My supervisor indicates that my IEPs are legally compliant

Appendix F

SAMPLE PROFESSIONAL GROWTH PLAN FOR CREDENTIALED SCHOOL PSYCHOLOGIST

Domain	Goal(s) Related to Domain	Specific Objectives Related to Domain	Evaluation: I will know I met my goal when . . .
Domain 1: Data-Based Decision Making and Accountability	• Increase knowledge of assessment tools appropriate for use with English language learners (ELLs) • Gain experience working in RtI/MTSS model	• Collaborate with district's bilingual psychologist to complete evaluation of ELL student • Attend workshop on assessment of ELLs at NASP convention • Participate on RtI data team • Assist with district-wide benchmarking in October, January, and May	• I have completed an evaluation with the district's bilingual psychologist • I have attended the NASP workshop • I have served on the RtI team for a full school year • I have participated in benchmarking
Domain 2: Consultation and Collaboration	• Become more skilled working effectively from an instructional	• Read about IC to gain background knowledge	• I have completed two cases following an IC model of consultation

(Continued)

Domain	Goal(s) Related to Domain	Specific Objectives Related to Domain	Evaluation: I will know I met my goal when . . .
	consultation (IC) model of consultation	• Complete at least two academically oriented consultation cases working from an IC model • Identify evidence-based academic interventions (EBIs) to address referral problems • Use progress monitoring data to evaluate EBI effectiveness	• Progress monitoring data indicated that selected EBI was effective for improving academic difficulty for student client • I receive positive feedback from consultee teacher
Domain 3: Interventions and Instructional Support to Develop Academic Skills	• Become more proficient at implementing interventions to support academic skills	• Create binder of resources on academic EBIs • Complete at least two academically oriented consultation cases	• I have completed two cases following an IC model of consultation • Progress monitoring data indicated that selected EBI was effective for improving academic difficulty for student client • I receive positive feedback from consultee teacher
Domain 4: Interventions and Mental Health Services to Develop Social and Life Skills	• Build skills applying motivational interviewing (MI) principles to school-based counseling	• Read about MI to gain background knowledge • Attend session on MI at NASP Convention • Apply MI principles in work with at least two student clients	• I have applied MI techniques in at least two counseling cases • I see evidence of clients making progress towards counseling goals • I get positive feedback from clients about their counseling experience

(*Continued*)

(Cont.)

Domain	Goal(s) Related to Domain	Specific Objectives Related to Domain	Evaluation: I will know I met my goal when . . .
Domain 5: School-Wide Practices to Promote Learning	• Contribute to improvements in school-wide positive behavioral supports (SWPBS) implementation	• Serve on the SWPBS team • Present workshop to SWPBS team and full faculty on key components of effective SWPBS • Examine office discipline referral (ODR) data from last year to identify most common types of discipline problems • Monitor ODR data to identify students in need of Tier 2 support	• I have presented an SWPBS workshop • I have observed an overall decrease in ODRs compared to previous school year
Domain 6: Preventive and Responsive Services	• Support improvements in school crisis preparedness	• Continue to serve on school crisis team • Complete NASP PRE-PaRE training • Deliver workshop to crisis team colleagues on fundamentals of PREPaRE • Identify areas in need of improvement in building/district crisis plans	• I am PREPaRE trained • I have participated in identification of areas in need of improvement in building/district crisis plans
Domain 7: Family-School	• Support efforts to increase	• Participate in planning of "Bagels, Books	• Records indicate that we had more parents attend

(Continued)

Domain	Goal(s) Related to Domain	Specific Objectives Related to Domain	Evaluation: I will know I met my goal when . . .
Collaboration Services	home-school collaboration	& Bananas" (BB&B) program during which parents read with their children in the cafeteria before school	BB&B than last year • Feedback forms indicate parents felt welcomed at school
Domain 8: Diversity in Development and Learning	• Increase knowledge of best practices for supporting LGBTQ students	• Attend professional development workshop on supporting LGBTQ students	• I have resources and knowledge for working with transgender students
Domain 9: Research and Program Evaluation	• Use data to evaluate effectiveness of SWPBS implementation	• Analyze ODR data to inform SWPBS team plans for improvement	• The SWPBS team has revised implementation plan based on ODR data
Domain 10: Legal, Ethical, and Professional Practice	• Build skills and knowledge for designing legally defensible IEPs	• Attend professional development session on legally defensible IEPs • Seek feedback from supervisor and colleagues for at least three IEPs	• Supervisor indicates IEPs are well written • Feedback from at least three parents is positive

Appendix G
INTERN EVALUATION FORM

1. Professional Work Characteristics Assessment

Please rate the intern's professional work characteristics based on the following scale:

Insufficient Data	Poor	Below Average	Average	Above Average	Outstanding
ND = No data	1	2	3	4	5

Respect for Human Diversity	
Takes time to reflect on the impact of own upbringing and background on view of the world and of others.	
Seeks out opportunities to gain experience working with clients who are culturally different.	
Is comfortable discussing issues related to diversity in supervision.	
Communication Skills	
Engages in active listening with clients, consultees, supervisors, and others.	
Communicates clearly with others.	
Is able to assert opinions in a respectful way.	

Interpersonal Skills

Relates effectively with teachers.	
Relates effectively with parents.	
Relates effectively with supervisors.	
Knows when to listen, when to ask questions, and when to share ideas and opinions.	

Adaptability and Flexibility

Can adapt when plans need to change.	
Remains calm when things do not go as expected.	
Listens to the ideas and opinions of others and can see situations from multiple perspectives.	
Possesses sufficient knowledge and skills to try a new technique when current approach doesn't seem to be working.	

Initiative and Dependability

Actively seeks out new learning opportunities.	
Is almost always busy doing something.	
Asks supervisor or other members of the team what can be done to help.	
Consistently follows through on tasks and meets deadlines.	
Is sufficiently organized and manages time and materials effectively.	
Limits personal communications and social media use during the school day.	

Ethical Responsibility

Possesses a thorough knowledge of NASP and APA ethics codes.	
Consults relevant ethics codes when faced with ethical dilemmas.	
Knows when to seek consultation with others regarding ethical dilemmas or practice that is beyond boundaries of competence.	
Uses a step-by-step ethical problem-solving model when faced with ethical dilemmas.	
Acts in a manner consistent with ethical standards.	

Technology Skills

Uses technology responsibly to enhance learning and build skills and identity (e.g., researches interventions online, follows school psychology social media sites).	
Uses technology effectively to promote efficient service delivery (e.g., competent with IEP writing software and student information databases).	
Communicates effectively and ethically via email or other electronic methods (e.g., protects confidential information when communicating electronically).	

2. School Psychology Skills and Knowledge Assessment

Using the Internship Training Plan as a guide, please rate the intern's development across the 10 Domains of the NASP Practice Model. Over the course of the year, it is expected that interns will have the opportunity to engage in an increasing number of activities; thus, fewer NA ratings will be given in spring than in fall. Interns are expected to develop entry-level competence in all domains by the completion of the internship. Students who do not receive ratings of 3 or above will complete remediation in collaboration with the university-based supervisor to support skill development.

Rating	Meaning
NA	Has not yet engaged in this activity.
1	Not yet able to successfully engage in this activity; exhibits deficits in this area.
2	Exhibits emerging skills in this area; is beginning to be able to engage in this activity.
3	Exhibits entry-level competence; adequately able to engage in this activity with supervision.
4	Exhibits well-developed skills in this area; can engage in this task with minimal supervision.
5	Exhibits superior skills in this area; is prepared to engage in this task independently.

Domain	Rating
1. Data-Based Decision-Making and Accountability	
Has knowledge of varied models and methods of assessment (e.g., standardized measures, CBA/CBM, interviews, observations) that yield information useful in problem identification, evaluating areas of strength and needs, and in monitoring progress.	
Uses such models and methods as part of a systematic process to collect data.	
Uses such models and methods as part of a systematic process to generate data-based recommendation plans about service delivery.	
Uses such models and methods as part of a systematic process to evaluate the outcome of services.	
Presents information gathered throughout this process in a way that is understandable to teachers, parents, and other members of problem-solving teams.	
Overall Domain 1 Rating[1]	

2. Consultation and Collaboration	
Has knowledge of behavioral, mental health, collaborative, and/or other consultation models and methods and of their application to particular situations.	
Establishes rapport with consultees (i.e., teachers, support staff, parents, and administrators).	
Collaborates effectively with others in planning and decision-making processes pertaining to individual students.	
Collaborates effectively with others in planning and decision-making processes pertaining to groups of students.	
Collaborates effectively with others in planning and decision-making processes pertaining to systems.	
Overall Domain 2 Rating	
3. Interventions and Instructional Support to Develop Academic Skills	
Has knowledge of human learning processes, techniques to assess these processes, and direct and indirect services applicable to the development of cognitive and academic skills.	
In collaboration with others, develops appropriate cognitive and academic goals for students with differing abilities, disabilities, and areas of strength and need.	
In collaboration with others, implements interventions to achieve these goals.	
Evaluates the effectiveness of these interventions and makes necessary modifications to interventions and goals.	
Overall Domain 3 Rating	
4. Interventions and Mental Health Services to Develop Social and Life Skills	
Has knowledge of human developmental processes, techniques to assess these processes, and direct and indirect services applicable to the development of behavioral, affective, adaptive, and social skills.	
In collaboration with others, develops appropriate behavioral, affective, adaptive, and social goals for students with differing abilities, disabilities, and areas of strength and need.	
In collaboration with others, implements interventions to achieve these goals.	
Evaluates the effectiveness of these interventions and makes necessary modifications to interventions and goals.	
Overall Domain 4 Rating	

5. School-Wide Practices to Promote Learning	
Has knowledge of general education, special education, and other educational and related services.	
Understands schools and other settings as systems.	
Works with individuals and groups to facilitate policies and practices that create and maintain safe, supportive, and effective learning environments.	
Overall Domain 5 Rating	
6. Preventive and Responsive Services	
Has knowledge of human development and psychopathology, and of associated biological, cultural, and social influences on human behavior.	
Has knowledge of universal supports, secondary and tertiary interventions, and crisis-intervention procedures and programs that promote the mental health and physical well-being of all students.	
Provides or contributes to prevention and intervention programs that promote the mental health and physical well-being of all students (i.e., universal supports).	
Provides or contributes to prevention and intervention programs that promote the mental health and physical well-being of at-risk students (i.e., secondary or tertiary supports).	
Provides or contributes to crisis-intervention planning and programs (e.g., member of school/district crisis team, drafting school safety plan, serving as counselor after crisis event) that promote the mental health and physical well-being of all students.	
Overall Domain 6 Rating	
7. Family–School Collaboration Services	
Has knowledge of family systems, including family influences on student development, learning, and behavior.	
Has knowledge of methods to involve families in education and service delivery.	
Works effectively with families, educators, and others in the community to promote and provide comprehensive services to children and families.	
Overall Domain 7 Rating	
8. Diversity in Development and Learning	
Has knowledge of individual differences, abilities, and disabilities.	
Has knowledge of the influences of biology, culture, ethnicity, experience, SES, gender-related, and linguistic factors on development and learning.	

Is sensitive to and possesses the necessary skills to work with individuals with diverse characteristics; exhibits cultural competence in rapport-building, interviewing, observing, testing, and counseling individuals with diverse characteristics.	
Selects or adapts strategies based on individual characteristics and uses knowledge of individual differences to identify best practices appropriate to specific situations.	
Overall Domain 8 Rating	
9. Research and Program Evaluation	
Has knowledge of research, statistics, and evaluation methods.	
Applies knowledge through evaluation of research related to educational and mental health issues.	
Understands research design and statistics in sufficient depth to plan and conduct investigations and program evaluations for improvement of services.	
Overall Domain 9 Rating	
10. Legal, Ethical, and Professional Practice	
Has knowledge of the history and foundations of various service models and methods.	
Has knowledge of the history and foundations of public policy development applicable to services provided to children and families.	
Has knowledge of the history and foundations of ethical, professional, and legal standards.	
Practices in ways that are consistent with applicable standards.	
Seeks ongoing supervision and professional development as needed.	
Overall Domain 10 Rating	

Supervisor Comments

Please comment on the intern's areas of strength:

In what areas could this intern benefit from continued professional development?

Additional comments:

_____   _____
Intern Signature   Date

_____   _____
Field-based Supervisor Signature   Date

_____   _____
University-based Supervisor Signature   Date

Note

1 This rating is meant to globally reflect general competence in a Domain; it need not be an exact average of all sub-skills within the Domain.

Appendix H

SAMPLE REMEDIATION PLAN

SUPERVISEE NAME: Sam Pseudonym
SUPERVISOR(S) NAME: Alex Anonymous, Ph.D. and Ryan McMadeup, Ed.S.
WORK/TRAINING SITE(S): Anytown Elementary School; Anytown High School
PLAN START DATE: January 3, 2019   **PLAN END DATE:** June 25, 2019

Target Behavior(s)

1. <u>Attendance</u>: Sam has arrived late, left early, or been absent without notice from his internship placement at Anytown High School.
2. <u>Assessment skills</u>: for his first four evaluations Sam has made administration and scoring errors on the WISC-V and WJ-IV.
3. <u>Professionalism/ethics</u>: Sam has failed to see students for some mandated counseling sessions and has not completed progress notes as requested by his supervisor at Anytown Elementary.

Present Levels of Target Behavior

1. <u>Attendance</u>: Sam's attendance was consistent and appropriate throughout September for the two days per week that he is scheduled to be at Anytown HS. However, he was absent for three days in October and three in November (six out of 15 scheduled days). For three of these absences he notified Mr. McMadeup that he would be out due to illness or emergency, but on three occasions he was absent without notice. He also

left before noon on two days and arrived later than 10:00am five times in two months. This inconsistent attendance has resulted in a lack of opportunities for regular supervision at Anytown HS.

2. <u>Assessment skills</u>: For his first evaluation using the WISC-V, Sam calculated the examinee's age incorrectly, did not observe time limits on the Block Design subtest, and did not write down the examinee's verbatim responses. Hand-scoring the protocol, he incorrectly calculated the VCI and WMI, resulting in an inaccurate FSIQ. After receiving feedback on these errors he did not record responses verbatim on his second administration of the WISC-V and continued to make addition errors during hand-scoring. Administering the WJ-IV at Anytown HS, Sam did not correctly observe basal and ceiling rules.

3. <u>Professionalism/ethics</u>: On at least three occasions, Sam has been observed alone in his office at a time when he was scheduled to be meeting with a student for mandated counseling. When asked about this he stated that he was confused about the schedule and did not realize he was supposed to be seeing students at the time. Dr. Anonymous asked Sam to complete brief progress notes for review at weekly supervision meetings, but after two weeks of bringing the notes Sam did not have them for the following three supervision sessions.

Actions Taken To Date

- Mr. McMadeup has asked Sam, both in conversation and via email, to notify him by email or text message as soon as he knows he will be absent from internship. He has also added Sam's name to the faculty sign-in/out book in the main office and required Sam to follow the same procedures as all other building faculty, noting his arrival and departure time each day.
- Both Dr. Anonymous and Mr. McMadeup have provided in-vivo supervision of Sam's test administration and have had Sam observe them testing students.
- Dr. Anonymous spoke with Sam about the legal and ethical importance of providing mandated services and keeping accurate and sufficient records.
- Dr. Anonymous and Mr. McMadeup met with Sam jointly to share their concerns. During this meeting Sam shared that he has been feeling overwhelmed by the pressures of transitioning to internship while also completing his final graduate school classes and maintaining a job in the evenings and on weekends. He disclosed previous struggles with anxiety and depression, noting that in the past he has had a tendency to withdraw during difficult periods.
- Both Dr. Anonymous and Mr. McMadeup participated in a phone call with Sam's university-based internship supervisor to share their concerns.

Supervisee Strengths

Sam is warm, personable, and engaging, and is skilled at building rapport with students and teachers. He has previous experience working as an aide in special education settings, which enhances his ability to consult with teachers about behavioral and mental health issues in the classroom. He has strong technology skills and has exhibited creativity in researching web-based apps for collecting behavioral data and implementing interventions.

Areas of Need

- Sam continues to lack awareness of some basic test administration requirements, such as basal and ceiling rules on the WJ-IV, time limits for subtests on the WISC-V, and the importance of writing down verbatim responses.
- Sam needs to build professional work characteristics with respect to the need to attend internship consistently and to inform his supervisors with as much notice as possible if he is going to be absent.
- Sam needs to appreciate and respect the legal and ethical importance of providing and documenting mandated special education services consistently.

Required Supports

- Sam needs additional supervised practice and feedback regarding the administration and scoring of cognitive assessment measures.
- Sam needs closer monitoring of his internship attendance.
- Sam may find it helpful to pursue mental health supports to help him manage the challenges he is experiencing as he navigates his internship.

Provision of Supports

Who?	Will Do What?	When?
Sam	Continue to follow faculty sign-in/out procedures at both school sites.	Immediately
Mr. McMadeup	Check Anytown HS sign-in/out book each day to confirm Sam's attendance.	Immediately
Dr. Anonymous and Mr. McMadeup	Provide in-vivo supervision of Sam's next two test administrations using the Assessment Administration Competencies form (attached) to document required competencies and any serious administration errors.	When next evaluation at each site is scheduled and started.

(*Continued*)

(Cont.)

Who?	Will Do What?	When?
Sam	Video-record test administrations (after obtaining parental consent) and review and self-evaluate the accuracy of his performance using the Assessment Administration Competencies form and submit completed forms to the building supervisor within five days of completing testing.	For all upcoming evaluations, until it is determined that this support is no longer needed (i.e., administrations are accurate and reflect competency).
Sam	Develop a personalized self-monitoring checklist targeting his most common administration and scoring errors to be completed for each evaluation conducted. Checklists will be submitted to the building supervisor within five days of completing testing.	Immediately
Sam and Dr. Anonymous	Review Sam's counseling schedule to address any areas of confusion. Each morning, upon arriving at Anytown ES, Sam will inform Dr. Anonymous of the students he plans to see for counseling that day, and at what time. At the end of the day Sam will confirm with Dr. Anonymous that he saw the student(s) and submit his progress notes for all sessions held that day.	Immediately
Sam	Consider consulting his university-based supervisor or other faculty members regarding the availability of mental health support services on campus, or referrals to community providers. At the present time, therapy or counseling is recommended for Sam, but not required as a condition for completing internship.	As soon as he feels comfortable.

Goals and Objectives

1. Goal: Sam will attend internship with consistency.

   a. He will arrive on time each day.
   b. He will stay on-site until 30 minutes past dismissal each day, consistent with the Anytown faculty contract.
   c. He will not be absent from internship for reasons other than physical illness or emergency. If he must be absent he will notify both field supervisors and his university supervisor by email as early as possible.

2. Goal: Sam will administer standardized cognitive assessment measures accurately.

   a. Sam will satisfy all required competencies on the Assessment Adminis-
      tration Competencies form.
   b. Sam will complete evaluations without making any serious administration
      errors indicated on the Assessment Administration Competencies form.

3. Goal: Sam will meet his legal and ethical obligation to see all students on
   his counseling caseload.

   a. Sam will hold all mandated counseling sessions each week.
   b. Sam will submit copies of progress notes to Dr. Anonymous at the end
      of each school day.
   c. If Sam is unable to hold a session due to client absence, or his own
      personal illness or emergency, he will inform Dr. Anonymous as soon
      as possible.

Progress Monitoring and Plan Evaluation

Sam and his supervisors will review this remediation plan and discuss progress
towards the stated goals and objectives during supervision each week. They will
also review Sam's performance using his university-provided summative evaluation form during the first supervision session of each month to assess how
effectively the plan is helping Sam to attain required competencies for internship. Dr. Anonymous and Mr. McMadeup will maintain regular (i.e., biweekly)
contact with Sam's university-based supervisor via phone and email to monitor
progress.

Consequences for Continuing Occurrences of Target Behavior(s)

Aside from limiting opportunities to gain experience and build skills, continuing
absences from his internship sites will put Sam at risk of not accruing the
necessary number of total hours to meet state and university training program
requirements. Should he fail to accrue the required hours, Sam will not be
eligible to complete the program and become certified to practice as a school
psychologist.

Should Sam continue to struggle to demonstrate adequate competency in
assessment despite employing the supports outlined in this plan, he will need
to pursue additional training in assessment before Dr. Anonymous and/or
Mr. McMadeup can approve him for successful completion of the internship
experience.

Continuing to miss counseling sessions and/or failing to complete required
session progress notes in a consistent and timely manner constitutes a deficit in

professional work characteristics and reflects a lack of appreciation for the legal and ethical obligations school psychologists have to provide mandated special education services. Dr. Anonymous and/or Mr. McMadeup would be obligated to inform Sam's university-based supervisor of such ongoing problems with professionalism and would document such concerns in their summative evaluations of Sam's internship performance. This could likely jeopardize Sam's successful completion of the internship experience and ability to be approved for certification to practice independently as a school psychologist.

Appendix I

DEVELOPING CULTURAL RESPONSIVENESS

Worksheet for Setting Personal Goals

Identifying, writing down, and routinely reviewing personal goals increases the likelihood that you will be successful. Complete this worksheet and update it regularly to reflect your ever-evolving efforts to practice in a culturally responsive way.

List your three most important personal goals related to enhancing your culturally responsive practice:

1.		This goal is . . . ☐ Immediate (this school year) ☐ Short-term (1–3 years) ☐ Long-term (3+ years)
2.		This goal is . . . ☐ Immediate (this school year) ☐ Short-term (1–3 years) ☐ Long-term (3+ years)
3.		This goal is . . . ☐ Immediate (this school year) ☐ Short-term (1–3 years) ☐ Long-term (3+ years)

Choose an immediate goal to complete the section below.

How will you know when you have met your goal?

```



```

List some potential obstacles to accomplishing your goal:

```



```

How can the obstacles listed above be overcome?

```



```

What resources will be required to meet your goal?

```



```

Which coworkers, family members, and friends can help you meet your goal?

```



```

What immediate action steps will you take at this time to work towards your goals and enhance your culturally responsive practice?

Action Step	Due Date
1.	
2.	
3.	
4.	
5.	

Notes

Date updated: _____

Appendix J

LETTER OF RECOMMENDATION FOR STRONG SUPERVISEE

Dear Dr. Jones,

I am so very pleased to write this letter of reference for **Jane Smith** as part of her application for a school psychology internship with the Yourtown Public Schools. Knowing what I do about Yourtown from the district school psychologists who are alumni of our program, I have strongly encouraged Jane to apply for this opportunity. Not that she needed encouragement; Jane has been thinking proactively about her internship experience for some time and has dedicated herself to securing an opportunity that will maximize her learning and growth as a school psychologist. I am certain that Yourtown will benefit tremendously from Jane's talents by extending an offer for next year's internship program.

 I first met Jane when she applied to our graduate program in school psychology. From the day she interviewed I was impressed with her intelligence, composure, and thoughtfulness. Since that time I have taught her in three classes, each of which highlighted her strong writing skills and academic aptitude. For instance, for my course on behavior assessment and intervention, Jane's final project was so outstanding that I saved it to serve as an example for future cohorts to follow. [Be specific] Furthermore, Jane has been my research assistant for the past three years and I am serving as the Chair of her dissertation committee. Her initiative and time management skills were remarkable as she led a team of graduate assistants at three universities in a complex data coding project while simultaneously developing a protocol for her dissertation research and collecting and analyzing her data. I knew Jane had the organizational skills to be a successful school psychologist the day she [Include a brief anecdote] introduced me to a website that built personalized planners! She always had hers with her and never failed to complete an assigned task, large or small.

It has been my pleasure to watch Jane grow and develop as a school psychologist and a researcher during the four years I have known her. She arrived with strong skills and good instincts and has honed these qualities by embracing challenges and opportunities that have allowed her to expand her repertoire. During her time with us at FDU she has balanced a full course load of graduate classes in addition to employment as an aide with the Nearby Public Schools, a research assistantship, a significant administrative role with our campus support program for students with autism spectrum disorders (ASDs), and even undergraduate teaching. She can handle virtually any responsibility that is thrown her way and, in my experience, delivers above and beyond expectations for every task she is assigned. I can speak for my program colleagues when I say that we could not think more highly of Jane. I know she will make us proud as she moves on to this capstone experience in her school psychology training, where she can continue to build on her unusually well-developed understanding of students with ASDs and adolescent development as she gains exposure to new settings, methods, and approaches.

> Highlight potential for growth

Jane possesses all the knowledge, skills, and professional work characteristics necessary to be a standout intern: she is incredibly organized, diligent, bright, motivated, caring, and intelligent. I would happily share more about my impressions of Jane or anything else that would support her application. Please do not hesitate to contact me by email at mguiney@fdu.edu or by phone at (201) 555–2000.

Most sincerely,
Meaghan C. Guiney, Ph.D. NCSP
Assistant Professor
School of Psychology

Appendix K

LETTER OF RECOMMENDATION FOR A SUPERVISEE WHO STRUGGLED

Dear Dr. Buckley,

I am writing this letter of recommendation at the request of **Sally Wells**, who is seeking her first position as a school psychologist after successfully completing an internship with the Quiet Creek Public Schools during the present academic year. I have known Sally since she entered our school psychology training program in the fall of 2016. During that time she was a student in two of my courses and I served as her university-based internship supervisor. I have observed substantial growth in Sally's knowledge, skills, and professionalism over the course of the three years I have known her, which suggests that she has the potential to have a positive impact on students, teachers, and parents as a school psychologist.

Sally has a warm, engaging and outgoing demeanor that allows her to quickly and easily build rapport with children and adults alike. As a classmate she was a clear leader who cared about the well-being of others, as she regularly organized study groups or outings for her cohort and made a concerted effort to connect with incoming students as a mentor. These efforts had a noticeable effect on the culture of our graduate program and speak to Sally's ability to function effectively in a school setting. I could easily see her serving productively on faculty committees and implementing initiatives to promote family–school partnerships. She exhibits the "soft skills" that are essential for school psychologists; these are typically difficult to teach or remediate.

During her time in our program Sally encountered challenges, but worked with determination to address them. Specifically, she had initial difficulty mastering the nuances of standardized administration

> Describe difficulties directly and specifically

of cognitive tests, such as observing basal and ceiling rules and recording responses in detail.

However, over the course of a structured remediation experience, Sally improved substantially in both her organization and test administration skills. Despite being initially disappointed in her performance and herself, she approached remediation with determination and embraced the chance to learn from supervision. She reframed this setback as an opportunity for growth and went above and beyond by seeking out additional field experiences with our on-campus clinic to help build her assessment skills in advance of internship. In the end, I was quite impressed by Sally's growth mindset.

> Highlight remediation efforts

As an intern, Sally continued to be actively engaged in supervision and cognizant of her training needs; she developed a clear plan for the year that built not only her fundamental testing skills, but also incorporated opportunities to learn new measures and integrate complex findings. Summative evaluations from her field supervisor, Dr. Jessica Clark, reflected that Sally demonstrated competency in all domains of school psychology practice.

Sally's interpersonal and communication skills will be a tremendous asset to her as she pursues a career as a school psychologist, along with her growth mindset and commitment to learning from supervision. I would be happy to speak with you further regarding my experiences with Sally; please do not hesitate to contact me by email at mguiney@fdu.edu or by phone at (201) 555–2000.

Most sincerely,
Meaghan C. Guiney, Ph.D. NCSP
Assistant Professor
School of Psychology

INDEX

active listening 16, 20, 104, 211, 224
administrative supervision 7, **8**, 174, **175**, 177
advanced school psychologists, characteristics of 11, 187–188
anxiety in supervisees: about being evaluated 42; about new roles 12, 29, 37; as a cause of PPC 86, *87*, 99; contracts as tools for reducing 32–33; due to lack of feedback 57; monitoring 15, **16**; resistance as manifestation of 62; as a symptom of burnout **127**

boundaries: and multiple relationships 25–30, 37; respecting as part of effective supervision **14**, **17**, 18, *90*, 121; setting to maintain work/life balance **11**, 133, 177, 180, 188
boundaries of competence 177, **212**, 225
boundary crossings 27
boundary violations 28
burnout: defined 126; preventing in ECSPs 180; rates of for school psychologists 127; signs of **127**; supervision as protective factor agains 187

climate assessment 107
clinical supervision **8**, 75, **175**, 177, 191–193
cloud computing and storage 148, 154, 156

collaboration: to address ethical dilemmas 120; with colleagues to provide learning experiences **17**, 49, 50, 73, 167; between supervisor and supervisee 7, 41, 42, 68, 88, 137; with university-based supervisors *87*, 162–166
communication: and boundaries 28–29; of feedback 55–66; of evaluation results 73; of expectations 41, 75, 80, 121, **163**; and remediation *90*; skills 44, 52; as a source of resistance 89; styles of 92, 105; and technology 147–148; with university-based supervisor 162–163
competence, boundaries of 177, **212**, 225
competence constellation 196
confidentiality: limits of for supervision sessions 35 75, 121–122; clients' understanding of 122; and telesupervision **152**; and group supervision 192
contacting university supervisor 162, 165
contract for supervision, sample 206–207
contracting for supervision 30–36
counseling out of the field 91
cultural competence 102
culturally responsive supervision: collaborative communication skills and 105; dual nature of 104; goal setting for 106, 237–239; multiple identities and 105; professional development and 103, 106, 109; relationship to outcomes 104; working alliance and 104

defensiveness 64, 71, 93, 105
DEP Supervisor Self-reflection and Supervisor Feedback Survey (DEP-SSFS) 77
Developmental Ecological Problem-solving (DEP) model of supervision 13, 166, 173, 181, 186
diversity dimensions 102, *103*
due process: and appealing evaluations 71; and personnel evlauations 75; and communication evaluations 80; and addressing PPC 83

early career school psychologists: access to supervision for 177; building supervision skills in 181; and the Novice Professional phase 176–177; supporting 178–180; transitions and 177–178
ecological factors 13
electronic file sharing 148
email communication 147–148
equality vs. equity 104
ethical problem solving model 118–120
ethics codes and supervision 116–118
ethics: and competence 116; and confidentiality 121; and evaluation of supervisees 118, 122; and providing feedback to supervisees 122; and multiple relationships 120; and socializing with supervisees 121; supervisors as role models for 113–115; and think aloud strategies 114
evaluation: by administrative supervisors 74; appealing 71; by clinical supervisors 75; cultural differences and 71; definition of 70; as an ethical consideration 118, 122; favorable conditions for 71; forms 72; of credentialed school psychologists 74; of preservice school psychologists 72
Experienced Professional phase 188, 190
expert school psychologists 189–190

facilitating entry 161–162
feedback: characteristics of 57–58; difference bewteen evaluation and 55; the feedback sandwich method of 59–61; feelings about providing 56; as an ethical consideration 122; importance of 55–56; motivational interviewing and 62–63; the Pendleton Method of 61–62; preparing supervisees to receive 63–65; techniques for providing 59–62
feedback sandwich 59–61
field-based supervisor responsibilities 163
formative feedback 41, 72, **163**, 180

gatekeeping **8**, 9, 70, 71, 174, **175**
goals: characteristics of 48; for developing cultural responsiveness 106, 237–239; and evaluation 71, 77; and planning supervision 34, 40, 45, 47; setting 38; and self-care 137; and the supervision relationship 56; SMART 48
growth mindset: and being reflective 21; and fostering resilience **130**; highlighting in letters of recommendation 170, 243; modeling for supervisees 72; and providing culturally responsive supervision 105
Guidance for Postgraduate Mentorship and Professional Support 174, 179
Guidelines for the Practice of Telepsychology 151
Guidelines for Supervision in Health Service Psychology 25, 31, 102, 181, 202

Healthy Lifestyle Assessment 73
hierarchical relationship 9, 22, 71, 194, 195
HIPAA 148, 153

identity development 105, **106**
informed consent: through contracting for supervision 32, 36; and telesupervision 154, 155

letters of recommendation 167–170
Lifespan Development Model 10, **11**
live observation 33

mentoring 174–175, **175**, 195
meta-supervision: for building competency as a supervisor 9, 17, 18, 116; for ECSPs 181, 188; through structured group supervision 193; as a means of professional support for advanced school psychologists 194–195
Motivational Interviewing 62–63, 221
multiple relationships 25–27, 29, 120–121, 125

NASP *Principles for Professional Ethics* 18, 28, 32, 116, 117–118

open-faced sandwich technique 61

peer consultation 152, 195–196, 198, 207
peer mentoring 196, 198
Pendleton Method 61–62

portfolios 73, 75
Position Statement on Supervision in School Psychology 186
postgraduate professional support **8**, 173, 174, **175**, 179
poverty 106
power (and culturally responsive practice) 103, 105, **106**, 109
power imbalance 9, 26, 28, 71, 120
privilege 103, 105, **106**, 108, 109
problems of professional competence (PPC): can't-do assessment of 85–87, **86**, *87*; collaborating to address 93, conducting difficult conversations about 91–93; contracts and preventing 34; definition of 82; ethical obligations and 81; evaluation and 70; examples of 82; guilt and 93; operational definitions of 83–84; problem analysis and 84–88, 96–97; problem identification and 83; prevalance of 81; remediation plans for 88–91, 98–99, 100–101, 231–236; resistance and 87–88, **89**; seeking support for addressing 93; self-assessment of 85; shame and 93; won't-do analysis of 87
professional disclosure statement 33, 37, 203–205
professional growth plan 76, 78, 191, 198, 220–223
professional networks 21
Professional Self Care Scale 136
professional work characteristics 20, 43, 44
proficient school psychologists 114, 188, 189, 198

racism **106**
reciprocal evaluation 77
reflective practice 13, 14, 21, 22, 96, 103
relational mentoring 196
remediation plans 88–91, 98–99, 100–101, 231–236
resilience 128, **130**, 132
resistance 87–88, **89**
restorative function of supervision 187, 189, 196
RIOT 44, **45**, 46

School-wide Cultural Competence Observations Checklist 107
self assessment 46–47, 80, 85, 190

Self-assessment Checklist for Personnel Providing Services and Supports to Children and their Families 107
Self-assessment for School Psychologists Survey 76, 179, 190, 198
self-awareness 57, 82, 96, 105, 128; *see also* self-reflection
self-care 128–138, 180, 187, 188, 190; assessment of 136–137, 140–141; definition of 128; methods of 132–136; mindfulness and 135–136; mindfulness-based positive principles and practices and 129; modeling 132; multipurpose ideas for 135–136
self-care plan 137, 142–146
self-reflection 46, 61, 103, 136, 180; *see also* self-awareness
Senior Professional phase **12**, 190
shortage of school psychologists 127, 175
site visits 163–164, 170
SMART goals 47–48, **48**
social networking 149, 155
socializing with supervisees 121
Standards for Graduate Preparation of School Psychologists 1, 166
structured group supervision 193, 198, 201
structured peer group supervision 193
summative evaluation 41, 72, **163**, 180
supervision plans 41–42, 47–50
Supervision Utilization Rating Form 73
supervision, defined 7–9, 174
systems change 107, 194

telesupervision 151–155
terminating supervision 166
text messaging 28, 148
think aloud 15, *90*, 114, 120, 180
transgender youth 106, 187, 223
trust 12, 32–33, **89**, 104, 196

university-based supervisor responsibilities 163

vicarious liability 35, 81, 174, 191
videoconferencing: etiquette for 154; software options 153

work-life balance **11**, 18, 73, 133, 180, 188

Made in the USA
Middletown, DE
20 August 2023